LIVE
*WELL*WITHIN
YOUR
MEANS

ALINE STRONG

LIVE WELL WITHIN YOUR MEANS
ALINE STRONG

This book is dedicated to my husband, Davis Strong,
for everything he has done and continues to do
to make my life peaceful, secure, and joyful.

Acknowledgements

I'd like to mention a few people who have encouraged me for the many years it has taken to write this book:

My sister, Jean Yashinsky, who has been a stalwart encourager of everything I do, and especially work in service to others. Pat Guillet who has been through years of supporting me by saying this was an important book and I could do it! Roger Halfacre who helps me out of distress regularly. Kelly Rico helped me keep to my dream schedule. A whole host of people helped me choose the title, including Gwynn Scheltema, who also did a crucial initial edit of the book. And my newest best friend, Shelley Schadowsky, who did far more than design the thrilling book cover. She shepherded me through the labyrinth of print and ebook formatting.

Then there are my willing victims first readers, Allison Elkin, Suzanne Moore, Jenny Schnoll and Charlene Lewin. Some major changes happened after that fun evening.

Finally, and most importantly, there is the emotional and technical support of my husband, Davis Strong. He is never unwilling to leave his own work to get me out of a technical tangle, and is always a calm advisor. My children, Michael Strong, Laura Howsen Strong, and Erika Strong, gave sensible perspectives, and guidance in the world of social media.

There are so many wonderful financial writers today and even in the past. Every one of them has wisdom and has informed my own understanding, and I am grateful to them all.

Is This Book for You?

As a kid, I was an arithmetic whiz. Those times tables were no match for me! However, I was always in the dark about the financial conversations at the dinner table: mortgage rates, the value of the dollar, pensions. When I hit high school, I fell in love with algebra, all that mess reduced to one neat number on each side. However, higher math was still a mystery, just like interest rates, and the stock market.

From my teens to my twenties, I made multiple, gross financial mistakes. I wracked up credit card debt, overspent on my checking account, wrote checks hoping money would appear, which it often didn't, borrowed from family and friends, and lived in constant chaos and stress around money. In desperation, I took an accounting course. I loved it; except, those year-ends and balance sheets did nothing to illuminate my personal finances. Then, I started to research every financial resource I could find. You probably know there is a lot of good money advice in books and the media. Unfortunately, none of it worked for long for me. It was worse than dieting. I couldn't even apply some of the ideas offered without far more money smarts than I possessed.

Finally, I turned to spiritual principles I was learning in other arenas in my life. And, holy cow, so to speak, financial things began to get better and stay better. The combination of practical action and non-religious spiritual support was the key to my financial peace and prosperity. I went from $5,000 debt on credit cards which I had no idea how I would pay, $800 monthly in overdraft on my checking account which no amount of money dumped in seemed to reduce, and hair graying faster than a young woman's should to a calm, realistic, comfortable personal and financial life.

With the determination of the desperate, I studied how these principles interacted, and applied them daily to the point where I repaid all my debts, I had money in savings, and I lived in peace around my finances. When I was sure my system worked for the long haul, I used my decades of teaching experience to show other women how to calm their financial chaos and live in prosperity. Now, I am sharing those solutions with you.

You can escape from financial chaos. You can establish a peaceful, prosperous life that you will be able to maintain. While neither money advice alone nor spiritual principles alone work permanently, a combination of practical advice balanced with spiritual support to make it stick will bring you relief from financial chaos and debt, to a financial life of peace, and the joy of lasting prosperity.

So, if you want to stop obsessing about money, and feeling ashamed to tell your family and friends about your real financial situation, read on. If you have already tried credit counselors, debt consolidators, money diets, home equity loans, family bailouts, friends' couches, church money programs, or bankruptcy, you have now finally found a permanent way to get on top of your money, and stay there!

How to Use This Book

You will find many exercises and self-tests in this book. Please do each before you read on. Simply cruising through the book, like a novel, won't bring you the benefits you want. I have nested each exercise, so that once you have completed it, you are ready for the next one. Do yourself a favour, do them as you meet them, and reap the rewards of increasing financial prosperity, and peace of mind.

It takes time for information to have effect. About six months after you finished reading this book, check in with yourself. While you may not have done everything suggested yet, are you better off than you were? Check your money, check your feelings, and check your outlook on life. Try this every few months. Then give yourself a pat on the back for the progress you are making.

There is a lot of information in this book. You may want to read certain sections more than once to get the concepts fixed comfortably in your mind before you start applying them.

The purpose of this book is to help you and your family recover from financial chaos and live in prosperity. However, there are times when your situation may be challenging enough that you need more specialized help and support, such as therapy, legal counsel, or professional accountants. Consult these experts in addition to using the suggestions in this book.

CONTENTS

1

RUN FROM EMPTY

Power Up!

Y ou are intelligent, competent, well dressed, often, and quite a charmer when you want to be. So, how can you be in such a financial mess? There are bills to the left of you, bills to the right of you, and collectors in your face. If not that, at the very least, you are obsessing about money for hours at a time. How could this have happened to a nice woman like you?

Many circumstances can create financial chaos. The obvious ones are losing a job, health issues, not finishing school, or trusting the wrong people. These are easy to acknowledge; however, there are also subtle reasons why you always seem to have money troubles. They hide deep in your emotions, working underground on the subconscious level. They are the ones which control you, distort your best thinking, and sabotage your best efforts.

Knowing about them won't change your money troubles overnight, although recognizing these forces are controlling you will help you accept the fact you need a permanent source of help.

SOCIETY PRESSURES

Take a look at today's society. It is awash in debt and doesn't seem to care. From the neighbours who hold lavish parties to the government who talks in billions, there is a shrug and not much else. *It's the way it is these days* seems to be the attitude. Society touts certain answers to quell financial fears however disastrous they may be for you in the future. Your peers are also a financial force against you which is hard to surmount.

Consider this: if you listen to friends, and society, your best chance at success in life is a higher education. If you don't have the funds, you can typically end up $25,000-$40,000 in debt to get a degree. Of course, banks give fifteen years to repay that loan; then again, you will be starting to repay it with entry-level salaries for the first few years. Now, do you feel afraid to go to university, and afraid not to go?

Home ownership is another societal value which is huge in North America. Yet look at the problems this has caused recently with people getting mortgages far higher than they'd ever be able to pay off. On the other hand, even sensible people buy homes these days which leave them house poor. At the end of the month, they use their credit cards to pay for the other necessities of life. Some end up at food banks. Though, they sure look good to the neighbours.

Clothes are a sure killer of budgets for women. Society says you need the right ones for work, and other right ones for love. If you ignore this, you may miss out on job opportunities, or in the dating game. Do you feel calm with the amount of clothes you have, or are you secretly proud or secretly ashamed?

And what about a status car? Depending on where you live, your car may seem more important than your house. If yours isn't in good condition, or you don't have a car, how do you feel about public transit? It's chic these days, but maybe not to you. Giving up the Lexus for a Mazda may feel like ripping your heart out. You are preening to an invisible audience at a huge cost to you.

Then there are the kids. Even their birthday parties can cause you angst and big spending urges. When the other kiddies have their fetes at Casa Loma with ponies and a circus, it's not easy to make your kid's party at Chucky Cheese. You cave in, and the budget gets whacked.

On top of all of that, the lives of the rich and famous have become a societal goal. Women you know go on cruises, and European jaunts, and visits to Thailand. How are they paying for them? Well, we know how-- credit cards. Even financial counselors encourage us to use credit as long as we keep it to just the one credit card for emergencies. This is counter human nature. Do you use your credit cards only for emergencies? I'm guessing the last thing you bought on your credit card was probably not baby formula.

Society's pressures have so invaded your thinking that the extravagant seems normal and necessary. It isn't so. Your real needs revolve around love. Simple as that. Stop buying into financial values which will bury you in debt.

EARLY LIFE INFLUENCES

Of course, maybe it started early in your life. If your family mishandled money, cheated, got into debt, or were severely underearning, that is what you absorbed. Your early childhood sets your perceptions of the world. Therefore, you have learned behaviours which are hard to overcome.

Children are like ducklings–they pattern themselves after the first adults they see. If your mother hid new clothes from your father, if your father got sick and you had to pinch every penny, if one of them was an addict and money disappeared into the bottle, your family distorted your money sense. As well if there was not enough rent money, food, clothes, you lost any sense of financial security: you feel the world does not provide enough for you. Coming from a poor home, you have lasting money habits which prevent you from enjoying a normal income if you are lucky enough to have that today. Also, if your home was unloving or unhealthy, your child's brain learned there is not enough love or safety in the world for you. This type of thinking also affects how you manage your money.

On the other hand, if in your home you got more things than affection, more permissiveness and neglect than boundaries and involvement, you learned to view the material world as your source of security and nurturing: money equals safety and love. Intuitively, you knew how untrue that was, so as a child, you erroneously concluded you must not be good enough, smart enough, or loveable enough to warrant the love and attention of your caregivers. Unfortunately, your adult mind still believes this.

Because you were raised with scarcity, either material, emotional, or both, you learned to become overly self reliant, never asking for help when you needed it.

INHERITED DISABILITY

Look inside yourself. It is possible you have a small, undiagnosed learning disability around numbers. No matter how many times you look at the number, is it sometimes higher or lower than you remembered? This is common, so you might as well acknowledge it if true. If you're sure you have $450 in your checking account, you'd better look again, and maybe again. It may be $540, $405, or even $45!

In addition to that, there's terminal vagueness. That same amount you think is $450 is really $350, but you can't be bothered to double check. You don't know your interest rates, or even how much cash you have in your purse, exactly. You don't pay attention. You don't *want* to! This is where you will *have* to lean on an outside help stronger than your resistance. More on that later.

SENSORY OVERLOAD

Have you ever considered you may be a Highly Sensitive Person? Some women are more susceptible to sensory overload.

Those bright store lights, the colours, the noise, the crowds, the multiplicity of choices--these things can overwhelm your brain, so that you drop your guard and go into a trance. Sometimes, your face feels flushed, your eyes glaze over, and though fatigued, you still keep shopping. Your body is reacting to excitement by pumping adrenaline. Once this chemical gets involved, it's like a drug—and it isn't easy to stop a buying frenzy. Company-hired psychologists have products placed for such impulsive purchasers.

When the body is in this wound-up state, your brain does not work properly. This shopping effect is akin to the syrupy feeling an alcoholic gets when drinking. Research even suggests shopping thrills are similar to sex – raised body temperature, quickness of breath, light-headedness. The brain gets befuddled and useless. Sad to say, elation during shopping is as short-lived as elation during sex. And in the morning, you may not respect yourself.

Stores know how to create atmosphere and ambience. Then again, if you can spot your physical reactions and get out of the environment, you can stop yourself before you go on a spending spree. Knowing what triggers you is the first defense.

SHOPPING FEELINGS

How about neighbours, friends and TV? Ain't it awful to see your neighbour use that new snow blower while you break your back with the snow shovel from hell? Doesn't it make you squirm when your best buddy goes on a winter vacation, a cruise yet, and you have to say you like using vacation time to putter around the house? Besides that, TV shows and movies depict people in lovely homes, with great clothes, eating at fabulous restaurants to which they drive in great cars. Images of other people's cool stuff emphasize what you don't have. It can make anyone feel inadequate, a failure.

Trained marketing professionals know how to persuade you to buy. They make things seem like the answer to your lifelong quest to quell that existential angst. In other words, to fill the hole lack of love left empty. Though rationally you know an advertised product will not make you feel wanted or connected, the primitive, emotional part of your brain knows no logic. The wounded part of yourself wants to believe it, and you buy.

Advertisers use Abraham Maslow's Hierarchy of Needs to reach your subconscious mind. He was the founder of

Humanistic Psychology, and he discovered our needs and wants are in levels. Once the bottom level is satisfied, we reach for the next level. To become a happy, self-actualized person, we need satisfaction on all five levels, in order.

<u>Maslow's Hierarchy of Needs</u>

Physical Needs: food, water, air, and sleep.

Security: safe job, protection of property, and family.

Belonging: friends, connection with family, and sexual intimacy.

Esteem: achievements, and respect from others for those achievements.

Self-Actualization: creativity, spontaneity, and tolerance of others.

Food or drinks will satisfy the physical cravings, burglar alarms for security, clothes, beer, even MacDonald's family themes address Belonging. Ads for cosmetics, cars, furniture, and fashion aim at Esteem needs. Interestingly, the fourth level is where ads stop. What, no ads aimed at people who are Self Actualized, who are creative, spontaneous and tolerant? No.

Advertisers are too practical. Since less than 10% of the population reaches Self Actualization, and these people aren't conned by ads, advertiser focus on the rest of the population who purchase stuff and more stuff, trying to buy security, love, and self-esteem. Becoming more creative, spontaneous (not impulsive!) and tolerant are the values which bring about the other positive emotions. Owning more stuff does not.

PRIMITIVE BRAIN FEELINGS

Advertisers also know we experience certain feelings when we shop, and they prey on that. Here are some of the less enjoyable feelings the primitive brain is busy with when you're in a store:

Shame: If you're at Payless buying shoes instead of the expensive David's, your primitive brain is saying, *Why do I have to shop for cheap shoes? I work hard, but I still have to shop where teenyboppers shop? Plus, winter is coming and my boots are a mess. Though if I buy some here, everyone at work will think I'm such a loser because they'll look cheap.*

You might feel ashamed if your peer groups are high achievers while you barely scrape by. Or, maybe your family situation brings up feelings of shame: the way they live, how they behave, how they treat you. You know it's not right, and you feel humiliated. Maybe you're different. Your ethnicity, religion, or sexual orientation set you apart from your circle and you feel shame. Unfortunately, this feeling comes into play when you shop, influencing you to make questionable decisions to feel better.

If you are a clutter bug, you are ashamed that you do not know what you have in all those piles. That's why you buy multiples of things. You can't remember if you have it, or not, or, you simply can't find it in all the mess.

If you are ashamed of your present financial situation, you may go out of your way to present a picture of the well-groomed, successful woman. Unfortunately, that takes money, which you do not have, so you go into debt. How has that worked for you up 'til now?

Fear: Safety is your major concern. You may not realize danger is the source of the fears you've stored in your primitive brain. Certain places, people, situations scare you. Purchasing things can bring on an adrenaline rush which overrides fear. Adrenaline may give you these sensations:

- Heightened Senses
- Sudden Boost of Energy
- Increased Breathing
- Noticeable Increase in your Strength
- No Feelings of Pain

While this might sound great, the reality is your behavior will become irrational because you're *not* in danger. Your mind will be clouded by this chemical, and make you hyper. That's why it's hard to stop a shopping spree.

Stop a Spending Spree

- To calm your body down, take long, deep breaths.

- Then rapidly walk out of the store. Taking physical action helps dissipate the adrenaline surging in your body.

Inadequacy: This emotion can also trigger you to attempt to reduce it with retail therapy.

You reduce feeling inadequate by concentrating on buying stuff, and the feeling of competence you get from making a smart purchase. *I am not the stupid idiot my boss thinks I am!*

But why does your primitive brain feel inadequate? Are you different in some tangible way from the norm? You may be a visible minority, disabled, or disfigured. Perhaps you feel different because you are poor, gay, less educated, or ill. These situations set you apart from the pack. You have felt the sting of society's negative attention.

At some level, you mistakenly believe your value depends on what other people think of you. As a result, you spend mightily on how you present yourself, trying to influence the world to see you in a more positive way.

Fantasy: *But, if I buy boots from David's, I'll look so fabulous when I saunter in tomorrow. Just imagine Cheryl's face!*

Fantasies while shopping are like mirages. You fast forward to you in the new, beautiful thing, and begin to imagine the reactions of others. Are heads turning? Is that office witch looking jealous? Are they all treating you with respect finally because of the new thing? Plus do you now feel a sense of belonging, of being in the group?

Some part of your primitive brain thinks this new item will change your life forever. Although, has any item actually changed your life for long? Earrings? Leather jackets? A condo you finally got then could not afford?

The problem with buying is the feelings are ephemeral. Yes, anticipating buying it will bring you a thrill, and owning it will add to that for a while. However, play the tape to the end. What happens after you've had it for a few weeks? Haven't you forgotten the good feelings, and gone in search of more? What is the final effect? You are more in debt than ever.

Playing the tape to the very end will bring a cooling dose of reality to any steaming fantasy.

Trance: Or, are you one of those women who relax so much when you shop, you end up having to go to the bathroom? You treat yourself to luxury items not on your list, if you even check your list. You are in a dreamy trance state, and your bill will reflect it.

MERCHANDISING

Buying magnets are everywhere you look. Movies plant products to advertise them. TV, radio, billboards, internet, transit, even clothes advertise products. When you're feeling tired, hungry, angry or lonely, these little ads burrow into your subconscious and *make* you act. Advertising encourages you to use your wallet to fill yourself with the care and love you crave. However, it doesn't satisfy, does it?

While all shoppers are the stock and trade of marketers, merchandisers aim at creating impulsive behaviour. They organize stores to get you to buy more than you intended. Ever had that experience? Who hasn't! They place items called point-of-purchase right at the cash register, ready for you to touch, smell, and toss into your basket when you're opening your wallet.

Merchandisers pay grocery stores to have their items placed on certain shelves. The closer to your eye level, the higher the price they pay. They place store brands, which are less expensive, on the bottom shelves. You have to bend down to save money at grocery stores.

Did you ever notice the dairy counter is at the back of the store? Merchandisers have created a route for you to follow, making you pass many products before you get to the milk. Next, what about those items at the end of the aisles? Prominent displays get your attention and you impulsively purchase them, thinking they are on sale, except, poor you, these items are getting stale or are slow sellers.

What is more, while you're moseying down the aisles, you're reacting emotionally to party items, big quantities, luxury goods. All of these create fantasies of friends, family gatherings, and fun times. Whether you can afford these things is not in consideration when you're operating impulsively. Furthermore, you are a vulnerable babe when it comes to warehouse stores, like IKEA and Costco. There are often no signs telling you where you are, so you have to hunt through all the aisles, passing tempting arrays of goods.

Instead of shopping impulsively to take the edge off your anxiety, try the old acronym of H.A.L.T. If you're feeling Hungry, Angry, Lonely, or Tired, HALT! How does a new pot help you feel less hungry? Maybe you need to buy better groceries, or to give yourself time to relax while you eat. If you're spending to get revenge on your husband, he may not make the connection between your overspending and his not paying enough attention to you. Having that talk or planning time together that you both will enjoy is far more likely to meet your real need. Call someone to talk, or pray. Otherwise, you'll be buying stuff to fill a need that stuff cannot fill.

DENIAL

Your own brain can sometimes work against you financially. Is the extent of your money problems a big secret from your partner, your family, and your friends? Well, guess what? You're also keeping secrets from *yourself.* For example, if you're paying

$600 to lease a car, do you tell yourself it is a necessary mode of travel when it really is much more a status symbol? You're keeping that little secret on yourself.

Self-delusion makes women distort the truth, so they can't see reality. Since they can't recognize what is really happening, they live in a fog, struggling against phantoms while ignoring the real wolf at the door. You're as sick as your secrets.

Secrets work in the subconscious mind, eroding confidence, affecting health, and damaging self-esteem. The first step is to recognize your habitual behaviours which will reveal many of your secrets.

For example, do you remember stealing anything? How about that gumball in Grade 1? How about the money from you know who? How about boosting things from a store as a teenager, or more recently? If that was you as a kid, maybe it's forgivable. Then again, if this is still your adult habit, folks, you need more income! See Chapter 4, *Claim your Income*.

If you take supplies from work without company permission and excuse it by saying your company underpays you, you're prevaricating. Stealing from anyone to make up your shortfall has consequences down the road. You cannot remain unharmed by this. It's that Universal Law: you reap what you sow.

NEVER ENOUGH

Somewhere early on, you missed getting what you needed: enough love, enough attention, maybe even the staples of life. Why me, your little self wondered? Unfortunately, your child's mind concluded there was something wrong with you. You were not good enough, smart enough, attractive enough, or loveable enough. Therefore, you did not deserve these good things. Now, as an adult, you're still living with these self-assessments, and using money as your whip.

This internal financial force makes you deprive yourself, or splurge, borrow and debt. You have read books, taken courses, and sought financial counselors, made resolutions, budgets, and promises, all to no avail. You're still powerless around your money.

Unwillingness to face reality has prevented you from facing this challenge of life and winning. Your internal resources don't feel strong enough to meet the problems head on, so you distract yourself with spending. One woman had this dream, or was it a nightmare:

I was about to climb Mount Kilimanjaro when a fabulous shoe sale at base camp distracted me.

Though you may understand why you do what you do with money, you feel trapped in old habits. You have an almost irresistible urge to perform the same old behaviours around your finances whatever the cost to you in turmoil, stress, shame, and defeat. Has it all become unbearable? That's good! Now, you're motivated to make changes.

PRACTICAL SOLUTION:
Money History

T o banish your demons, you must first identify them. You can do this by writing a Money History. It records your earliest memories around money. Putting this information down in black and white clarifies it, and shows you that your money troubles had a beginning and therefore they can have an end. The past may have been bad, very bad, but it wasn't worse! You will see patterns which will explain some of your present habits, avoidances, and fears around money. Awareness is a huge leap forward in conquering old habits.

Reviewing your financial history may reveal other compulsions with alcohol, drugs, food, sex or tobacco that have gotten out of control and are costing you a lot of money. Alternatively, maybe you will see you spend when you feel lonely: buying things at the same stores or eating in the same restaurants can give you an illusion of relationships. Or, maybe you splurge after arguments, or visits from certain people, at the beginning of a new job or relationship. Discovering these secrets which have been influencing you for much of your life is the first step in changing.

There are many ways to do a Money History: chronological, backwards, or events.

CHRONOLOGICAL MONEY HISTORY

In the chronological approach, you view your past like a TV series, one episode at a time. You can look at your early years, 0-9, and then every seven to nine year period after that to your present age. For example,

Major Money Events/Attitudes:
Age 0-9
My father got sick when I was about 7 years old. This wreaked

havoc with the family budget. I thought we were poor so never asked for things I needed, even clothes. One day, the teacher sent me home from kindergarten for wearing my mother's high heels because I didn't have shoes. I never mentioned it to my mother.

Age 10-19 etc.

BACKWARDS MONEY HISTORY

In the backwards approach, you view your history starting from today. Where are you now around your money? Then, work backwards, a year or two at a time. You can also look at groups of years, like in certain cities if you moved around.

Major Money Events/Attitudes:

Today: I'm presently $72,000 or so in debt. This has crept up on me over the last six or seven years.

Last Year, I broke up with my boyfriend of several years. We sold our house, but lost money on it. My share of the loss was $15,000. This increased my debt from $57,000 to $72,000.

Four Years Ago, I met my boyfriend. At the time, I was $20,000 in debt and renting an apartment on my own. After a few months, he and I bought a house together. Then he lost his job.

EVENTS MONEY HISTORY

If you prefer, you can simply think back to your first memory of money and go on to your next memory.

Major Money Events/Attitudes:

1. My first encounter with money occurred when I stole gum from the corner store when I was four. My mother hit me far beyond the necessary to teach me a lesson. Even though she apologized the next day, because she didn't look me in the eye, hug or kiss me, I thought she didn't mean it. It ruined our relationship.

14

2. *The next thing I remember is whispers around the house about my father losing his job. Then I saw my mother crying.*

Your Money History is limited to facts around money. Be as honest as you can. You will not have to show this to anyone.

There is no need to delve into deep psychotherapy here unless you feel the need. In that case, do it with a professional therapist.

SPIRITUAL SOLUTION:
Ask for Help

C all it what you will: Nature, HaShem, Love, Buddha, God, Goddess, Jesus, Friendship, Psychotherapy, or Reality itself, you need a positive, powerful force to help you clean up your money life.

To each of you, whatever your previous experience, I suggest you keep an open mind about a God. Is there an acceptable spiritual source for you? Maybe the God of your childhood was one you don't want in your life now. If your childhood taught you to believe in a punishing God, you don't want to go back there. Then again, perhaps you grew up in an environment which labeled religious women as weak or dependent, calling God a crutch. Alternatively, your family may never even have discussed such matters, and so a relationship with this concept seems foreign. Or, maybe you are religious, but the God in your life proved unable to handle your financial woes even when you prayed for help. Saddest of all, maybe you have been deeply disappointed in God based on experience.

The answer is you need to be practical, too. Without paying attention to the realities of your finances, no matter how much praying is going on, you'll never get out of hock. Paying attention to the realities is your job, your footwork.

Where do you go for help once you admit you live in financial chaos? Paid financial counselors, competent family friends, websites, blogs, psychologists, even medication can help; all the same, not one of these can stop you from making your next money mistake once you're in the trap of your own mind. Women in 12-step groups like Debtors Anonymous, Gamblers Anonymous, Workaholics Anonymous and of course, the granddaddy of them all, Alcoholics Anonymous , have been there and gotten out of the bad neighbourhood they call your mind.

Conversely, if such groups don't attract you, where are you going to turn?

When you are in mental and emotional turmoil, God can intervene, bringing calm so you can make better money decisions. God, alone, can intervene on your behalf if you call out when you are about to spend, and stop you. Really.

AN IDEAL SPIRITUAL SOURCE

If your present memories are not of a pleasant, supportive God, write a better description. What would you wish your God to be like? Start with that. Be sure your definition creates a benevolent concept, more powerful than you, which is interested in everything you do. Make it up!

The perfect helper can be male or female, or a concept like beauty, nature, or even truth. It can reside inside or outside you, or both. Funny as it may seem, more than one person I know says Whoopi Goldberg is their model for a Spiritual Helper. They see her as someone who is kind, intelligent, and humorous, traits they want in their Spiritual Source.

Choose a Power with qualities you want, and cancel out any qualities you don't want. Give it a shot. You have nothing to lose but your misery.

MY IDEAL SPIRITUAL SOURCE

WANT these Traits	NOT These Traits	Name
On hand at all times	Punishing	God
Smart	Critical	
Forgiving	Grudge-holding	
Humorous	Scary	

God will set you straight in your financial thinking, and tell you the truth, without harming you. God will help you make better decisions in all areas of your life including money management, and inspire your best life.

ASK

Now that you have a positive source in mind, *use* it. *Ask* God to break the magnetic tractor beam that keeps you buying too much. Ask your God for help to stop trolling store aisles to see what's what. Ask for Help to remove the buzz in your brain, so that you decide in advance what to spend, spend it, and leave the store having spent only what you planned. When was the last time *that* happened?

Connecting to this Source of your own design may feel foreign at first. But that's all right. The process grows on you gradually. Just quit saying *No*. Resign from the debating society. Allow your life to transform from restless, irritable, and discontent, from feeling shame, fear and remorse to one where you feel peace and joy and live in abundance. Now, give yourself permission to enjoy the abundance available in the world. You think others can have it, but not you? You need relief from this type of thinking. Furthermore, you deserve to live in prosperity. Yes, you do.

As you begin to take care of your money, God will shower you with unexpected gifts. It may seem strange; all the same, the more positive attention you pay to your money, the more you get of it. It's almost like God says,

Since you are taking good care of the resources I've already given you, I'll give you more!

Nevertheless, the thought of facing all your life obstacles is scary. That's because, up until now, you have been relying on a wonky mechanism—your own thinking. Isn't it true your best thinking got you where you are today? Now is the time to get guidance of a different kind. Your income will improve and your debting urges will stop.

No one enjoys being under the thumb of a dictator. Credit and debt have become your dictators. In such situations, women sometimes get sick. How is your health, emotionally, physically, mentally? Are you able to pay your fair share of an expense, or separate love from money?

No matter who is to blame for your money chaos, you are the one left suffering, holding the bag with a receipt in your hand. You can't help it. If you know you cannot fix this alone, realize now you are *no longer alone.*

Wouldn't it be wonderful if you felt less pressure around money today? Ask for Help with this. Wouldn't it be great if you were able to relax, and enjoy yourself today? Ask for Help to bring peace of mind, even if only for a few minutes. Wouldn't a break from the obsession around the bills feel like a two-week vacation? Ask for Help to filter your thoughts.

You can have all of this and more by tapping into a positive source of Help, called any name you like, just *not* you. Try one or more of these words, silently or out loud, once or a thousand times:

Please help me! Please help! Help-Help-Help! He-e-e-e-lp!

Don't tell anyone what you're doing. Though your early life made it difficult to interface with the world, the retail environment manipulates you, and your inborn temperament makes it hard to swallow reality, there is a way to fix your financial problems for good. You can experience permanent prosperity, and financial peace of mind.

Ask God for Help. Then, watch for it.

2

❦

NAME THAT DEBT

Power Up!

There are myriad opportunities each day to go deeper into debt and our society smiles benignly while you do it. You start the morning with the newspaper or internet news service paid for on your credit card. This is a debt because the total at the bottom of your credit card goes up, not down.

- As you drive to work, you gas up and pay with a credit card.

- On your lunch hour, you go out to shop for a gift. You use a store credit card.

- You need $5 to donate to the next baby shower and don't have the cash, so you borrow it from your friend. You'll pay it back tomorrow, or the next day.

- You get a phone call from the dentist reminding you about your last unpaid bill.

- You also make a few photocopies of an article for a friend, using company resources.

- You sneak out an hour early because you realize you want that mattress which is only on sale until tomorrow. That's theft from your employer, isn't it?

- You rush into the store as it's closing and buy the mattress using your line of credit. What a great deal!

- You pick up the mail at home, and throw the electricity bill in a drawer. It's due sometime in the month, maybe near the end? You never get it right. Always have to pay a darn late penalty.

- You rent an online movie which is charged to your credit card, and settle down for a nice evening.

It's been a busy day of spending money you do not have. Each one of these is adding to debt. If you used cash in each of these situations, would you have made the same decisions?

Vagueness is the enemy of Clarity. Without seeing clearly, you can go on behaving unconcernedly. Which means, you will get the same results as you've always gotten, and who wants that?

So Many Ways to Debt!

Debt is a hallmark of our modern times. In the pantheon of ways to debt, the two most common, credit cards and personal loans, are the tip of the iceberg.

CREDIT CARDS

While some women manage their credit cards well, paying off their balance monthly, how many women do you really know like that? Anyway, some of them lie and say they do when they don't.

People euphemistically refer to credit cards as plastic. That's like calling a hurricane a summer shower. Did you know the banks are relying on your making a mistake? They admit to making more money on fees and penalties than on interest.

If you want to know how long it will take you to pay off your credit cards, Google a debt reduction planner. Here is how long one of these sites says it would take to pay off $25,000, at 19% interest, and a minimum payment of $400 a month: 100 years.

That's a heart stopper! Did you know research shows when banks do not print the minimum payment at the bottom of a credit card bill, people pay more? However, if you can no longer pay even the minimum on your myriad credit cards, keep reading.

Reality Dose #1: If you can't afford it now, you won't be able to pay it off later. If you are tight for money now, you'll be tighter after this new purchase. If you want to make yourself feel good with some retail therapy, buy a pair of scissors. After that, cut up your credit cards. Don't faint! I heard the thud from here.

Reality Dose #2: You cannot spend money you do not have. Repeat this mantra next time the urge to splurge hits you. What you need is to manage your money so you will have a pile of it for the next purchase. You can do that. There is hope. Stick with me here. You can go from red to black, from poverty to abundance, and from sick and tired of never having enough to grateful and grinning in prosperity and peace.

Let's talk about how most women use credit cards. You start out feeling rich or relieved because credit feels like savings. It feels like this money is yours to use in any way you wish. That is your first mistake. This is *not* your money. This is a loan. If you're using it to eat out, or buy diapers, you feel shame because you can't afford what others can. The credit card gets you out of that humiliating situation. Or, you fritter the money away.

> One woman told me this story: *I can remember my college roommate ordering pizza on her credit card when she didn't have two cents, literally, to buy groceries. True, she did get a meal, but the cost of that pizza was more than the few groceries. What about her next meals?*

Reality Dose #3: Credit card purchases are hard to keep track of. I knew one fellow, a paramedic, who subtracted from his checking account balance every time he used his credit card. What a revolutionary idea! Do you know anyone who does that?

Most women charge, and then charge again, and at the end of the month, feel punched in the stomach by the total.

This is where the minimum balance blisters begin. If you don't pay off the card before you use it again, the blister gets bigger. It gets more painful. You keep spending. The blister breaks, and takes so very long to heal, if it is not aggravated again. Unfortunately, some women go out and push down the pain by buying something else on their credit card. This is the medical model for a serious financial illness.

Reality Dose #4: Emergencies, passing fancies and exaggerated needs blur, and play havoc with your mind. Many women are grateful for their credit cards. How else would they have paid for their unexpected car repair? How else would they have paid for all those school expenses back in September? *And,* how else would they have gotten a dress for the party, or the vacation they so needed to relieve some of their stress, ironically, often financial?

Using credit cards hides your income deficit, mismanagement of what you do have, or painful decisions you need to make, often called Facing Reality.

Where's the Sugar in Life?

Scientists created an experiment with children under five to see if they would balance out their eating if left to pick their own food. For a month, the children had access to a large variety of foods left on a table. Some ate bananas, only, for a week, but then started on another food. Others ate a little of this and a little of that. At the end of the month, the researchers concluded the children did balance out their nutritional needs when left to themselves.

Then, the experimenters added sugary foods to the options. In no time, the kids' diets went haywire. They chose the sweets over all other nutritional foods. Since sugar has no vitamins or minerals and in fact, needs minerals and other body resources to break it down, it would have adversely affected these kids' health over time.

Compare sugar consumption to credit card use: credit cards rob your financial life of other, healthier things.

SPURN CREDIT CARDS

Our society is set up to receive credit card purchases lovingly. It is so easy, so seductive, so much a siren call to our own destruction.

Online Shopping

Shopping online is easy and so convenient, that's for sure. This is probably why your credit card bill is so high. Though we think we are clever in getting cheap goods, are we? Remember travel agents? Travel agencies have experts in travel. They work with the airlines, cruise lines, hotels, and car rental companies every day. They know things you do not, and will not likely find out.

A friend of mine recently went through a travel agency to book her ticket to India. She and her husband thought they had only a choice of two routes and two carriers. Neither was appropriate. The travel agent pointed them in the direction of a third option, with shorter flight times, a better route, and lower cost. She had to pay the travel agent $35. Well worth it. Also, she could pay for her travel arrangements any way she wanted. She paid by debit. No credit cards were harmed.

You could use debit or PayPal, right?

Travel Arrangements

Credit cards are ubiquitous. Everyone not only has one, but they seem mandatory for certain things, like hotel reservations and car rentals. Except, how often do you rent a car and stay in hotels? Is it once a year or once every few years? If it is often for business, can't your company supply you with *their* company credit card?

Anyway, you really do not need a credit card to rent a car. If you let them know in advance, you can leave them a cash deposit. Mind you, it's a large deposit, about $500. However, you get that money back when you return the car. If the rental car company you choose insists on a credit card, find another rental car company who will accommodate you, let your travelling companion use theirs, or set up a secured credit card. More on that in a minute.

You don't have to use a credit card to rent a hotel room, either. You can send them a check for one night's stay in advance. That works. It's kind of old fashioned—writing a note and including a check. You do remember pens. They might even write you back! More likely, they will email you. No need to get sloppy with nostalgia.

Secured Credit Card

This is one way women can use credit cards, not incur debt, and pay no fines. You put an amount of money on your credit card, say $200, and then you spend up to that limit. It's like a debit card, though with the convenience of a credit card. You are simply paying up front. Your bill balance will always be either a credit or zero.

A zero balance on your credit card. Now, that fantasy can be yours! The challenge of this system is that you have to track carefully. If you go over the amount you have placed on your card, you will be in debt, and subject to the same interest, fees and penalties of a regular credit card.

Cancel Your Credit Cards?

Why not cancel your credit cards today? Don't throw up! You can do this. You will need to do two things: cut up the cards, and call the bank to cancel the account. You can do this even if you have a balance owing.

1. Cut up all the cards.

Once she cut them up, one woman made a dragon collage of the credit card pieces, and stuck it on her fridge as a reminder she was free from the debt monster.

No keeping one for emergencies. You know that new shoes can seem like an emergency if you have a big event to attend.

Freezing the cards, hiding them, or giving them to someone to hold generally does not work. You'll take one back, you know you will. Your habit is like a devil with horns, a hot runny nose, and slathering jaws wheedling you into using your credit card *just this once. After all,* the devil voice says, *you really need that thing to have a perfect life.* Beat that rat at his own game. Cut up the cards.

2. Cancel the accounts at the bank.

You can cancel no matter what your balance. It means you will make the payments, but put no new purchases on this account. If you do not cancel, the bank will send you a new card on the expiry date, and you'll have to cut it up all over again. Will you have the strength to do it one more time?

Later in the book, I will show you a way to save. You'll have a Clothes category for emergency shoes, and an Emergency Fund for bona fide traumas, like car repairs or a new stove.

You have no need for a credit card.

LOANS FROM FRIENDS AND FAMILY

Your family and friends may have stepped up to the financial plate more times than they should have by now. Do you live in agony, shame, and anger because of it? Yes, they may be the first in line to loan it to you. After all, they love you. However, at every family gathering, every friend's dinner party, do you avoid eye contact with the person to whom you owe money? Do you even leave the room, or do they?

Assuring your parents they no longer need to bail you out, nor do siblings, or friends will do wonders for your relationships.

When one man told his mother he was coming home for Christmas, she offered, as usual, to pay for his airfare because, as she always said, she and his father could no longer travel to see him. When he told he had his fare, and to keep her money and buy something for herself, she burst into tears.

When parents see their children prospering, behaving as adults around money, they feel they have raised a self-sufficient person. At least, in that way. It is soul satisfying.

Asking parents for advice without your hand out will be a new experience for both of you. In addition, remember, you do not have to take their advice now that you are paying. That may also be a new experience for both of you. Friends are only slightly different. If you have had a supporter who has given or loaned you money in the past, there is an out-of-balance power relationship between you. There may even be hidden resentments, on both sides. It will be a relief to your friends that they are no longer banks. A simple thank you for all their support in the past and an invitation for a dinner on you will begin to rebalance things.

Family and friend debts are the most emotionally charged. This is why some women prefer to pay them off first. By first, I mean after you have read Chapter 9, *Make Things Right* on debt repayment and know what you have available for debt settlement.

Emotions aside, the money you owe them is part of a business transaction. You have used their money for a certain time, and you're going to pay them back every cent they've loaned you. Don't kid yourself into believing people don't remember the money you owe them, however large or small. It is not a gift unless they said so *and* you didn't ask for it.

However, if you begin to arrange to pay these people, and they say *you do not need to do that,* you will have to think it over. Does this gift feel peaceful, or do you feel you got away with something? Do you feel like an adult, or do you feel like a dependent? Repaying personal loans makes you feel independent.

If your family or friend-creditor refuses to take repayments, ask again a little later. They may have had time to realize they need the money, or want it. If after a reasonable length of time, and a couple of offers from you to repay them, they still say they do not want the money, you can do one of three things:

1. Find out if their financial circumstances have changed, that is, they have more than enough money already. If so, thank them for the gift.

2. Donate the sum to a charity in their name, asking them what charity they'd like.

3. Otherwise, you can thank them, commit to not taking unsecured loans again, and tell them so.

Do what makes you feel like an independent adult.

LINES OF CREDIT

A line of credit is not a cool credit card. It is a credit card in a different skirt. Debt with a new hairdo. You're using money you did not earn and will have to pay back, with interest. That is not cool. You still have to make monthly payments from your future earnings for things you bought in the past. You're mortgaging your future. Not cool.

Nor are you special if the bank wants to give you a line of credit. Call it what it is—a loan. You have to pay it back. If the bank gives you a lot of credit, they are hoping, as with the credit cards, you will mess up and they will be able to charge you fees and penalties. It's rather like a parasite/host relationship. The bank wants you to keep enough of your money to be able to pay the fees and fines, yet wants to suck as much of your money as it can while still keeping you alive enough to work.

You think I'm exaggerating. Surely, you say, banks are not that Machiavellian, are they? Be sure: banks are in business. Their business is selling money. What is their goal? To increase their bottom line. And whose money will help them do that? Any more questions?

The only use for a line of credit is to roll over the balances of your high interest credit card debt if the line of credit interest is lower. You do not need a line of credit any more than you need a credit card, less in fact. Furthermore, you can cancel it even if there is a balance owing.

An Emergency Fund will help you out of tight financial spots. Start one today, no matter how small. Put a dollar in an envelope or in a savings account. Your Emergency Fund will make the bank pay you interest rather than the other way.

PAYDAY LOANS

A payday loan is a short-term loan for under $1500. You can borrow up to 50 percent of your next paycheck. You must pay back the loan, plus interest and fees, from your next paycheck — usually within two weeks of borrowing the money.

Besides interest, payday lenders may charge many other fees, such as set-up, administration, processing, verification or convenience, broker fees, collection, loan repayment, return or non-sufficient funds fee, finance or additional fees. That's a lot of fees, and they can add up very quickly, making the original loan balloon:

> *This couple took an $800 payday loan that, in a matter of months, morphed into four loans with an overall balance of $2,200. They were carrying some loans with annual fees of 800%.*

Users sometimes cannot repay the full loan in the short period they agreed to. Life happens. In order to avoid the excess charges, they go to a different payday loan store, and take another loan to pay off the first. This is how people get into the debt trap.

The industry says it's cheap to borrow from them since it's such a short-term loan. Let's compare how cheap it is against other loan options.

Payday Loan Cost vs. Other Ways of Borrowing

Based on a $300 loan taken for 14 days

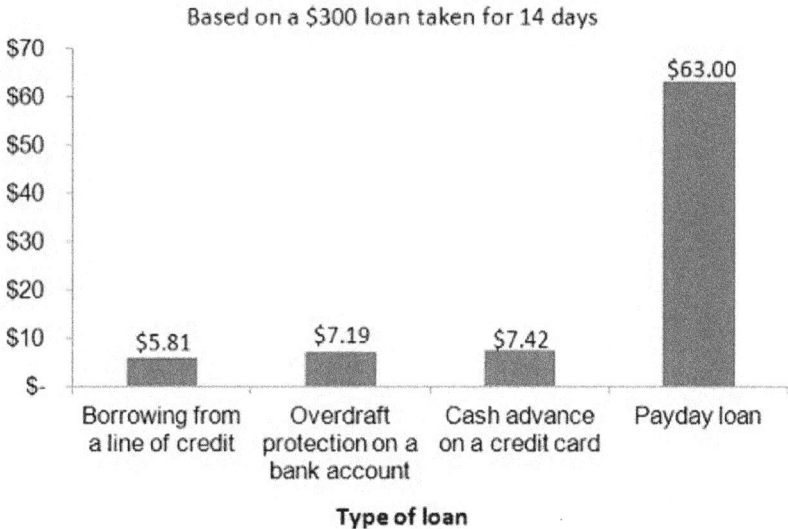

Source: Financial Consumer Agency of Canada

Federal usury law in Canada prevents lenders from charging more than 60 per cent interest, but makes an exception for short-term loans, leaving it up to the provinces to cap the amount charged. Maximum fees per $100 lent range from $17 in Manitoba to $29.85 in New Brunswick; Quebec bans all payday lenders outright. All the same, at those capped rates, a two-week loan can yield annualized payments of more than 500 per cent.

Found on a payday loan site: *PAY2DAY Inc encourages responsible borrowing. An Ontario Payday Loan of 14-days incurs an APR of **521.43%**. Payments made after the due date may result in a returned item fee and returned item interest at 59% per annum. If your account becomes severely delinquent, it may be turned over to our internal Legal Department or external third party collection agency that could impact your credit score. In accordance with government regulations, your loan must be* *paid in full by the due date and may not be extended, refinanced or rolled over.*

As a consumer in Canada, you have rights. Here's a checklist to keep in mind if you presently have a payday loan.

- British Columbia, Alberta, Saskatchewan, Ontario, New Brunswick, and Nova Scotia do not allow payday lenders to roll over payday loans. This means a lender cannot extend or renew your payday loan, charging you additional interest and fees in the process.

- In British Columbia, Alberta, Saskatchewan, Manitoba, Ontario, New Brunswick and Nova Scotia, payday lenders cannot ask you to sign a form that transfers your wages directly to them.

- No payday lenders or loan brokers may communicate with a consumer in a manner that constitutes harassment: They can only contact you a maximum of three times a week only (not counting regular mail), they cannot use threatening or intimidating language, and they cannot use excessive or unreasonable pressure.

If you are being treated unfairly, *complain*. Refer to Chapter 10, *Slay the Dragon* for guidance.

Alternatives to a Payday Loan

Here are cheaper, *preferred* alternatives to getting a payday loan:

- **Make a secured loan**: If you have an item you can use for security, like a piece of jewelry, a musical instrument, or something else of equal value to the loan, use it as collateral for the loan from a friend or family. If you are unable to repay the loan, your creditor will keep the item, but you won't be in debt to them. Look around your place and see what you can use as security and use your item as security for the loan from someone you know and trust.

- **Sell your unwanted items:** de-clutter and turn items into cash.

- **Credit Counsellor:** See a not-for-profit credit counsellor.

- **Cut Back:** Reduce any bill you can renegotiate, and use that savings to pay down more than the interest on the payday loan.

- **Negotiate a Payment Plan:** Some payday loan companies will help you get out of debt by agreeing to *stop* further interest and fees, and set up a payment plan which slows down how frequently you repay, but eventually pays off all you owe. See Chapter 10, *Slay the Dragon* for more debt negotiating techniques.

- **Work** overtime, or ask for an extra shift.

- **Pawn** things you don't need, preferably at specialty stores. Sell your Xbox to a game store as opposed to a pawnshop, and you'll get a lot more for it.

Wiser, yet sadder users say that if you can't afford the expense you need the loan for now, it's unlikely you'll be able to afford it once you get your paycheck, and have to pay all your usual expenses plus the entire loan plus interest. Although governments are clamping down on the payday loan industry to improve their practises, it's not safe in those waters, yet. If you're not in trouble around payday loans now, avoid that route.

STUDENT LOANS

The most pernicious, dream-destroying debt of them all! Many financial advisors will tell you student loans are good debt. Hear this loud and clear: no unsecured debt is good. Student debt is debt.

Run the tape to the end: once you graduate, you will be starting your career at the bottom of the corporate ladder; don't think you won't. In addition, your student loan repayment starts six months to a year after you leave school. The banks give you fifteen years to repay that loan for a reason: you don't have a high paying job for much of that time.

You will also be trying to live a life. That includes rent, food, transportation, and entertainment. Unless you still want to live at home with the parents. Not much glamour or independence in that.

All the same, everyone cries, I need a higher education to make a career for myself, and earn big bucks down the road. Not! You can earn more money as a tradesperson over the course of your life once you subtract the costs of your education. You can go to a one or two-year college diploma course and earn a good living rather than go to university.

I do not dispute the value of an education, just going into debt to get it. You can get that degree and graduate debt-free. If you are clever at school, you can fund your education with grants, and scholarships. If your family is hard up financially, you can apply for bursaries. You can work to save the money before you go. You can also go to school part-time, at night, in summers, and/or through correspondence.

Time is the variable. It may take you longer to graduate, though when you do, it will be without a noose of debt around your neck.

SERVICES TAKEN YET NOT FULLY PAID

This goes for any bill, including utilities. Once you get the bill, you need to pay, in full, by the due date, or you're adding to debt. If the dentist makes payment arrangements with you, though you have completed the full treatment, it is debt. This goes for your car mechanic, or the friend who bought the concert tickets. Once the mechanic has fixed the car, you need to pay for it. Once you have the ticket in your hand, you need to pay for it.

In order to do this right, you will need to know the whole cost, upfront. You need an estimate from the dentist, the garage, and the friend who is buying the tickets. Add in any services charges. If you do not have the money to pay for these things, do not take the service.

For example, if you're having your car repaired and the estimate is higher than your cash on hand, ask what must be done right now. Attempt to lower the bill. If that doesn't work, do not get the repair done now. Rent a car, take the bus, car pool.

If you need dental work done, use the same technique. Find out how much the work will cost. Find out what the dentist needs to do now, and decide if you can afford it. Do not make payment arrangements. If your dentist regularly gives discounts to women without dental insurance, ask for that discount. All the same, do not take the whole service if you cannot pay for it. You will be surprised how you can arrange for only what you need done and not go into debt.

If you have friends who are getting tickets for some entertainment, you owe them the money before you take your ticket. Once it is in your hand, your money needs to be in their hand. Otherwise, you're incurring debt--a personal loan from friends. What if you don't have the money for the concert now? Then, don't go. Save up and go to the next one. There will be a next one. On the other hand, what if you will have the money in a couple of weeks, when you are paid? In that case, do not take the ticket until that time. The thing is your friend can always sell your ticket. Then you owe nothing. On the contrary, if you have the ticket, and haven't paid, your friend is out both the money and the collateral.

Be strict about this. You cannot take things from others when you haven't paid for them. Who wants to be in debt to a friend or a dentist? They notice, and worse, so does your self-esteem.

UNAUTHORIZED TIME OFF

This may seem more a moral issue than a financial issue, unless you are the business owner!

A company fired a technical editor for cheating on her time card. This clever, devious soul had figured out how to position her time card so that the stamp didn't show her two-hour lunches.

Don't ask how. They never figured it out. Most people's minds are not that clever, or devious. She suffered for it in another way. She would be outed by this company if a prospective employer called; or, she'd have a big gap to explain in her employment record.

Unfortunately, there are a few ways to fool yourself into thinking you're being honest when really, you are cheating your employer. For example, if you work overtime, but your boss doesn't pay you for it, and you take time off for personal things during the workday, you'd better track your hours. It may be you're cheating your employer, or maybe you're cheating yourself!

One airport agent worked overtime at night, so he took time off during the day. Since he never recorded it, after awhile, he lost track of how much overtime he was working compared to how much time off he was taking. He was exhausted, though.

The solution is to keep a black and white record of hours worked. Don't cheat yourself or your company by creating a false reality. Clarity and honesty about your work hours is the best way to see clearly what your working and non-working hours are each week.

COMPANY MATERIALS

Office supplies purchased with company money belong to the company. Taking them for personal use is theft. Harsh words, nevertheless, clear. If you take a few things now and then because the company doesn't pay you what you're worth, ask for a raise or get busy finding a new job.

Your integrity is in question. Can you be trusted? Are you honest? You cannot remain unharmed by taking what is not yours. This behavior is a type of debt since you now owe the company money for what you have taken, and you haven't paid them. If you have done this, and cannot repay the company because they have no mechanism for it, try what this woman did:

> *This teacher used the photocopy machine at school for flyers for a personal group. When she realized she shouldn't have done this, she tried to pay the school. Except, they did not have a mechanism for taking payments for office supplies. So, she figured out how much she owed, and donated the money to a charity the school was supporting. After that, she determined to make the additional effort to use copy stores.*

SELF-TEST: ARE YOU TRIGGERED TO SPEND?

Respond with True or False to the following Statements.

1. I overspend in particular stores.

2. I am embarrassed to put things back in front of certain store clerks.

3. After I see this relative, I find myself shopping as soon as possible.

4. When I shop with a certain friend, I buy more than I wanted or needed.

5. I overspend at Christmas or birthdays fearing others will judge my presents.

6. I think that living in a better apartment or house will make people like me more.

7. I have a one-track mind where shopping is concerned. If I want it, I have to have it.

8. I have lost my ability to do arithmetic accurately, if I ever had it.

9. I forget my bank balance minutes after I've looked at it.

If you answered True to four or more of these questions, you are triggered into splurges. It's time to bring those thoughts up to the light of day, and show them for what they are: splurge triggers.

CERTAIN SITUATIONS

Certain places bring up emotional issues which can lead to debting. Knowing about these slippery places can help you avoid them, or protect yourself.

For one Mom, it was health food stores. How could she not have enough money to buy this especially healthy food for her children? It was no deterrent that each item was double or triple the grocery store price. She felt shame she did not have enough money for the most basic of all mother-jobs—buying healthy food. Consequently, she regularly blew the budget in that store.

What to do about that? In some cases, it is wisest to simply avoid the store altogether. If you cannot do that, decide what you want to buy beforehand, make a list, buy only that, and get out. Oh, and be sure to check you have enough money before you head off to shop. Better yet, bring either cash, or the amount written down. Memory can play funny tricks under pressure, and you might remember a balance of $16.39 as $39.16.

CERTAIN PEOPLE

Every time this woman got together with her more prosperous friend, she ordered an expensive lunch, which she could not afford.

Are there certain people who get you into such an emotional stew you can't think clearly? When your father comes around, do you overspend, trying to show him you are more successful than you are? Or, is it your ex? Your in-laws? Your job friends? Your sister? It can even be the unnamed *them,* the strangers in the street. You think they care about what you wear as you walk past them, that they admire you or judge you. Probably, these strangers ring an old bell in your head, harkening back to the kids in the hall at school. That'll send a shiver down anyone's back.

If your credit card or even your debit card starts smoking from overuse around certain people, it's best to do a little prep work before you meet up.

- Write a gratitude list about all the good things in your life. This will bulk up your self-esteem. Then, try not to start conversations that lead you into the abyss, like comparing their lives to yours--compare and despair, every time. Don't fall into that self-abusive trap.

- Remind yourself of the negative things you know about them. No life is perfect, not yours and not theirs.

- Leave their presence. Go to the bathroom!

- Focus on the other people around you. Determine to be of service to someone there, and that will immediately help you forget about your own problems.

- If you can do none of these things, avoid that person for a while.

CERTAIN EVENTS

Do certain events catch you sleeping financially? Lunches and gifts for the colleague who's leaving the company, office parties, wedding invitations, or holiday celebrations are a few of the irregular but predictable money suckers. Special holidays are notorious for incinerating bank accounts: Christmas, vacations, and school start-up. New clothes, hair appointments, airfare, and gifts. All these cost big bucks. The less money you have available, the more inadequate you feel, the more likely you are to overspend to avoid looking and feeling like a loser to *yourself.* Complex!

Instead, you can plan for them. Set up a calendar of the events that normally cost you quite a bit. Use standard monthly calendars, or download interactive calendars. Mark in cyclical events, like Christmas, and other special events for this year, like a wedding. As others come up, put them in.

Initially, this might scare you. Where will you get all that money? Here's where: set up two savings categories: Special Events, and Gifts for Others. The Special Events category will have money in it for those and the Gifts for Others will take care of the rest. Even if you only have a little money to put into those categories, it adds up week by week.

ADRENALINE ADDICTION

I've alluded to this already. There is a physical component to shopping for many women. Their faces flush, their eyes brighten, and their breathing speeds up. The rush is akin to that of gamblers or extreme sports enthusiasts.

Once the body has gotten its hit of adrenaline, it's like a drug fix. It can become an addiction, and hard to give up. There are other ways, more acceptable ways, to deal with adrenaline hunger:

- Do a sport

- Exercise

- Work on a project which excites you

- Go somewhere you have never been, even on a bus.

How to Avoid an Adrenaline Rush

However, if you are in the middle of a shopping trip, here are some ways to get and stay calm.

1. Pray before you enter the store. Try this one:

God, guide and protect me as I shop in this store.

2. Make a list before you leave the house, or certainly, before you enter the store.

3. Once you have a list, check how much money you have to spend. That'll sober you up. Do all this before going in the store. What with the lights, and noise and crowds, it is not an atmosphere conducive to sane thinking.

4. With your list in hand, and money accounted for, get the stuff, and get out. Do not troll through the aisles seeing what's what. The stuff will hook you. Psychologists whose only job is to make you want to buy the stuff have engineered item placement on the store shelves. Will you let

Machiavellian minds control you? Think of it as a video game. Avoid the evil traps.

5. You're trying to overcome a bad habit. Impulse shopping is like cigarette smoking. An unhealthy habit can be broken, although with effort. Doing your shopping this way will get home with what you wanted, and not one more cent of debt.

6. Then give yourself a no-cost, well-earned reward, like a self-hug or a drink, a healthy drink. We don't want to substitute alcoholism for shopping addiction. Good grief. Help us, Lord.

7. There is also another way to deal with the adrenaline hunger. Get calm. Adrenaline is the fight or flight response of the body and it exhausts the adrenal glands. That is why we don't get that feeling too often. So, learn to meditate.

Meditation

What was once a silly-looking posture made fun of in cartoons has now become a growing movement. There are books galore, tapes, videos, schools, even countries where meditation is encouraged. The one statistic that always fascinated me was the experiments done with Buddhists monks who meditate for hours each day. In testing their brain waves, researchers discovered monks had a much happier brain pattern than most anyone else. What's more, it was solely attributable to meditation. Now if that isn't an encouragement, what is?

Don't worry. Meditate. Get happy! More on this in Chapter 11, *Prosper Now*.

FAULTY REASONING

1. *You need a new dress because everyone has seen the old one at the last party.*

2. You deserve a new car because at your age, you should have one.

3. A better address will get you better friends or dates.

4. A bigger house will make your family fight less—well, that one may be true if you stick each person in a room alone.

Each of those common but painful thoughts implies you are not enough. What you look like, what your personality is like, your accomplishments, your character, none of it is good enough or as good as other women. Then again, you know that is not true.

Though some women have more than you, some women have less. Some women are better looking than you, but others aren't. Some women are smarter than you, sweeter than you, or more talented than you, then again, many aren't.

Face it. You're a normal person, with assets and defects. The plain truth is you're neither better nor worse than most of the women in the world. We all struggle with our character flaws, and so we should, to improve as human beings. All the same, we have delightful parts of ourselves.

Therefore, you don't *need* a new dress because several people saw you in the old one, once. Strangely enough, you are not the center of everyone's attention. Instead of dressing to impress, you might look forward to talking to the women who will be there. What a novel idea. Change the focus of the evening from dressing beautifully to behaving beautifully, showing interest in other people's lives, listening if they have a problem. Boy, will you get invitations after that!

As for deserving the material things at your stage in life, look around you. Do you have a roof over your head? Do you have food in the refrigerator? Do you have clothes in your closet? Then, you're all right today. Rather than focusing on what material possessions you don't have at this stage, try looking at the quality of your relationships. How attentive are you to your friends, spouse, kids, siblings, parents? Are you an honest, hard working employee, boss, colleague at this stage in your life? If you are, great. Then again, if not, time to pay attention to *that* rather than distracting yourself with material toys to put you further into debt.

Here is more faulty reasoning.

a. Can't pass up a good deal

Ask yourself if you would buy that sale item if it were full price?

b. Can't buy just one.

If the item is practical, or beautiful, and you have decided, *in advance*, you want it, could you buy just one?

This client once bought her husband five pair of pants on sale, a good sale: $5 each, for men's slacks! How could she pass that up? When she got them home, two pair fit fine, but the others did not work out for various reasons. As a result, she'd ended up buying two pair of pants her husband liked, had to donate the other three to the Salvation Army. They appreciated them, no doubt.

If you can pass up a good deal, or buy one of an item, you won't end up with a house full of bargain basement junk. That is a sure way to save money.

OBSESSIONS

Obsessing about things you want can be another trigger. Once the mind turns to having a certain item, it locks on like a magnetic tractor beam. Furthermore, once the shopping begins, without a list that is, buying things creates its own electric current. There is very little you can do once you're in the middle of the shopping obsession.

Like the 12-step program, Alcoholics Anonymous, points out, *one drink is too many and a thousand isn't enough.* Any alcoholic will tell you the thinking is so seamless before that first drink. Sometimes there is unhappiness, or a happiness that begs for a celebratory drink. Sometimes, there is nothing at all. The alcoholic enters the restaurant, orders a glass of pop, thinks that rye would go nice in that, and orders one. No thought to the outcome. It's almost like there is a devil on their shoulder, waiting for a mindless moment. Once the rye is in the coke, and that goes down easily, the alcoholic thinks, another would be fine, too.

For some women, the brain works like that around shopping. Likewise, there is no defense against that first debting urge except to have decided *in advance* you will not use credit cards, you will check your funds to see if you have enough money, and you will have a list of the items you want, and you have asked for Help.

What are your present obsessions? Do you want that car, house, apartment, tool, or dress to impress? Who is it you are trying to impress? Is it someone alive, who is critical of you, or someone dead who was critical of you?

One travel agent I know got a call at work from a woman who wanted to fly to New York City first class. She wanted to rent the biggest car she could, a Cadillac, and stay in the most expensive hotel on Fifth Avenue in the bridal suite. She kept saying she wanted the most expensive of everything. Her voice sounded tight, controlled, as they went through the reservations. Finally, she heaved a great sigh, and cancelled everything. Then she told this story:

*She had gone on a visit to meet family in New York City the year before. She'd had to do it on a tight budget, but she got there. Unfortunately, she felt the poor relation. When she returned home, she determined to go back the next year, except in **style**. All year she scrimped so she could afford the most expensive of everything. However, after ordering it all, she realized she could not erase the bad experience of last year this way. What she decided to do was to book a nice sun vacation for herself later that winter, and she hung up.*

That is a healthy ending to a story of obsession. Facing reality, saving for those things you want, nice things, lovely things, is fine! Create a savings fund called Mediterranean Cruise, or Harley Davidson or Prada purse, and start plugging money into it from every paycheck. Start with one dollar a pay if that's where you are right now. Seeing you are honouring your fondest wish is soul expanding. While you won't get on the cruise or a motorcycle or that purse at one dollar a month, you will find you can portion off a little of any windfall moneys that come your way.

Now that will give you a healthy adrenaline rush!

INACCURATE ARITHMETIC

A real splurge trigger may be your inability to accurately add and subtract, multiply and divide. Since shopping can cause a strange haze to come over your brain, while in normal circumstances you're a reasonable mathematician, while shopping, you may make big mistakes.

So? Use a tool. Carry a calculator; use your phone, iPad, Blackberry, or the technology of your choice. You will be the envy of all the shoppers in the store, believe me, when you whip out your adding tool, total up your potential purchases, add the tax, and begin to take a couple of things out of your shopping cart. Additionally, you will be your own best friend when you step out of that store, having a bag of stuff you really like, and no new debt.

SHORT MEMORY

This is an odd yet common splurge trigger. You think you know how much money you have. You had $45 a while ago, and you haven't bought anything new recently, so you should still have $45. If you dare to check yourself, you may see you only have $23. You forgot about the watch you bought. Memory is a funny thing. I think mine is about three seconds.

For some women, numbers do not stick. Maybe it's wishful thinking, or maybe it's an undetected disability. That is why we have that high tech invention called print. Write down what you spend so you can subtract from what you have. The balance is available for shopping. Not rocket science, but practical and valuable to you.

PRACTICAL SOLUTION:
Splurge Triggers

B ecome aware of your slippery places. Awareness is the first step when you are trying to change. Track your behavior and your thinking to increase your defense against sneak splurge urges. Starting from today, go back to the last time you splurged because of one of your triggers. Using what you have learned, ask for Help to think of new ways of managing these situations in the future.

Once you have good ideas for resisting a spending urge triggered by your slippery places, write them down. Carry the ideas with you for easy referral. You'll see the next time the urge to splurge comes up, your mind will suddenly consider a healthier alternative.

SPLURGE TRIGGERS

Splurge Triggers	When	What To Do Instead Of Splurging
Certain events: names	Christmas. Trying to compete with the in-laws.	Remind myself that gifts are not love.
Certain people: names	Old school friend, Cheryl. When we go out to dinner, she likes the fancy places.	Suggest we take turns choosing the restaurant.
Certain Stores: names	Middle Earth health food store.	Go in with a list and get out!
Faulty Reasoning	Can't pass up a good deal.	Buy only *one* thing, *if* it's on my list.
Inaccurate Arithmetic	When buying clothes, I forget the tax, or add incorrectly.	Carry a calculator in my purse.
Obsessions	I love leather jackets and can't stop thinking about a green one.	Start a savings category for this item.
Poor Impulse Control	Once I start buying, it's like frenzy.	Pray for protection before I enter a store. Go in with a list and pray for Help to get out.
Short Memory	I can't remember how much I have in any category.	Bring my spending Plan with me in my purse.

QUICK FIXES

How many of these popular fixes have you tried already? Yet, have any worked for long? If you've skipped one or two, don't bother. Take this short cut: read where they fail women, and learn how you can do better yourself.

Tighten Your Belt Tighter?

Some money gurus recommend deprivation as the ideal debt-repayment strategy: They say to cut out movies, restaurants, cable TV, new clothes, and vacations, that is, the pleasures of life. After all, they argue, you want to pay off that debt fast, don't you?

Belt-tightening can only go on for a so long though, before the buckle breaks, and the pants fall off. Dieters know this. When they stay on a strict diet for long, at some point they rebel. Then they wolf down a whole whack of forbidden foods, ending up weighing more than before they started. The truth is the human spirit cannot survive constant deprivation. Fight it if you will, human nature rebels against lack of enjoyment. Yes, you need pleasure in your life to get lasting prosperity.

> *When this mother began her Spending Plan, she included both a Debt repayment envelope, and an Entertainment envelope. To her, entertainment meant a movie and snacks for her husband, herself, and their two kids. Accordingly, every pay period she put $15 in an envelope marked Entertainment. She saved for a couple of months and then used her $60 for a family outing.*
>
> *No doubt, she could have paid down her debts faster without spending on Entertainment. However, to her, this category meant play. She avoided the pattern of all work and no play making her a resentful and about- to- debt-again woman.*

If you were a car, would you be the stripped down model? How stripped down? No air conditioning? Radio, CD player? Moon roof? Leather seats? Cruise control? Would you have the econo model because you really could not afford the bells and whistles, or because they were too frivolous for you?

Some women have forgotten looking pretty isn't only for their partner's benefit. Makeup can be only for them. It is not wasted money.

During one counseling session, as soon as I asked, "Where is money for you?" this woman began to cry. "There is no money for me," she said, "not even for a tube of lipstick."

We lowered her Debt Repayment to her mother by $10 a pay. Her mother was perfectly all right with that though it would take a little longer to pay off that debt. In the meantime, she had a personal allowance. First, she saved for a lipstick, then for magazines, and then for lunch out with friends.

Mind you, some women pride themselves on their parsimony. For them, being frugal is a valued lifestyle choice. In spite of this, there is a difference between thriftiness and deprivation.

SELF-TEST: Are You an Anorexic Spender?

Answer Yes or No to the following questions:

1. **Do you wear your kids or spouses' items rather than buying your own?**

2. **Is your purse or underwear falling apart?**

3. **Do you need to go to the dentist or medical practitioner yet haven't because of the expense?**

4. **Are your shoes or boots in poor shape but you wear them anyway?**

5. **Are the bulk of your clothes old, by your friends' definition of old?**

6. **Do you hold it in instead of going to the washroom when the first urge hits?**

7. **Do you serve yourself last in most things?**

8. **Do you deny yourself small pleasures, like entertainment?**

9. Every time you think of spending on a nice treat, does a voice bellow: '*Who do you think you are???*'

If you see a pattern, having answered Yes to four or more of these questions, you are budgeting yourself within an inch of your life, an abundant, joyful life.

You have many reasons why you do this. Maybe you are not living the life you desire. I am not talking about the mansion, the servants, and the trips; I'm talking about the real life you secretly dream of. It may be a family of your own, working as artist, or running a business; however, it is your place in the world. Are you filling it?

While understanding why can be fascinating, it will not change your behavior unless you take action. You need balance, and the key to balance is considering your needs, and wants. Acknowledge you deserve a pleasant life.

Your spending habits are at their best when they realistically reflect your needs and wants. It is the best insurance for avoiding new debt. It's just everything will happen a little slower. Your Play category may start at $3 a pay. You can choose to go for coffee, buy a comic book, or swim at a community pool. On the other hand, you can save for something else you want, not need.

This is how a Spending Plan, discussed more later, differs from a Budget. A budget restricts options; a Spending Plan chooses between options. Stop tightening the belt so tight it strangles you, and welcome a balanced life without deprivation.

Credit Counselors

Many financial gurus suggest seeking help from credit counselors. Here's what these people can do for you: they can contact your creditors, and negotiate repayment terms, such as less interest. It sounds good, doesn't it? Because credit counselors hide you from the real consequences of your debting behavior, they rank up there with your parents bailing you out if you promise never to debt again. Have you had that experience? And did you debt again?

The problem is hiding like a little kid behind a Big Brother. What do you learn? If credit counselors get you out from under, making it easy for you, you will debt again. Why not? You still have that big brother to fight your battles. That's not exactly how adults behave.

Also, as parents, we want to model adult behaviour for our children. Would we want them to avoid personal responsibility?

Unfortunately, human beings tend to learn more from pain than from easy solutions. What you need to do is face the hard consequences of your poor money handling like a grown up. Scary though it is, it is the beginning of becoming a money-wise woman.

What is the difference between a woman and a girl? Is it only the physical, or is it also an attitude. It is easy to spot a woman vs. a girl by her choice of words, and her decisions. She is attractive, and like attracts like. Men who are also responsible and mature notice.

Is this *Really* Normal?

Other common advice from money articles suggests what the *average* family of four should spend. Where do these percentages come from, some mysterious, otherworldly place? Here's an example:

NORMAL? MAXIMUMS

FAMILY INCOME OF $3,000 NET A MONTH:		
HOUSING rent or mortgage, property tax	35%	$1050 per month
UTILITIES heat, electricity, water, phone, cable TV, internet	5%	$150
FOOD meals at home, lunches for school or work	20%	$600
DEBT car loan, line of credit, credit cards, loans, etc	20%	$600
SAVINGS University or college funds, vacations, Christmas, emergencies	10%	$300
REST OF LIFE clothes, hair, cleaning supplies, car insurance, birthdays, car registration and license fees, charity, computer, cosmetics, entertainment, entertaining, pets, garden, home décor, vitamins, magazines, office supplies, professional fees, vacation, alimony, exercise, classes, books/CDs	10%	$300

Look at the *Rest of Life* amount. Can you really pay for all 21 items out of 10% of your income? Car Insurance, alone, would eat up half of it. That leaves very little for your enjoyments in life. This is nothing short of impossible, and demoralizing for most women's families. While the Rest of Life is low, we can see why: Debt Repayment is high. By this point, you know depriving yourself to pay down your debts fast is a sure way to debting again.

Pay It All Off

Another solution seen in the media about debt repayment is the 'real-life' story of a family who suddenly gets a large money gift, like a dividend, a bonus, or an inheritance. With a flourish of trumpets blaring, they use it to pay off all their debts. Then they wipe their brows and say, '*Whew, wasn't that debt awful? Well, we've certainly learned our lesson.*" Cut to the bright sun shining down on a darn nice house in the suburbs. This is less a money management strategy than an object lesson in how some women are lucky and you're not.

Still, is it even appropriate to dump all of a windfall on debt? Once the pain of the debt is gone, and the flood of relief is over, you might think it's o.k. to debt, a little. After all, aren't you debt-free? The devil is hissing in your ear!

One deprivation guru bragged about a family who narrowly missed declaring bankruptcy by ploughing all windfalls into debt repayment, depriving themselves of everything along the way. Then he had to tell the whole truth: within two years, the family was back in debt to the tune of $42,000.

Instead of dumping all the bonus or inheritance on your debt, split that windfall into thirds.

WINDFALLS

To spend, save, and keep your windfall all at the same time, divide the money using the Rule of Thirds. Deposit a third to the Past, the Present, and Future categories. The Past refers to debts still owed. The Present refers to needs, wants right now, or something you will be buying in less than a year. And the Future refers to long-term savings, like a house, a car, investments, or building up your Emergency Fund. Vacations often get a share of the money from either the Present or the Future.

You won't feel deprived because you are going to spend some of the money on your family, soon. You won't leave yourself vulnerable to emergencies in the future because you have an abundant and growing Emergency fund. In addition, you will see your debt melting slowly away.

Now, you may never get a large inheritance, but you most certainly get small, unexpected sums of money now and then: a rebate you'd given up hope on, a tax refund you didn't expect, a bonus or cash birthday gift. Split all windfalls into thirds. Nothing dramatic. A little here, a little there. Sane spending, calm money management. That's one of your financial goals.

Latte-a-Day Debt Repayment

One book makes debt repayment seem like child's play. The author says break your debt down into a daily number. It's not that this isn't a good perspective. Its aim is to lower the panic around having to pay off so much debt, and to make it seem doable. But, is it? Take a debt of $20,000. That's $55 a day you need to cut from your daily spending. Surely, it is realistic for your family to do that! Really? Let's try it:

PROPOSED DAILY SPENDING REDUCTIONS

DATE	ITEM	SAVE	GOAL: $55 a day
Monday	No latte	$5	$5
	Bag lunch	5	10
	No cookies in kids' lunch	.50	10.50
	No bacon for breakfast	.57	11.07
	No pop for lunch	1.50	12.57
	Pasta with no meat in sauce for dinner	2	14.57
	Turn out lights in house more	1	15.57
	Turn down thermostat	2	17.57
	Think out errand route to save gas	1.50	19.07
Short of Goal: $55-$19.07 = $35.93			

You are $35.93 short of your goal. So, maybe today you avoid clothes shopping. Although, can you do that everyday? What if your spending is cut to the bone already? This system seems so easy, but it doesn't work in real life. And when you can't make yet another quick fix work, it brings on a sense of hopelessness.

The fact is there is a way out of debt. Balance debt repayment with other parts of a pleasant life. Addressing your needs and wants, figuring out your spending plan, contacting creditors and negotiating a longer term for debt repayment, these are the real steps to lasting financial solvency and prosperity.

Line of Credit

Say your roof springs a leak, and the car breaks down. In a recent article in Reader's Digest, a financial counselor, herself a former debtor, advised readers to use a line of credit. She did not believe in keeping a large sum of money in a low interest bank savings account as an Emergency Fund.

Some people think a line of credit is safe to use at will because it is a secured debt, usually against your house. This is true, though there is a danger here. Simply because there is money available to you doesn't mean you should use it. Buying a new outfit for a wedding, unless it's yours, is not an emergency. Redecorating your house is not a sensible use of a line of credit while finishing your basement for rental may be. In every case where you think you want to take out a loan on your house, and that's what you are doing when you tap your line of credit, talk to a trusted advisor or two, not someone at the bank!

By the way, did you know if you have a bank account at that bank, and you're slow to pay or miss a payment on your line of credit, the bank can go in and take the money from your checking account without consulting you? They do not need your permission. Word to the wise.

If your roof does spring a leak, and the car breaks down, imagine having that money in an Emergency Fund that is in a flexible, liquid investment paying you interest, like a GIC which is a Guaranteed Interest Certificate or a TSA which is a Tax-free Savings Account. Instead of having to go into a line of credit, and more debt, expect one emergency every year or two, and get going now on an Emergency Fund; even $1 a pay is more than you have now.

Debt Settlement, Consumer Proposal, Bankruptcy

More than 118,000 Canadians declared insolvencies in 2012, that is, declaring bankruptcy or filing for a consumer proposal. The numbers that are creeping up most are in the pre-retirement segment, ages 50-59. I discuss Debt Settlement, Consumer Proposals, and Bankruptcy in Chapter 9, *Make Things Right*. Suffice to say that some advisors recommend them when situations warrant. But, which one is more likely to net you permanent restraint from debting?

> *When this woman asked her father to bail her out of debt twice, he did. However, the third time, he refused. So, she declared bankruptcy. This brought her the relief from creditors she desperately wanted. However, a few years later, she was back in debt more than before. More than 10% of people go bankrupt more than once, that's 12,000 people a year.*

None of these temporary techniques will work for you, permanently. How many money books have you already read, how many money seminars have you already attended, and how many guaranteed, sure-fire systems have you already tried? Your heart is in the right place, your motive is excellent, yet are things fixed?

SPIRITUAL SOLUTION: Debt Reduction Attempts

Y ou have chronic issues around money which you have been battling for years and years. So, it does not make sense to expect a solution which is a band-aid to heal your raw wound.

Prove it to yourself: quick fixes do not work for women who have chronic money problems. Look at this woman's efforts; then create your personal chart:

Sample DEBT REDUCTION ATTEMPTS

TYPE	WHEN	HOW MANY TIMES	RESULT
Belt tightening	In my 20's, when first married, when the kids were born, before I went back to work full-time,	8, at least	Never lasted. Had binges of spending, especially on vacations
Line of credit	Considered but not taken	0	Afraid of it
Credit counseling	Once the second child was born	1	Couldn't apply it to my real life
Bankruptcy	Considered but not done	0	Afraid of it
Normal family expenses	Before we bought first and then second house	2	Got depressed. Did not apply to our family
Windfalls	Lawsuit payout	1	Money disappeared, think it went to groceries, general expenses
Daily debt repayment	recently	1	Could not take that much money out of our daily spending
Family bailouts	25 years ago, 15 years ago, and several other times	4	The money melted away into something. All gone. Still wracked up new debt.
TOTAL ATTEMPTS		16	OVERALL RESULT: Money disappeared. I felt badly about myself. Debted again, and the debt grew.

It's sobering to do your own list. The good thing is you're trying your hardest to get better at this money thing. The sad thing is to see how all these attempts ended up in bad feelings about yourself, and little progress in the right direction.

Assess advice you are willing to try:

1. Does this system work for women, or is it false hope sold with a catchy jingle?

2. Is it possible this solution will work, but not permanently?

You no longer need to deprive yourself, humiliate yourself, or fail trying one quick fix after another. Reality is neither good nor bad; it depends on how you cope with it. The Chinese character for crisis contains two concepts: danger *and* opportunity. This is where you are now. On the road of healthy and happy money management, there are no quick fixes.

A permanent fix is both practical and spiritual. With that approach, you can start to live your dream life.

3

SPLURGE ON DREAMS
Power Up!

You may or you may not remember what you always wanted for your life. With time, and encouragement, you can dream again. You can discover what work you'd love to do, what you'd like to achieve, what things and what experiences you'd like to have in your life. For one woman, it may be to have a family or live in the country. For another it may be to create a book of poetry, or paint landscapes. For you, it may be to play sports professionally, go into medicine, own a sailboat, travel abroad, open your own business, or go back to school. Allow yourself all your visions. They motivate you.

At the same time, some women use money as an excuse for not doing something. Removing the financial issue does not always change the behavior. Consider any Dream you have. You think the money is your real limitation. On the other hand, if it were free, are there other reasons you might not get it, or do it?

Let's say you want to go back to school, except you don't have the money. O.k., imagine the money is there, granted by a government program. Would you jump at the chance, or would you start worrying about your poor study skills, your intelligence, or past failures?

On the other hand, maybe you aren't sure what you really want because you're thinking about what you *should* want.

Elizabeth Gilbert, author of *Eat, Pray, Love*, knew she *should want* to stay married, have kids and live in the suburbs, except she didn't. She wanted to pursue her career. It was as simple as that, yet socially less acceptable. Because she was killing her spirit by not living as she wanted, she chose to get a divorce in spite of many obstacles, wrote her successful book, and today, is a happy woman. Didn't she deserve to be happy? Don't you?

ENDURING DREAMS

I can't repeat often enough how crucial it is for you to put money towards your dreams. Without this, your money plans are budgets. Budgets limit. The human spirit rebels at such restrictions. Your dreams cannot come second to your bills. They are the *reason* you pay your bills in the first place. Bills give you a place to live and food to eat *while* you follow your dreams.

ENDURING DREAMS CRITERIA

You may be a newbie at this, all the same, it will absolutely work for you. Some people call Enduring Dreams their Goals, or their Real Needs, or Real Wants. The key is duration. This is not a fad, or an impulsive idea. This is an important idea, which, though perhaps small, will move you in a positive, new direction, or reaffirm your present good direction.

Enduring Dreams all have the same characteristics:

- In quiet moments, often by yourself, this vision pops up. It may scare you to think of it, or it may give you pleasure, but every now and then, it returns to your conscious mind, reminding you of its existence.

- The dream lifts your spirits when you think of it. You aren't overexcited, or manic, yet you do feel a smile spread through you at the idea of it.

- You have considered how you might get on with accomplishing it, even daydreaming about the details and work involved, not just the results.

- At some point, you have wanted to weigh the costs and benefits. You may be too afraid to do this now; nevertheless at least you have *wanted* to consider the good this realized dream will afford you.

- Though the dream may or may not be what others think you should do, in analyzing it, you see it is positive for you.

- But, the dream does not only benefit you. Though it may or may not benefit your family, it does benefit others in a positive way.

- And, finally, the word 'enduring' means two things: it has been around for a long time, and the effects of it will be long lasting, and positive.

Dream Fears

Sometimes you're afraid to move towards your Enduring Dreams for fear you won't get them anyway, so why bother. On the other hand, maybe you no longer know what your dreams are. It's been so long, you've forgotten. Or, maybe you never formed any. Don't worry. If you can't even think of any or if you have buried or shunted them aside, you can uncover lost dreams, or create new ones.

But, does it seem selfish to go after your Dreams when other family members have needs? No! You're role-modeling self-esteem for your children or others watching you. Not to mention your being happy and fulfilled makes you a mighty nice person to live with.

Once you begin to pay attention to this deep part of yourself, visions surface. You have the right to have dreams at this point in your life.

Multiple Dreams

However, what if you're one of those women with the opposite problem: you have so many visions you don't know where to start? First, be sure to apply the Enduring Dreams criteria. Using the criteria will help you separate small goals from real dreams. De-clutter your mind. Focus on the enduring dreams.

Then, if you still have a load of visions for your life, ask for the courage to take the next step to fulfill them:

1. One at a time, begin to research and pray about each dream.

2. Talk to a few relevant people to find out their experiences around your dream.

3. Investigate the options and costs of each.

4. See what free services are available to help you, e.g. Your old schools or the government.

5. Ask to feel more enthusiastic, or less enthusiastic about each dream to remove some or prioritize them.

God, please bring me more enthusiasm for this dream, or more uneasiness about it.

6. Put money aside from each pay in a fund until you have the amount you need to start at least one of them.

7. Unexpectedly, though you are paying attention to it, you may find your interest in a particular dream fades. Maybe it's a dream you have outgrown. But, it still has value as a starting point for a new dream. Don't ignore it.

8. Be alert, and notice how your Enduring Dreams are starting to come true!

IMPULSIVE WANTS

But, what if your dreams change every few weeks? You might be dealing with the fleeting impulse of an impulsive want. Here are some examples of impulsive wants: taking a trip with a friend without checking on how this will affect your other needs. Going to a movie, a bar, or a restaurant without planning for the money in advance. Buying an outfit without acknowledging the balance in your checking account, and that the rent is due.

IMPULSIVE WANTS CRITERIA

- Impulsive Wants are always recent ideas.

- They have not been given much sober thought.

- They are likely not good for you in the long run.

- Impulsive Wants may originate from over-influential, or excited friends or family.

- It is a Right Now idea that satisfies a passing desire, but has no lasting value in your life.

- The negative result of an impulsive want can be lost time, lost money, and even lost relationships.

SELF-TEST: DREAMS VS IMPULSES

Review the Impulsive Wants and Enduring Dreams criteria below, then see if you can decide which is which in the two following questions.

IMPULSIVE WANTS CRITERIA	ENDURING DREAMS CRITERIA
Are always recent ideas.	Have been in your mind for a long times.
Have not been given much sober thought.	Have considered how you might get on with accomplishing them.
Are likely not good for you in the long run.	At some point, you have wanted to weigh the costs and benefits.
May originate from over-influential, or excited friends or family.	In quiet moments, often by yourself, these visions pop up.
Is a Right-Now idea that satisfies a passing desire, but has no lasting value in your life.	Though the Dreams may or may not be what others think you should do, they are positive for you.
Often has negative results: lost time, lost money, and even lost relationships.	Benefit not only you, but are positive for others, too.
	Lift your spirits when you think of them.

Which of these ideas is an Enduring Dream, or an Impulsive Want?

1. *You were walking down the street when it hit you: get a PhD in American Literature! You're so tired of your low-paid, stupid job. You love literature. Moreover, isn't your father is a professor and wouldn't you love to show him you can excel in life, at something, at nearly 40? Not sure how to pay for it, but it would be fantastic to be a professor at some prestigious university. Why not apply and see what happens from there?*

2. *You hate your job. You were at a concert last month and are still thinking about the guitar player. That's what you really wanted to be, a musician, not a French teacher. But, could you earn a living? A friend mentioned a music school that hires part-time, so you could keep your present job for now, and move gradually into the music biz. Wouldn't the kids love to have a Mom who is a jazz musician? It would show them you could live your dreams. What a thought!*

Answers:

1. Other than momentarily lifting your spirits, Idea 1 is recent, ill thought-out, and unlikely to be good for you since a PhD is a long haul, often 10 years, expensive, and jobs are severely limited. Sounds like Dad is over influential. It is not that you can't act on the moment sometimes, be

spontaneous, but be sure one financial transaction does not negatively affect other areas of your life. Deciding to apply without assessing how it will affect your other needs makes it an impulsive decision.

2. Idea 2 has been in your mind for a long time, and you are starting research by talking to others, seeing how you can solve some of the problems. Of course, it takes courage to pursue a career in the Arts, and your kids would be sure to notice what it takes to succeed in life. And doesn't the idea make your eyes sparkle! It is an enduring dream.

TYPES OF DREAMS

You're a multi-faceted person, and so you will have dreams for many areas of your life, and dreams for other people. Initially, physical needs come to mind. There is nothing wrong with having a lovely home or beautiful things. The world is an abundant place. And seeing you with wonderful things makes you a good role model for others who may want to emulate your positive, new lifestyle.

Therefore what creature comforts would you love to have? It may be a simple thing like a new mattress, or a grander thing, like a new car. Write down any things you have been wanting for a long time.

CREATURE COMFORTS

Make a list of things you'd like to have. Over time, you will add to or delete from this list. Once you start paying attention to real needs, more forgotten ones will surface.

reliable car
warm winter coat
better neighbourhood to live in
new bed
dance classes for daughter

EXPERIENCES

Next, make a list of the experiences you'd like to have: the places you'd love to visit, or things you'd love to do.

visit Newfoundland
go to Paris
climb a mountain
go on an African safari
road trip to Yellowstone Park
sail on a catamaran

WORK

Are you working in your ideal field? Does it pay you enough to live a comfortable life? If enjoyment and prosperity are not present in your work life, you're not doing the right job. If you have given up on your perfect job, the world is worse off, too. Happy people creating products or performing services they love make the world a better place.

If you studied something you loved while you were in school, you are on the right track. The fact your acting jobs don't pay the rent says you need to manage your life more realistically, but not get rid of the acting. You need a part-time job that pays you steadily while allowing you some free time to do the acting. It's possible. People are living like this today. If you did not study what you wanted to in school, there is nothing stopping you now. There are night courses, correspondence courses, and government and company-training programs.

On the other hand, maybe you do not know what it is you want to do. You used to know, maybe, as a little tyke. Or, maybe you got a hint at some point in your later life, yet thought the idea too ridiculous, or too much work, or too hard. Getting that vision for your life is the single most important thing you can do to save your sanity today. It may or may not be what others expect of you, but it is healthy, and you feel drawn to it consistently.

Find Your Dream Work

Would you like to know what work would make you feel alive again, enthusiastic again? Think of all the jobs you've ever wanted to do, no matter how crazy. Ballerina, anyone?

1. Search for an online calendar from a community college or university.

a. Read the list of programs they offer.

b. Highlight and save those that sound interesting to you. You may like several, and they may be vastly different from each other. And one or two may remind you of old interests. Highlight them all.

2. Look in the job ads online or in the newspaper for job titles that give you a thrill when you read them.

3. Listen to comments from strangers that come unexpectedly. For example, sometimes, people will say you look like a teacher, a minister, or a cop. Don't take these comments too seriously; on the contrary, don't ignore them. Put them on the list to research.

4. Think of what you're good at. If you have a gift, maybe that's where your real work lies.

5. Use your intuition if you're in touch with it.

6. Go for professional career testing

Let's say you have come up with a starter list. For example, each of these, at one time or another has greatly appealed to you: stand up comic, carpenter, banker, web creator, psychologist, college professor.

Once you have a list, begin testing out each one. Once you know more, which jobs still appeal? In the example, this woman picked three to test out: stand up comic, web creator and psychologist. Then she narrowed it down to becoming a psychologist.

A caution. If possible, job shadow people in the fields which intrigue you because not all jobs which look good on the outside are good for you on a daily basis. Here's a case in point:

One woman, desperate to find meaningful work, went for career testing. When the title of artist came up, she got excited. Except, when the next question referred to working with smelly paints, alone in a small room, for little or no pay, she quickly lost her enthusiasm. She was in love with the aura of being an artist, not the real practice.

A Backwards Goal Setting Plan will help with seeing how feasible and attractive the dream is to you.

BACKWARDS GOAL-SETTING

Once you've settled on a major dream, give yourself a chance to see what it takes to succeed with it.

1. Set a date to complete it. eg. *Psychologist. 7 years from now.*

2. Below that goal, write down what you would need to getting to the goal above. Put a date on that. Eg. *Complete PhD internship in Psychology, 6 years from now*

3. Below that goal, write the things you would have to accomplish before you get to the goal above. One at a time, think it out, and put a date on each action.

Eg.

Complete PhD dissertation. 5 years from now
Complete class work. 3 years from now
Get admitted to PhD program. 8 months from now.

Complete admission application. 4 months from now.
Start admission application. 2 weeks from now.
Download admission application. 1 week from today.
Research training options. Start that today.

Soon enough you are at the present day, and you have a course of action for the next several years on route to realizing your dream. This and this alone will put fire into your life. When you funnel your money into realizing your dreams, you will be a much better money-manger.

OTHER GOALS

For You

What else do you want in your life that has little to do with money? Are there latent talents you want to develop, like dancing or building something, or discovering something? Are there relationships you want to create or enhance? Think about areas of your life which can use enrichment, maybe excitement. How about these:

- creating an aerobics routine,

- learning how to make stained glass,

- learning to drive, *finally*,

- finding a reliable love partner.

For Others

You may have visions for other people, but which involve you. Perhaps you'd like to contribute funds to them, or volunteer your time or knowledge. Think in terms of your spouse, children, relatives, friends, your religion, your field of work, or society. Here are some ideas:

- create college fund for my kids

- create retirement plan for spouse

- counsel kids on career choices

- help new mothers with their babies

- help church with new building fundraiser

After you have finished your lists, review each item against the criteria for impulsive wants or enduring dream. Is each good for you in the long run?

Exercise: YOUR ENDURING DREAMS

1. Read the following chart, a sample of one woman's dreams.

2. After reading the chart, make a list of your own dreams.

3. Measure each against the dream criteria.

4. Write the ones that pass that test into your own chart.

5. Answer the questions for each. It will motivate you to move forward on your dreams.

Sample ENDURING DREAMS

Describe the Real Dream	When did you first think of it?	How often have you daydreamed details of it?	Who thinks you should not do this and why?	How is it positive for you?	How is it positive for others?
Be a teacher	5 years old	Once or twice a year, on and off for several years.	Family and me. Too costly to retrain.	Respected profession. Good pay. Good service to others.	Time off when kids off, so no daycare. Pass on many years of knowledge.
Go on an African safari	9 years ago	Once or twice a year	Husband. Nervous traveler.	Get away from technology, see animals in natural habitat	If husband comes, good for him. Otherwise, gives others a role model of courage in travel.
Study reiki	15 years ago	Once a year every three or four years	Family. Might embarrass them.	I can be useful.	I can help them, especially the very young and the very old.

PRACTICAL SOLUTION:
Fund Your Dreams

I t is core: pursuing your visions will motivate you to work; otherwise, you are trudging through life. Start to fund every enduring dream, even if it's pennies from each pay. Over time, when unexpected money comes in, and it will, you will deposit some of that for each dream.

Even if your income barely covers your basics now, starting a savings plan for your dreams is a promise you are making to yourself.

Once you state your intention to accomplish your dreams, and start the ball rolling, sometimes God steps up with unusual solutions. Take this example:

One woman shared that she wanted a horse. She loved horses, but lived in an apartment, worked at a clerical job, and saw no way to make this dream happen. Despite this, she researched and prayed, calling every riding stable, and voila, she found a part-time job riding boarded horses. The owners were thrilled their horses were being exercised, and she got to ride every weekend.

PARALLEL SAVINGS

Here's how to pay for your dream life. Not all dreams have to come true at the same time. Some need to happen in two years, some in five years, even some in ten years. It's best to save for all of them, though, at the same time, in parallel savings. This means saving for each and every dream, from every pay. It may mean a little money for this one, and a bit more for that one, nevertheless funds go to each.

The amount you put into each dream depends on your other financial responsibilities and your income. I'll discuss how to create a balanced Spending Plan in Chapter 5, *Spend the Proceeds*. In the meantime, start saving for your dreams.

STEPS for PARALLEL SAVING
for DREAMS

1. Do internet research, and put a cost beside each dream. Catch your breath. There is a way to save even *that* much money.

2. Create a timeline for each, that is, how soon you want to realize the dream. Adjust for reality. Give yourself more time; though, stay positive.

3. Finally, divide the total cost by the number of pay periods you'll have before you need the money for each dream. For example, if you are paid every two weeks, divide by 26. If you are paid twice a month, divide by 24. If you prefer to do your finances monthly, divide by 12.

How much would you need to save each year, and each pay period, to save the full amount?

Sample PARALLEL SAVING for DREAMS

Dream	Savings Needed	Yearly Breakdown	Save Monthly
New car within 2 years	$4,000 Down	$4,000/2=$2,000/yr	$2,000/12 = $167 month
House within 5 years	Down payment: $10,000	$10,000/5 years =$2,000/yr	$2,000/12 = $167 month
College tuition for son within 10 years	$16,000	$16,000/10 years = $1600/yr	$1600/12 = $133 month
TOTAL			$467 savings per month

Using this plan, you will live your dreams. If each month you save $467, you will fund a new car within two years, the down payment for a house in five years, and college tuition for your son in ten years. The money will be there.

If all that seems like a long time to wait to get what you want, it is a lot sooner than never! Parallel saving will fill your heart with joy because all your Enduring Dreams get attention and money. Therefore, they will all come true, in time.

SPIRITUAL SOLUTION:
One-Day-Soon
Spending Plan

T o coordinate your dreams with the practical aspects of
your life, create a One-Day-Soon Spending Plan. It is
not a budget. Budgets restrict. Spending Plans make choices. Big
difference.

There are two types of Spending Plans: Realistic and One-
Day-Soon. A Realistic Spending Plan encourages you to choose
between options you have considered. Though you may not be
able to have everything you want all at the same time, with a
Realistic Spending Plan, you can have everything you want, in
time.

On the other hand, a One-Day-Soon Spending Plan reveals
what is important in your life. You can see if important areas are
underfunded, or where you might be overspending on things you
do not fully enjoy. A Realistic Spending Plan takes income and
unsecured debt into account: unsecured debt is any debt you have
not backed up with collateral, so a car loan or a mortgage is
secured debt. However, a One-Day-Soon Spending Plan is free of
those concerns, opening up your life. It is important to know
what you'd like to be spending in *all* areas of your life.

When I was growing up, we used to ask a well-dressed girl if
her family were rich, dripping with envy. Children are so nosey
and rude. Often the response was, *"We're not rich, but we're
comfortable."* Your One-Day-Soon Spending Plan wants to find
your comfort level.

You do deserve good things in your life, a balance between
your wants and needs. Remember, this is not a *realistic* spending
plan; it is a goal to which you aspire. Once you acknowledge your

comfort level, you'll be surprised to find one-day-soon comes sooner than you think!

1. Using the Spending Category Ideas table below, write in how much you'd feel comfortable saving each pay in each category. For example, in your Clothes category, you may want to write $100 a month. This would be $1200 a year. If that's the number you feel comfortable with, not afraid of, or thrilled by, put it down. Alternatively, perhaps you feel more comfortable with $50 a month, or $150 a month.

2. Do not ignore any categories you'd like to have, like subscriptions.

3. Look to your feelings to help you determine the point at which you feel peaceful with the amount.

4. Mind you, if every amount makes you feel nervous, or overexcited, try this prayer. You may have to say this often as you proceed until the peaceful feelings come.

God, bring me a feeling of peace as I record comfortable amounts of money in my categories.

5. Keep in mind this is not considering your *real* income or debts. That comes later. It's more to do with loosening the tight purse strings you have been living with, or, noting overspending in some areas.

6. For Bills, though you may want to write down zero, restrain yourself. Instead, highlight any bills which you think are too high now, and write down what you think would be a more realistic number. Soon, you will negotiate to reduce the costs of all your bills.

Caution: Once you are finished, do *not* total these numbers. It may give you a heart attack. Trust in the process for now.

7. Next to your comfortable sum, write in what you presently spend in each category, on average, monthly, even if it's zero.

ONE-DAY-SOON MONTHLY
SPENDING PLAN

Item	Present $	One-Day-Soon $	Item	Present $	One-Day-Soon $
Books	0	50	Vacation	0	50
Gifts	5	20	Vet	10	15
Massage	0	20			
Tithing	10	20			

SPENDING CATEGORY IDEAS

Business Personals: $	theatre	Investments: $	sightseeing
bank fees	Emergency Fund: $	contributions	souvenirs
cell phone	Food: $	RRSPs	taxis
computer	coffees/teas/drinks	retirement	tips
legal fees	hosting dinners	wedding	train
internet	fast food	Taxes: $	Debt Repay: $
paper	groceries	income taxes	family/friends
postage	restaurants	GST tax	back taxes
supplies	snacks	property tax	banks
trade magazines	water	Transportation: $	credit cards
Clothes: Family $	Gifts: $	airfare	line of credit
accessories	anniversaries	car /payment	Other: List $
alterations	baby	gas	
dry cleaning	birthday	insurance/rental	
garments	cards	maintenance	
jewelry/repairs	celebrations	parking	
laundry	Father's/Mother's day	public transit	
shoes/repairs	holidays	registration	
Children/ Pets: $	weddings	repairs	
pet care	work	taxis	
outings/parties	Health: $	trains	
school	chiropractor	Self Care: $	
sitters,	dentist/insurance	cosmetics	
special foods	disability insurance	gym	
sports	doctor/specialist	hair	
transportation	glasses/contacts	manicures	
veterinarian	health insurance	massage	
Education: $	long-term care insurance	pedicure	
books	prescriptions	toiletries	

parking	therapy	Spiritual:	
supplies	Housing: $	books	
travel	cable TV	CDs	
tuition	condo fees	classes	
workshops	maid/contract labour	donations	
Entertainment:$	décor	meetings	
books	electricity	tithing	
CDs	furniture	Vacation: $	
concerts	heat	cell phone fees	
houseguests	rent/mortgage	entertainment	
dates	house insurance	hotels	
DVDs	maintenance	meals	
hobbies	moving	mini-emergency fund	
magazines/newspaper	storage	tips	
clubs	gardening	transportation	

8. Compare what you're presently spending in your categories with what you thought would be comfortable. Highlight any categories which are way out of whack when you compare Present with One-Day-Soon amounts.

Compare ONE-DAY-SOON to PRESENT

Item	Present $	One-Day-Soon $	Item	Present $	One-Day-Soon $
Books	0	50	Vacation	0	50
Gifts	5	20	Vet	10	15
Massage	0	20			
Tithing	10	20			

Your One-Day-Soon Spending Plan numbers are important, but so is their relationship to other categories. If you see you would like twice as much money in Vacations as in Housing, then you know you'd be willing to live in a smaller place in order to go on more vacations.

A VISION FOR YOUR LIFE

What is your God's vision for your life? Note, I did not say, what is *your* vision for your life. Maybe you want to be an actor, while God needs you to be a teacher. Hey, there is a lot of acting in front of a class. In addition, as a teacher, you'd be able to pass on some of your hard-won wisdom.

The truth is God needs your help to heal the world. This may be God's way of meeting both your needs and that of the world: you want to be in front of an audience, and those students need an exciting teacher who has wisdom and knowledge. Win-Win. Enjoyment is part of any vision God has for your life. Therefore, part of your vision for your life needs to include enjoyment.

In addition, God would want you to have love. Your love relationships may or may not be what you want, but you will absolutely experience the giving and receiving of love if you follow God's vision for your life.

Take a little time now to think of your life from God's point of view. Write down this question and wait a few minutes for an answer.

God, what is Your vision for my life?

Write down what came to mind. A picture of a vacation? An arm hugging you? A desk with a whiteboard in front of it, and marketing ideas on it? Write it all down. It's a direction. Talk about it with someone you trust. You are getting guidance on an important life path.

Don't leave your dreams on a back burner while you struggle to make ends meet. They are as important as your rent or groceries. In fact, they may be more important.

Here is a meaningful story which circulated after World War II.

A man found two dollars. His family was starving, and he needed to buy food. Bread cost one dollar. He bought one loaf. With the other dollar, he bought a rose. When his wife castigated him for this, he replied, "I bought the bread to live. I bought the rose to live for."

You fund your needs to live, and you fund your enduring dreams to live for. As you consistently place money into all your categories, you will feel more motivated and joyful.

4

❧

CLAIM YOUR INCOME
Power Up!

Working, yet not earning enough money to live a pleasant life is one of the most demoralizing and frustrating situations there is. This is a main reason women debt. Except, you do not have to continue this.

The first principle of becoming compatible with your money is to change your thinking. You can have your every enduring want, though maybe not all at once. But, you will start to get some things you want almost right away as you do the exercises in this book. And while you're enjoying those, others will gradually come. Patience will become your new best friend, yes, even you.

Try this prayer:

God, please bring me wonderful work where I do wonderful service in a wonderful environment for wonderful pay.

Even if you work at home, this prayer is helpful. Make it your mantra for the next month. Say it often, with a smile. Then, expect a miracle.

Face Your Income

More income will not solve your money problems. Does that statement shock you? How is it possible that a big influx of cash

81

right now would not fix everything in your life? But, if money solved money problems permanently, then no high-income earners would be in debt or go bankrupt. I'm sure you have had the experience where money came in. You got some breathing room, but in a few short months, you were back in financial hot water again.

Money *alone* cannot solve your debt problems permanently. It requires the help of spiritual guidance, funding your Enduring Dreams, and income generation.

In order to increase your income, you have to know how much you're netting now, *exactly*. Here are sources of money. List any amount your family gets, adding others if appropriate:

MONTHLY INCOME SOURCES

Alimony	$	Annuities	$	Bonus	$
Canada Pension Plan		Child Support	$200	Commissions	
Contract Fees	$400	Disability Payments		Dividends	
Freelance Fees		Gifts		Gig Fees	
Government Child Allowance	$116	Guaranteed Income Supplement		Inheritance	
Interest		Loans Repaid		Old Age Security	
Pensions		Refunds		Reimbursements	
Rent		Royalties		Salary	$1008
Sale of Assets		Social Security		Teaching/Tutoring Fees	
Other Incomes: $					
Other Incomes: $					
Other Incomes: $					
Other Incomes: $					
TOTAL INCOME: $1724 GROSS.		TAX: 15%		NET INCOME: $1465.40	

Has this list given you any new ideas? Star which of these sources of money might net you income which you haven't considered, like getting back that loan your sister-in-law owes you.

INCOME TRACKING

Know what you have. That is the first part of your job. It's as important to track your income as it is your spending. You'd be surprised at the number of women who watch expenses to the

82

penny, and approximate when it comes to income. It's a quirky mind that ignores income while obsessing about debt.

If you have one or two regular sources of income a month, it is simple to track. If your income is more complicated, like a full-time job and a part-time job, and maybe the Canada Child Tax Benefit, as long as it is arriving every month, you can still calculate your income accurately. Then, use that information to set up a realistic cash flow situation.

While you may think you can recite every penny that comes in to your house, it is unlikely you do know how much comes in yearly. For example, do you receive sales tax rebates or small amounts of interest paid on savings accounts or investments? You can save these small sums and earmark them for special events. You can save them in your Income category to cover expenses or unexpected bills throughout the year. Every little bit helps, right? Therefore, focus on tracking your money and write it down. Comb through your memory for the past year, and record all sources of income and when paid, to the best of your ability.

Knowing exactly how much money you get each month will make it easier to plan your savings, and spending. It is a spiritual exercise because you can start to believe you are on the way to more money because you're paying attention. There's a motivator for you!

STEADY INCOME

If your funds come in at a regular time, in about the same amounts during the month, it's easy to keep track of it.

INCOME TRACKING : ONE OR TWO SOURCES

SOURCE	DUE DATE	AMOUNT	MONTHLY INCOME
My paycheck	1st	$768.19	
His paycheck	3rd	1000	
My paycheck	15th	768.21	
His paycheck	17th	1000	
TOTAL			$3536.40

If your income comes from multiple courses, and arrives in dribs and drabs throughout the month, but still at regular times, in regular amounts, tracking is not complicated once you write it down.

INCOME TRACKING: MULTIPLE SOURCES of REGULAR PAY

Month: March 1-31, 2xxx			
SOURCE	DUE DATE	AMOUNT	MONTHLY INCOME
The Star, part-time	Mar 4	$600	
Disability Assistance	Mar 15	180	
Wal-Mart, part-time	Mar 23	340	
Baby Bonus	Mar 31	100	
TOTAL			$1220

IRREGULAR INCOME

It's when you don't know from one week to the next how much money is coming into the household, and you want to be able to pay for your Basics, you especially want to track your income to start beating the bushes for more money if you can see you're coming up short.

Perhaps you work on a freelance basis, on commission, or own your own business where you have a paid project for a few days or weeks, and then you don't. You have good weeks and bad, certain seasons are better than others, or it's feast or famine as one paying job ends before another begins.

In this case, it is even more vital to track your income to see how much you have received, and what you expect to be earning this month. To get a feel for this, fill in a table with your income from last month, as best you can remember. Blank forms can be found on my website at www.stopdebting.com

IRREGULAR INCOME TRACKING

Month: Jan 1-31, 2xxx			
SOURCE	DUE DATE	AMOUNT	MONTHLY INCOME
The Star	Jan. 4	$600	
Sharon's Place	Jan. 17	375	
Toll Agency	Jan 23	300	
Transportation Toronto	Jan. 24	100	
TOTAL			$1375

you can see this woman's income came mostly in the last half of the month. Knowing this, she can plan to pay most of her bills when she gets most of her money. That will help her cash flow situation.

COMBINATION OF STEADY AND IRREGULAR INCOME

Irregular income is hard to handle because it seems the bills are very regular. If you are in the situation where you have a small, steady income and you make money irregularly as well, track it one month at a time.

DRAW FROM INCOME

You may have weeks where you get a huge check, then other weeks where you have no income, slow income, or less-than expected income. The system best for this is a Draw. A Draw is technique where you take out a set amount of money from a source, in this case, your checking or savings account, on a regular basis. The cost of your Basics needs plus savings, determine the Draw amount.

Deposit all your incoming checks into one account, and on the first and the fifteenth of the month, or every other Friday, or some other suitable, predictable date, withdraw a pre-determined amount of money.

For example, every two weeks, on Friday, you withdraw $500 cash from your account. If there is more than $500 in there, you ignore the balance, and take out just $500. There cannot be less than $500 or you cannot withdraw that amount. In this case, you will have been watching your income during the days before, and either made concerted efforts to earn more money, or used some of the saved money in your Emergency Fund to top up your Draw.

Do not create a business line of credit, as some financial experts suggest. That will simply mean you go into debt when your income is less than your draw. What if your income is less for a few months in a row? You'll be deeper in debt, and have to dig out once again. It is far wiser to be alert to your income situation with an Income Tracker, and then find more work if it looks like you'll fall short. It's the *only* way you will reach your true income potential.

Even if you get a large income check, you always deposit the whole amount into your Income Account, and withdraw only the pre-determined Draw amount. That way, you will build up a surplus *float* in that account which you will use during low or no paycheck weeks. It's the Joseph and the Amazing Technicolor Dream coat savings plan: use the fat checks to fund the lean checks.

Here is an example of a woman who has a part-time contract as a College Human Resources Administrator, and a freelance photography business as well.

You can see though her money is coming in here and there, she deposits each check into the Income Account. On March 15, she takes out her regular Draw of $500. That leaves a balance of $230. She leaves the balance in the account. When the next check arrives, she deposits that. Two weeks later, on March 31, she takes out another Draw of $500. And that leaves a balance of $170. She leaves that in the account, and so it goes.

DRAW FROM INCOME

Client	Invoice # & Date	Billed Amount or Part-time Pay Earned	Due Date	Projected Monthly Total	Amt Paid & Date	Draw $ & Date	Running Balance
The Star	M3-04 Feb. 15	$600	Mar 2	$600	*$550 Mar 11		550
Sharon Place		$180	Mar 15	780	180		730
						$500 Mar 15	230
Toth Inc	M3-05 Mar 10	$440	Mar 21	$1220	440		670
						$500 Mar 31	170
COMMENTS: *The Star didn't use one of the pictures, so paid $50 less.							

Fill in a table like this on a coloured piece of paper so you can find it easily, or place it in a coloured file folder called Payment Owed, or Accounts Receivable —make it green!

Where to Put Draw Money

It is best to have two separate bank accounts:

1. The first is an Income Account where you deposit all money paid to you. It can be either a savings or a checking account.

2. The second is a Spending Account. If you think of the Draw as your *paycheck,* then you will start another account, likely a checking account, where you deposit the Draw money you have taken from your Income Account. Since the Draw money is what you use to pay your bills and living expenses, a separate account will make it clear how much money you have to work with every two weeks.

Short of Draw Money?

The amount of the Draw cannot be larger than your income, of course. Consequently, if your earnings aren't keeping pace with your expenses, you may not have enough in your account to pay yourself the regular Draw. By checking your Income Tracking sheet daily, however not *several* times a day, you will soon know if you will be short of money.

Act quickly! Use one or all of these ways to beat the bushes for extra income:

- **Call late clients** one day after they were to pay you, and speak to their Accounting Department.

- **Ask for overtime** or extra work or shifts at your part-time job.

- **Temp work**: get in touch with a Temp Agency, and schedule yourself to work enough to make up your shortfall.

- **Call former clients** and present clients to rustle up work.

- **Sell something**: Look at what you own. Do you have jewelry, an expensive watch, a musical instrument, stocks, or artwork? Go online to eBay, Kijiji, or Craig's List and sell it. Response from these sites is quick, so don't worry about lag time.

- **Take a secured loan**: If you're unable to meet your Draw amount still, offer one of the valuable items you own to a friend or family member as security for a loan. This means you agree to repay the money by a certain date. If you do not, they own the item you left in their hands. Be honest about this. If you cannot pay them back by the agreed upon date, insist they keep the item. Once it is theirs, they may sell it or keep it; it is no longer your concern. The good news is, you will have made money, and you will not have any new debt.

PRACTICAL SOLUTION:
Get Out of Underearning

Has this tracking made it crystal clear that you do not earn enough to pay your bills and the other expenses of your life? Women in business for themselves, those on contract or commission, those with minimum pay jobs, and many others fall into this ugly reality. Maybe you are a chronic underearner.

SELF-QUIZ: ARE YOU UNDEREARNING?

Answer True or False to the following statements:

1. I earn less than other women with my education or skill level.

2. I use debt to augment my income.

3. Many of my clothes, shoes, and other items are in poor condition.

4. I volunteer more than I can afford.

5. I have financial emergencies more than once a year.

6. I often feel guilt, shame or fear, especially around money.

7. I have trouble meeting my bills.

8. I have a pattern of good earning then dropping way down in income.

9. I put off what must be done.

10. I create chaos when things are going smoothly, even starting conflicts.

11. I feel I have to constantly re-prove my worth and value at work.

12. My underearning is causing problems for other people.

13. I deflect ideas to improve my money situation without investigating them.

14. I have poor boundaries with people who then take advantage of me.

If you answered True to seven or more, you can identify as an underearner. This is good because now that you see the truth, you can begin to focus on making changes which will bring you abundance. You're not living a full life if you're pinching pennies.

INCOME IMPROVEMENT

If you need an influx of money right now, there are quick ways to get it and techniques that are more lasting.

QUICK CASH

Secured Loan or Sale: As mentioned previously, if you have an item of value, offer it as security for a loan from a friend or family, or sell it outright. Consignment stores sometimes take good-condition, stylish clothes.

Cash in an Insurance Policy: Some policies have a savings portion. See if you can cash that.

Welfare: They have temporary funds for emergencies. There's no shame in reaping what you have sowed in the past when you worked. In addition, if you feel you really must, you can pay the money back. For more details, see the Government Payouts section later in this chapter.

Babysit: Many mothers like adults to watch their children.

Dog Walk: Visit local pet stores to put up a notice, and speak charmingly to the receptionist so she'll remember you. Put up notices on your communal mailbox, grocery stores, and door to door in your neighbourhood.

Hobbies: Do you love your hobby? Get weekend work there.

House Clean: Molly Maid-type services are always looking for people. It's only temporary. They pick you up at your home and provide all supplies.

House Sit: Let friends and family know you're available to water plants, feed cats, and pick up newspapers when they go on vacation. You might even be able to live in their home for several days, saving you food money, maybe even rent.

Landscaping: Doing the neighbours' gardens can relieve them and bring you some needed cash. Also, landscaping companies always want help in season.

Teach or Tutor: See if you can teach at community centers, or through Continuing Education in your Town or local college.

Visions: If you haven't filled out your Ideal Job vision, do that now. Then, research and pray.

LASTING INCOME INCREASE

These options will be a source of continuing higher income.

If You Have a Full-Time Job:

Raise: The easiest way to improve your income is to get a raise at your present job. When did you last get a raise? What is the process for requesting one? Check it out. You can see if your employer is paying you the industry standard by looking at wage comparisons with online salary guides . Show that and an updated resume to your boss and ask God for the courage to help you ask for a raise.

Keep on eye on the job market. Each year that you have more experience, you're more valuable to other employers. Don't be shy about contacting a recruiter, trolling the online job sites, or letting friends and family, although *maybe* not work friends, know that you're in the market for a higher paying job.

Benefits: Ask for benefits like health or dental care if a raise is not possible. Even more vacation will reduce your commuting costs, lunches out, and stress. Furthermore, and more importantly, it will increase your enjoyment of life. Ask for more vacation time if a raise is not possible, or even if it *is*.

Shifts: Ask for more shifts, either from your manager, or from other employees who might want time off.

Overtime/Extra Projects: Is there something you can do that will earn extra income at your present company? What about overtime, or extra projects where you work outside of regular hours? Ask your boss.

One woman began an office cleaning service, starting with her own office!

Promotion: Is there any chance of your getting a promotion? Check out the job postings in your company, or ask your boss. If you think your direct boss will feel threatened, thinking you're after their job, ask your boss' boss.

Lateral Move/ Change Departments: If you make a lateral move to another department, might that get you in line for better pay down the road?

Change Companies: If all of the above fail, find other companies in the same business as you're presently in, and with an updated resume begin a job search.

Is time a resource you have more of than money right now? If so, trade time for money as you work to get a raise, or move up into management.

If You're Working Part-Time:

Ask for Full-time: The easiest way to increase your income is to ask if there is full-time work in your department, in another department, or even at Head Office. Check out your company's Human Resources postings, or ask your boss.

Extra Shifts/Projects: Ask other staff members or your boss for extra shifts. Ask about extra projects, for pay.

Sales on the Side: Start an entrepreneurial sideline, like Avon, which you can sell to your colleagues. Of course, you'd leave the catalogue on your desk and let them come to you. After all, it is during work hours.

Re-train: Of course, you may have to upgrade your skills to get a better job. Look into government education programs before you put out your own money. Also, ask your company if they co-pay for courses. Speak to a college Financial Aide officer for other suggestions, not a loan. No more debting, no matter what!

Second Job? Taking on another part-time job is not as profitable as hunting for a full-time job. Your commuting costs will be higher if you work two places, and often there are no benefits for part-time work. Use your energy wisely. Pound the computer for a full-time job elsewhere if none is available at your company.

If You're Working on Contract:

To increase your income as a contract employee you can do several things:

Increase your rates. Are you undercharging? I bet you are. Find out what the going rate is in your industry. Check online salary guides to see what you should be getting. Rest assured, you won't get it if you don't ask for it.

Charge for *all* your time per job. How much time do you actually work on each job? Remember, lawyers charge each client for every phone call and letter. Shouldn't you?

Ask for a higher fee at each contract renewal.

Update your Resume. If your company pays more for people with more experience, run your updated resume by Human Resources to see if you have moved up in the pay grid. You most assuredly will not get more money if you don't ask for it.

Ask for benefits. If you're working for a unionized company, you may be surprised to learn there are benefits for part-time and contract employees.

Create a Business Plan. If you're working on contract, think of yourself as running a business. This entails tracking your income, your expenses including transportation, and your time. Create a Business Plan? You may be surprised at how it will focus your work, and generate more income.

If You Work Straight Commission:

Track your Own Commissions. Do not trust the company to be as interested in what they have to pay you as you are. If you cannot do this, get help. If you have to hire someone to set up a system for you, it is a deductible expense. More importantly, it will add to your peace of mind; you will know when you are being paid, and how much.

Sales and Marketing Plans. You're a business owner if you're working on commission.

Joe Girard, the greatest car salesperson in the world, according to the Guinness Book of World Records, had a sales plan, a marketing plan, and a tracking plan. He sold cars, up to six a day, one customer at a time. However, he planned and tracked to be sure he was paid!

If You're a Business Owner/ Self-Employed:

Get a Part- time Job: For now, take a temporary, part-time job. Add that income to your business income and you'll be laughing! This may even generate more business as you make new contacts, or learn new ideas.

Focus on Profitable Areas: Track all income to see its source. Then, channel all activity into building up the part of your business that is most profitable. Spend less time on parts of your business that aren't bringing in any income, like shuffling paper.

Present Clients: Ask your present clients what more you can do for them.

Former Clients: Contact former clients to see if they have new projects, or suggest new projects to them. Ask if they know anyone else who might benefit from your services.

Networking: Even online, there are groups who help each other with contacts or leads. Get in touch with people in your field, people who know you, and wave your flag.

Focus: Get your present work done without getting distracted, and then do other things.

Time Management: Spend your time on moneymaking activities, not paperwork. Set weekly priorities, like this: Urgent and Important, Urgent but Less Important, Important but Not Urgent, and Not Urgent and Less Important. Then use an hourly time planner to schedule all your appointments, obligations and routines, like meal prep and exercise. Oh, don't forget commuting time. Once that's done, you'll see how much time you have left in the day. More than you thought. That's time to follow your dreams.

If You're Unemployed:

If you're not working, let's start from the beginning:

Resume: If you have sent out resumes and not been invited to any interviews, there is something wrong with your resume. Resumes are sales letters. If you're new to the field, put your education first, assuming it is relevant. If you have experience in the field, highlight those jobs. If you have neither, there's your problem! You'd have to see what skills you do have which are transferrable to the new field, and highlight those.

Also, use keywords from the job description. Employers say what they want in the job ad. Tell them you can do each thing they want, or, are a quick learner!

Interviews: If employers are calling you to interviews, then your resume is doing its job. But, if there are no job offers, there is something wrong with your interviewing technique.

Clothes: First, look at your interview outfit. Interviewers make decisions about perspective employees in less than one minute. You haven't had a chance to say much, have you? It's how you look that they are judging. Do yourself a favour, and read the book that coined the phrase "dress for success", the *New Dress for Success for Women* by John Malloy. It's an oldie but a goodie since business fashion does not change.

Standard Questions: If you're dressing appropriately for the type of job you want, and still aren't getting job offers, ask someone to videotape you in a mock interview. Be sure and rehearse your answers for standard interview questions like," What are your best and worse experiences working?" Check the internet for other typical interview questions. Be sure to think out your answers so they show you in a good light, but are honest. They train interviewers to spot liars. Scary, huh?

Body Language: Once you have practised these kinds of answers, and you *have* to practise, look at your body language. Is it odd?

An older man came to me for coaching on interview skills. I videotaped a mock interview. He had a noticeable body tic. He slumped between questions. He said he was waiting for the interviewer to lob the question at him. Then he popped upright, caught the question, answered, and slumped, waiting for the next one. Once he saw the videotape, he stopped that, learned to lean forward to appear enthusiastic, and got two job offers in the next week.

Job Search: The experts recommend you spend at least four hours a day on job search. Get up at the regular work time, shower and dress as if you were going to work. Then head to your computer, or to the library, and hunt. You can even take a coffee break after a couple of hours, like the good old days when you had a job.

Apply in person: Cafes like Starbucks, fast food places, and temp agencies like to see you.

Call Past Employers: Remind them of your services, and see if there are any suitable openings

Friends and Family: Let them know you're looking for a particular type of job, though are open to ideas

Home-based Jobs: Look for work you can do out of your home if you need to stay there. Computer-related work or childcare come to mind.

Employment Agencies: Sign up with *several* employment agencies.

Troll online: Check job posting sites, including Kijiji, Craig's List, and non-profits, such as Charity Village, government jobs sites at the city, provincial, and federal levels, and general or specialized recruiter agencies

Set Goals: Try for jobs at a higher level than your past jobs. Set a number goal: apply for a certain number of jobs each day.

Daily Applications: Send out applications for jobs everyday.

GOVERNMENT PAYOUTS

Fortunately, there are government programs for those who qualify for financial assistance. Go after them!

AGE BENEFITS

Canada Pension Plan

The Canada Pension Plan or CPP, pays back the contributions you made when you worked, and adds money to it, payable once you're 60 years old. Many women prefer to wait until they are 65 to collect the maximum though you can wait until you're 70 and older to get even more. It is a benefit which is relatively painless to arrange. You can apply online. And if you have worked in other countries, CPP will co-ordinate your benefits with them, too.

Old Age Security

Once you turn 65 in Canada, you will get Old Age Security or OAS. Combined with Canada Pension Plan, it is similar to the American Social Security, though not quite as generous. If your income tax form indicates you presently earn over $40,000 a year, the government will claw back the OAS, though you will still receive CPP benefits.

Guaranteed Income Supplement. If you earn less than a predetermined amount, and you'll check the amount as it changes, there is the Guaranteed Income Supplement or GIS. It is *in addition* to CPP and OAS for low income households. The GIS benefit is based on your annual income, or the combined annual income of you and your partner.

FAMILY BENEFITS

Child Tax Benefit

Canada Child Tax Benefit is a tax-free monthly payment made to eligible families to help them with the cost of raising children under age 18. It is an income-tested program, yet the income limits allow middle class families to qualify. For example, net income over $42,000 only has a small reduction, so you can earn as much as $100,000 net and still get a partial payment.

Scholarships, Grants and Bursaries

You can find scholarship listings at the high school guidance departments. If students don't apply for scholarships, they won't get any. As obvious as that seems, students are loathe to apply for them because it is quite a lot of work. They have to write essays, arrange references, and often, show financial need. Force them. Think of it as a part-time job which could net you $10,000 a year, for about ten hours of work. Nice hourly wage.

The government is in the school grants business. Ontario Student Assistance Program or OSAP distributes $350 million dollars a year to post-secondary education students. There are new programs all the time. Presently, there is a 30% off tuition sale! Is your heart beating faster? To get that benefit, students need to apply for OSAP, and be evaluated financially.

Unfortunately, the amount of grant money awarded is seldom enough to pay fully for tuition, books, and living expenses. Therefore, you need to apply for funds from more sources.

Bursaries are an option if you can show financial need. You never have to pay those back. Sometimes, it is wise to apply for a student loan in order to qualify for a bursary. But don't spend the loan money. Student loan money is debt, and you have to pay it back, starting six months after finishing school. Banks charge a regular interest rate, and need to be repaid in full within fifteen years. Remember, students start at the bottom of the salary food chain when they are new graduates. That is not the time to have extra debt payments.

It bears repeating: Do *not* take education loans. Education debt is *not* an investment; it is debt. Go to school part-time, at night, in summers, or online through correspondence. It will take longer, no doubt, but you won't be in debt when you graduate. Believe me on this, if nothing else: education debt repayment is a painful 15 years.

MEDICAL BENEFITS

Disability

Some provinces have a disability program where, if you're unable to work at any job, there is a financial support. In Ontario, it's the Ontario Disability Support Program . You will not receive a princely sum; still, it will keep body and soul together if you cannot work anymore. While Welfare assumes you will get on your feet and become employable later, Disability accepts that you can no longer work. You also get a disability tax credit which is money, too. Once again, we are grateful we have a compassionate society which supports those disabled permanently. It does not mean you cannot be productive. Volunteering, even on help phones, for short periods, may be a boon to your spirit, and a great benefit to others.

WORK BENEFITS

Employment Insurance

If you have lost your job through any means except being fired, you may qualify for Employment Insurance or EI. Actually, with a good explanation, even if your employer fired you, you might get benefits. Quitting without good cause would probably not get you an entitlement. Good causes might include harassment, or bullying. Write it up, and talk with an EI counselor. Other than this, EI is anxious to help you get back on your financial feet. The claim has a two-week waiting period, so you will not get any money from them during this time. If you got a severance package, or vacation pay, they will factor that into when they will start paying you benefits.

EI benefits are based on what you earned, although there is a maximum. The government deducts taxes before they send you the check. Of course, EI is a temporary measure, about a year. EI offers many retraining programs, some of which are great. Lately, EI has come up with programs to support career change if laid off in certain industries. If you think you qualify, check into it now. They don't always last, so call now.

Another thing EI can do for you is help you get to interviews out of town. If you can drive, take a bus or train, they will pay for that. In rare cases, even airfare is possible.

EI also has a program for those who are unemployed and want to start a business. In order to qualify for the program, you need to create a business plan, and if the idea has merit, EI will give you financial benefits for about a year while you also earn money from your business.

Welfare

Check out the facts around Welfare before you reject the idea, or get too eager. It's a hand up with the hope and intention it will be temporary.

You can work and still receive this benefit, depending on the income. You may even be able to keep your assets, like your house. As well, if you are on welfare, you get medical and dental benefits. It is worth considering.

Something few people know about is if your EI payments are due to start, but not for a while, and you're facing financial distress, you can get Welfare temporarily until your money starts to flow. Also, if you're applying for disability, and have to wait but cannot work, you may qualify for Welfare.

Think of it this way: maybe receiving Welfare payments will allow you to do good works you could not do otherwise. Perhaps you will volunteer on a help line for distressed women, visit shut-ins, or read books for the blind through the Canadian National Institute for the Blind.

Welfare is not for everyone, obviously, still it is there for those who need it and want it. Keep an open mind while you investigate.

Food Banks

If things are bad, you can always access food banks. Many of the women now volunteering in food banks once used them. Their situations have improved, and yours will, too. In the meantime, the folks at food banks are non-judgmental, and friendly. No questions asked. When you get back on your feet, you can donate back to the food bank in thanks, as so many former users have done before you.

OTHER INCOME SOURCES

You may not think of the following things as sources of income, all the same, any money that comes into your home is a source of income. This means you need to tend to it, making sure it continues. All of these are income: alimony, child support, company benefits, discounts and refunds, and expense reimbursements, like car allowance.

ALIMONY AND CHILD SUPPORT

Without getting into the vitriol of the thing, let's hope you do get the payments, and on time.

One woman told her departing husband that if there were any trouble about getting the money, she would get a job as a server in the café where he met with his friends. Was he willing to call her bluff? There has never been a problem with the money.

If you have an Income category, whenever this money comes in, stick it all into that pot. And every payday, take out your pre-determined amount, leaving the balance in the pot. If the money is late, this is a job for your Emergency Fund. While you're waiting for your support check, draw out the amount you should have gotten. When the support check comes, repay the Emergency Fund, and deposit the rest in the Income pot.

However, if your partner does not pay *at all*, take legal action. If you want your ex to go to jail for nonpayment, be aware that in jail, they won't be able to support you and the children at all.

If there is no way you're able to get money from your absentee spouse, you will have to improve your own income.

B-JOBS

If your situation is one where you have erratic paychecks, consider taking a B-Job. Many women in the Arts live this type of life. It is wise to sign on with several Temp Agencies in your field, if possible, or simply do office work. You can also sign on to work temporarily in department stores, or fast food restaurants.

No, these are not the ideal jobs, they are your B-Jobs; except, if they support the family, they are honorable.

COMPANY BENEFITS

Health and dental benefits can add 30% to your wages. This is why finding a full-time job is far better than two part-time jobs. Mind you, there are companies who do pay benefits to part-time workers, Starbucks being one, and Home Depot. If offered, it is important to add in this 30% when deciding between two jobs.

FAMILY GIFTS

If your family regularly gives you money for your birthday or Christmas, you can probably count that as income. Of course, the one year they do not do this, it will come as a shock; then again, you have an Emergency Fund, so all will be well. However, family donations should be limited to *unasked-for* gifts. If you ask for a gift because you're short of money this month, that is a loan, an unsecured loan, therefore, a debt. Remember, you are not debting anymore, no matter what!

To be an adult in an adult world, to be self-supporting through your own contributions, to have self-respect and maturity, family donations are best limited to gifts at appropriate gift-giving times. A few bucks slipped to you as you leave is not an appropriate gift since it implies you need financial support, and cannot take care of yourself. Refuse this type of gift. Regain your self-respect.

One middle-aged woman planned a vacation with her mother, assuming she would pay for them both as her Mom had in the past. When she accepted that at age 47, she could pay for her own vacation, and maybe even treat her Mom, she began to save. Good thing she did. For the first time, Mom didn't offer to pay.

INSURANCE PAYMENTS

If you're not in touch with the benefits your insurance company offers, talk to your insurance agent or your company Human Resources person right away. Some policies have little-known perks. For example, Foresters Insurance has a cash payout after a number of years of holding the policy if you want to claim it. It's a one-time payout; still, it is an income source if you need it.

Speaking of insurance, check to see how much insurance you have. Might you be over-insured? If your company has a policy on you, find out what it covers. And if it's enough, do you really need to be paying for more? If you cancel your private insurance, you have saved the monthly premiums, and that is income.

INVESTMENTS

You don't need to be a high roller to have investments. Yes, it is excellent if you have lots of stocks, bonds, market index funds, Guaranteed Investment Certificates or GIC's, Registered Retirement Savings Plans or RRSP's, Tax-Free Savings Accounts or TFSA's, and any number of other initials which we can't translate into words anymore. Alternatively, you can start small. Small investments build your confidence in your ability to handle such things.

Do you have a knack for investing? Some women do. Their intuition and good sense, their research and reading, make them excellent investors. If you can free up some money in your Spending Plan for this, do it, although keep to an affordable amount. The benefits can be astounding.

Dividends are a wonderful source of income in the right hands. Warren Buffet had to start somewhere, after all. Keep a boundary around how much money you will risk, and stick to it.

Women who are vague about their money often forget to count interest paid on investments. A check for $35 once a year may not cause a blip on your radar, except that $35 can buy a dinner out, or a concert ticket.

Then again, are you tracking the income? Do you have a file which records when you should get the dividend, and when you actually get it? Does your file show how much you received last year, or the last few years? Your investment interest is extra cash. Pay attention to the pennies, and watch the dollars grow.

This author came up with a brilliant idea for an investment. She created an Investors Club and sold shares in herself. As a professional writer, she has ups and downs in monthly income, yet over the year, does a respectable business. She asked investors to send in monthly payments for a yearly payout. It took a couple of years to get that business off the ground, but it worked.

Are you in the Arts: an actor, writer, musician, or dancer? Could a variation of this idea work for you?

Some call going into debt for your education an investment. No. It is unsecured debt. It will take 15 years to pay off, if you're lucky enough to get a good job. See the section on *Society Pressures* in Chapter 1 to find ways to complete your education without debt.

RENTAL INCOME

Keeping your house up so it will get a good price on resale is an investment, but the sale proceeds are not part of your monthly income right now. If you need money today, can you make a room available for a foreign student? Can you rent to a college student? Is your basement rentable, maybe with a few, small changes?

Big changes need municipal approval. Be sure and check out what the realistic rental incomes are in your area before you act on this. Still, a basement apartment in your house will add to the resale value down the road, and give you a monthly income boost now.

MONEY DUE TO *YOU*

Search your brain's database for any money owed to you that you have forgotten to request, or given up on from past colleagues, family or friends. Money owed to you may make you feel like a bill collector. But, requesting repayment of a loan, at the right time, in the right way is simply a business transaction. As you intend to repay every cent you owe, and will feel the better for it, your borrowers want the same thing for themselves.

Try this script:

Hi _____: I am getting my finances in order, finally! And I see I loaned you $_____ in April 2xxx. I'd like that repaid. Let's negotiate a schedule and an amount, called a payment plan, that is doable for you, but also respects my need to have the money back.

If you arrange even a small amount paid back each month, say $5, it will be income for you, and a weight off their backs. Of course, if you know they are living a prosperous life, ask for higher monthly payments or even the whole amount right now.

Follow up with them if they miss a payment. Find out what went wrong, and if necessary, re-negotiate the terms of your agreement. You will not abuse your borrower, of course, still do not give up.

Repeat the request:

Let's negotiate a schedule and an amount that is doable for you but also respects my need to have the money back.

Ask God for the courage to do it.

PAST EMPLOYERS

Does a company owe you money for work done some time ago? Can you come up with the details: dates you worked, and hourly wage, and number of hours? You can send them an email saying you will be calling at a certain time. Have your facts and figures handy. Tell them the amount they owe you, and arrange to pick up the check. You can ask a friend to accompany you if you feel uncomfortable or afraid.

If they insist on mailing you the check, ask what date you can expect it. Then follow up if you don't get it by then. Don't be afraid. If you did the work, even if they fired you, they owe you the money. The only exception to this is if they fired you over theft. However, if you stopped working for any other reason, the best you can do for yourself and your wallet is to ask for the money.

Be sure and track who you speak to and when, and get the arrangements in writing. A confirming email from them will do.

REIMBURSABLE EXPENSES

Women who have the company benefit of health or dentist care and auto expenses often have to send in requests for reimbursement. While you are really only getting back your own money, if you also get an automobile allowance, you are paid a mileage amount which is more than you spend each month. You are supposed to be putting the extra into a category for car repairs. Do you? That is, are you asking for *any* money your company or the insurers owe you?

She was a highly paid consultant to a Human Resources firm. All her travel expenses, office supplies, phone bill, and car mileage were reimbursable, as long as she gave in records of what she'd spent. At one point, this woman had more than eight months of expenses not turned into her company, or the health insurance and the dental insurance companies. The details of tracking all this overwhelmed her.

Who can't identify with that? Feeling overwhelmed by financial details is a common problem for many women; nevertheless not submitting your expense reports means you will be out-of-pocket. This caused that consultant to use her credit card to pay for her income *shortfall*, and that meant she was also paying interest on money owed her.

All that being said, tracking those expenses can be a bear. You may find the whole idea so overwhelming, you'd best set time aside, tonight, and begin to get this part of your income organized.

Have you ever tried using a 12-pocket file folder? You can file the receipts by month all in one place. Or, how about an expense tracker online? Working a little at a time, you will get through this. Add two simple file folders and you can keep track of what reimbursements you have requested, and which ones have been paid.

Hired Help

However, if filing your expense report is actually horrible for you, perhaps you could subcontract it to your partner, one of your older kids, or to an accounting student from a local college. Though you'll have to pay them, it won't be more than the expense money you're out.

You can also see if you can get free help from the company accounting department. Throw yourself on their mercy. They'll love showing off their expertise. You may be surprised to learn that banks will even assist you with this. Ask for help. You'll love getting those reimbursement checks.

Insurance companies are pleased to have *you* pay for services and never claim them. Let us not be benefactors of the insurance industry.

SPIRITUAL SOLUTION:
Tall Poppy

T he mind is a strangely dangerous place. It can sabotage you while you're blithely going about your business. For example, you may unconsciously reject ideas that might make you money without investigating them. Or, you may overwork to the point of exhaustion, and then have to stop working completely. Some women are even very uncomfortable at the thought of being the center of attention, and they hide from life and work opportunities.

Re-form Yourself

In ancient China, there was a lovely field surrounded by a high fence behind which was a meadow full of flowers, and especially the elegantly tall, brilliant poppy. Because the fence was so high, the tall poppies were the only flowers the villagers could see, but they were enough. As they walked along the country roads, they marveled at the beauty of these flowers. However, one day the evil emperor ordered all the flowers destroyed. He hated them because they drew the villagers' attention away from admiring him. He sent his men to mow them down. But, it was only the tall poppies which hit the blades. The short flowers escaped. Though they escaped, the villagers who could not see them behind the high fence ignored them.

The sad truth is many women are afraid to grow to their full potential because they will be noticed, and vulnerable, and in the line of fire. What a tragic loss. Then again, there is a way to be all you can be!

1. Do not sell yourself cheap. Checkout the online sites which list salary ranges for women in your field. Place yourself at

the mid-point, or higher if you have any experience or the education for it. Do not ask for the lowest amount, *ever.*

2. Do not take work which underpays you, except as a temporary measure, that would be less than three months, or you will perpetuate your debting.

3. Do not say *no* to money from any legal source.

4. Do not debt, *no matter what.*

5. If you're under-employed, and underearning, revamp your resume with a professional service, practice your interview skills, ask God for courage, and start applying for better jobs.

6. Stop wasting time. Track what you do each day, and then plan your week to meet your goals.

7. Pray for God's vision for your life, rather than yours. What would your God have you do to earn a living?

8. Draw or describe your ideal work, the atmosphere in the workplace, the commuting time, the use of your talents, skills, and knowledge, and who you will be helping along the way. Invite God to change this description to reveal the perfect job for you, at this time. Then, list how much money you'd like to earn, referring to online salary sites.

9. Try saying this prayer:

God, please put your protective light and love around me and let the talents You gave me flourish. Please bring me wonderful work, in a wonderful place where I do wonderful service for wonderful pay.

That should do it!

5

SPEND the PROCEEDS

Power Up!

Right now, you do not have a healthy relationship with money, a healthy balance in your checking and savings accounts, a nil balance on your credit cards, or a healthy savings account for emergencies. Furthermore, you may not feel healthy yourself. You're tense and irritable, or worried and depressed. You may have physical problems from prolonged stress. As well, unfortunately, you may not have healthy relationships with some of your family, love interests, friends, or colleagues.

As the Chinese saying goes, No money, no life. Money is the grease you need for social occasions, as well as subsistence. The problem is, you have no money, and have not had for a long time, and your life has suffered for it. You have made financial decisions, yet were more often wrong than right.

Naturally, you'd have done better if you had known how, except you have tried many ways to get the help you need. Nothing has worked for long. Here's an example of one woman's thinking.

Where's That $40 I Took Out This Morning?

Follow the dark labyrinth of a typical shopping day:

9 am. I merrily go to the bank machine, take out $40 in cash, and feel, what, loaded? Healthy? Happy?

10 am. I hit the gourmet grocery store for a bottle of mustard. You know the gourmet kind with the seeds. I leave the store with three apples, a quart of milk, a chocolate bar, a magazine, and a dazed smile on my face.

11 am. Stop at the library to get two videos for tonight. Oops, how did I get that fine?

12 pm. Lunch at the fast food place, a snack really. I'm on a diet. Again.

1 pm – 3 pm. Have to answer those emails, don't I?

3 pm. Forgot the darn mustard! Back to the gourmet grocery store. Leave with a bottle of mustard, a bag of onions, and a bar-b-q'd chicken for dinner. Too tired to cook tonight.

4 pm. Hit the emails, again. Where do people find this stuff? Love the music things.

5 pm. Call from friend to go out to dinner. Put bar-b-q'd chicken in the fridge. Put on my coat. Get in the car.

5: 05 pm. Count money left in wallet. Hey! Where's that $40 I took out this morning?

6:15pm. Drive to bank. Take out $40 I was saving for the rent, except I already accepted the dinner invitation. I promise myself I will not do this again!

I'm depressed just reading this. However, I can rewind that day and create a happy conclusion:

9 am: I check the Spending Plan I developed at the start of the month. How much is left in the Grocery category? I write a list of the things I need, starting with gourmet mustard. I go to discount

grocery store. I pay with a debit card, subtract what I spent from the balance in the Groceries category on my Spending Plan page. I feel ...not too much. It wasn't that exciting.

11 am. Get one video from library. Who has time to watch two? I have no fine because I get stuff back on time. I am not vague about due dates.

12 pm. Go home for yummy lunch from healthy food I just bought. Mmmm.

1 pm. I check my Spending Plan in the Restaurants category. I will have a nice lump in there after this Friday's pay. I contact a few friends or family members on the phone. I make a date to spend time with them, maybe go out to dinner. I feel excited and have something I can look forward to.

4 pm. Check emails. Where do people find this stuff? Love the music things.

5 pm. Call from friend. Dinner invite. I know my Restaurants category is low until Friday, so I do a quick check in my Entertainment category. Yes! There is enough for a movie instead. Friend agrees! All set, I hum while making dinner.

6:10pm. The new mustard tastes weird.

7 pm. Meet friend at movie theatre. What a crowd! Pay for ticket and popcorn with debit. Subtract from my Entertainment category. Only $1.17 left. Fortunately, my pay comes this Friday, so I'll put my pre-determined amount into the Entertainment category, and be ready to spend again! As for issues with the rent, what issues? The money is in my Rent category, untouched.

Well, today, you will learn this way to lasting prosperity. God will do for you what you have not been able to do for yourself.

TRACK SPENDING

Be a detective for a few days. Your distorted thinking tells you taking care of money is boring, picky, beneath you. All the same, not taking care of money is wreaking havoc in your life. The first step in controlling your money, as opposed to it controlling you, is to look at what you value in life by seeing what you spend your money on. I know you think you know from your Money History; however, there are still some surprises in store for you. You may not be spending enough money on things that really matter to you, and too much on things that don't.

For example, do you buy a practical coat if it's on sale, while you haven't bought a beautiful coat, one that you love, for years? In contrast, do you buy many clothes, yet do not allow yourself to look in that college course catalogue? Do you deprive yourself of life's pleasures as if this is a virtue? You drive an old, beater car, live in a tiny space, and never order what you really want on the menu?

Deprivation is to debting what anorexia is to overeating. It is a manifestation of distorted thinking. Often women in financial chaos think they put their money where their hearts are; however, really, they do not. Find out what kind of life you have been living by tracking what you're spending your money on.

Your initial Spending Record is a diagnostic tool to show where you're spending your money, and if that is where you want to be spending your money. As the old saying goes, 'Take care of the pennies and the dollars will take care of themselves.' I'd like to rephrase that: Note the pennies, and the dollars will take note, too.

Though you may want to get better around money, you need help to overcome bad habits of long standing, a penchant for vagueness. This keeps you from consistently doing the small tasks which form the foundation for a stable financial life.

Start a pattern of awareness around your money. Begin to note where that $40 you took out of the bank this morning went by this evening. Make a simple Spending Record. It can be a piece of paper in your wallet or a small notebook from the dollar store where you write down expenses as they occur.

Some women scoff at writing down the exact amounts they spend. They call it nickel and dime-ing themselves to death. On the contrary, that's an excuse for being vague. Every cent does count. Write down the $2.13 for the coffee instead of $2. You'll see being precise about your money brings in a big reward—more money!

Another benefit of being accurate is other people are very accurate around your money. If you're out by one cent at the bank, you'll hear about it. If you give your daughter one dollar less than you promised, well, we know about that. Appropriately, other people expect you to be accurate, in return.

It can take a while to get in the habit of jotting down each purchase. Ask your spiritual source to help you consistently record what you spend. So many women start out with good intentions, but slack off for numerous reasons. It isn't a hard task; then again, consistency is never easy. In spite of this, if you pick up where you left off, repeatedly, in a short time, you'll have a true picture of where that $40 went you got from the bank this morning.

Make no self-judgments on your spending habits. This is simply a record of what you value shown through what you spend your money on. For now, don't show this information to anyone. This is for you to become aware of your spending choices.

Psychologists say it only takes 21 days to form a habit, though it can be hard to keep going for that 21 days. Why not turn this burden of recording your money over to God. Be willing to do it, yet ask God to help you be consistent, one purchase at a time. You will get used to the new habit of sharing your money challenges with this Power which is willing to help you succeed. Your life will get better every day. Can't get no worse! Record for six weeks at least, or better yet, three months. God will help you be persistent and accurate. No simple task!

RECORDING SYSTEMS

A Spending Record can be as simple as a piece of paper or, as high tech as a spreadsheet on your phone.

Paper and Pencil

Paper and pencil have worked for millennia. It will work for you, too.

Take this little story:

It's 3012 and a central computer controls the world. All is perking along nicely until something happens to knock out the computer. The world leaders run to the smartest woman in the world. She stays up in her ivory tower for three days until she figures it out. On the third day, she's got it! She races down the many stairs to the boardroom, shouting, "Watch this!" Then, she takes a small pencil and a little piece of paper. Carefully, she prints 2 + 2 = 4. The world leaders gasp. "Yes," she shouts, "and it works every time!

Fold a regular piece of paper into quarters. In each quarter, draw seven squares, one for each day of the week, as in the sample. Keep a pen handy, and jot down everything you spend, to the penny. If you'd like something bigger, hit the Dollar store and buy a small spiral, lined notebook. They're less than a dollar each. Date each page, and write down your numbers. If you don't have the time to do it before you leave the store, ask for a receipt. In fact, always ask for a receipt! More on that in a minute.

Sample SPENDING RECORD on Paper

Feb 1-7, 2xxx			
Monday	Tuesday	Wednesday	Thursday
Coffee 3.53	Coffee 3.53	Coffee 3.53	Coffee 3.53
Gum 1.17	Magazine 6.87	Car payment	
Groceries	Car Gas 25	221	
156.60	Phone bill 45		
Rent 750			
Friday	Saturday	Sunday	
Coffee 3.53	Movie 16.57	Donation 5	

One sheet of paper will actually last you two months. But, if you want to use separate pieces of paper, that's o.k., only remember to dump the completed ones somewhere you can find them later. Try your night table, or a kitchen drawer, anywhere consistent. You'll be glad you did when you want to review your overall spending patterns.

Computer Spreadsheets

Depending on your comfort level, there are computer programs which can help with a spending record, or you can create a simple table in Word to make a neat, all-in-one record. With a USB key, you can even use the computer at the library.

Record what you spend as you go if you are using your phone. If you're using a home computer, record what you spent that evening.

A Strange Bonus

One of the odd things about keeping an accurate Spending Record is sometimes, almost mysteriously, your spending decreases. While this is not the initial goal of a Spending Record, time and again women have reported this side bonus.

Paying attention like this highlights which choices you are making. When it's written down in black and white, you notice your patterns, and sometimes you change your mind. Instead of a

Starbucks snack, you choose to buy a small bouquet of fresh flowers.

SPENDING RECORD TALLIES

Once you have a record of what you have spent in one month, find the total for each category. But, before you begin, set up some music to listen to. Listening to music is an excellent way to stay calm while figuring out your finances.

Emotions are in the right hemisphere of the brain, and so is music appreciation. If you want to be happy recording your numbers, turn on music. Like a spoonful of sugar, music will make the medicine of your tallying go down better.

Sample CATEGORY TALLY

Category	Monthly Spending
Car Gas	40 + 35 + 25=$100

If you do this for each month, you will have three figures which reveal how much you spent in each category each month. Take an average of the three months, and you can now see how much you spend on each category, as an average, each month.

Sample SPENDING RECORD TALLY

Category	Month 1 Spending	Month 2 Spending	Month 3 Spending	Average per Month
Car Gas	$100.00	$70.00	$90.00	$86.67
Car Payment	306.00	306.00	306.00	306.00
CDs, Magazines, DVDs	31.14	19.57	35.18	28.63
Clothes	119.34	89.67	99.34	102.78
Debts	421.00	421.00	421.00	421.00
Entertaining	114.22	117.11	74.29	101.87
Entertainment	50.26	35.13	65.86	50.42
Gifts	22.18	9.09	32.11	21.27
Groceries	832.00	987.00	892.00	903.67
Kids' Activities:	388.00	94.00	238.00	240.00
Rent/Mortgage	750.00	750 .00	750.00	750.00
Snacks	105.44	72.72	95.94	91.37
Utilities & Phones	320.00	350.00	304.00	324.67
TOTAL	$3559.58	$3321.19	$3403.72	$3428.16

Once you tally the numbers from three months, and take an average, you will see the big picture on your spending behaviours. You will see spending patterns which are neither right nor wrong, simply reality. You will be the judge of whether or not you want to stay with these patterns.

These figures are reality. It is not a number plucked out of the air by someone who says this is how much you *should* be spending, or what the *average* person spends. You're a unique individual, and enjoy your life in your own way. This Spending Record average reflects how you actually live your life. Once the first four weeks has elapsed, tally the results. You will now see how much or how little you spend on coffees, clothes, and snacks. That can be a revelation!

RECEIPTS

If you don't record your purchase amounts at the point of purchase, you'll need receipts for everything you buy. It won't sound odd to ask for one; cashiers are used to giving receipts. They won't know why you want one, or care!

Stick them in your wallet until you have the time to deal with them. At the end of the day, pull them out, record what you bought on your spending record. Now, should you throw them away or keep them?

Most of the receipts you collect in a day are simply garbage once you record the numbers. Only keep the ones which are for items you might have to return, or which have a guarantee. For example, if you have purchased gum, that receipt will go in the garbage. If you have purchased clothes, that receipt will go into a keeper file. Repeat this procedure the next day, and the next until it becomes a habit. Then, keep on doing it. Remember, being consistent isn't a skill that comes naturally to many; still it is a habit you can acquire, with God's help.

The danger with receipt collecting is if you forget to record the numbers soon, you're going to have a big pile of receipts when you do get around to it. Still, it's better than forgetting what you spent your money on.

If you use computer spreadsheets for your spending record, keep the receipts and log them in at the end of the day. If you have a portable device, you can record your spending on the spot.

Some payments may not come with receipts, like donations, or even automatic deductions, like gym memberships. Record those payments on the appropriate date. You want an accurate record of where all your money is disappearing!

If you wait too long to record your purchases, or forget to ask for a receipt, no meteor will crash into earth. Write down the numbers when you do remember, to the best of your recollection.

Ask God to help you record better next time. Then, you will not get lost in old habits of self-sabotage. Though maybe never perfect, in recording your spending, ask to be more consistent. It takes the intervention of God to get you to take good care of yourself.

God, please give me the willingness to record my spending.

PRACTICAL SOLUTION:
Monthly Spending Plan

U nlike a budget, which restricts and deprives, a spending plan brings a life you truly want to live, and the money to fund it. It brings clarity so you're no longer spending by rote, using up all your available funds on the basics, and never getting to your dreams. A Spending Plan is a blueprint to overcome vagueness. It also brings pride, perhaps for the first time in a long time, as you begin to handle all your financial responsibilities. However, a Spending Plan also acknowledges and funds your Wants. Now is the time, and without the use of credit, you will have money for new clothes, vacations, classes, and gifts.

In Chapter 3, you experimented with a One-Day-Soon Spending Plan. You figured out how much money you thought you needed in each category of life to feel comfortable. At that point, the plan did not consider your income. Its purpose was to help you expand your vision for your life, what you'd like it to be in the not-too-distant future. *Now*, you're ready to create a realistic spending plan based on your present income.

The best thing about the Spending Plan is conscious spending in a balanced life. You are not only paying bills with your earnings, but also planning things like vacations. When was the last time you had a nice vacation? Even if you only put $1 or 1% into a Vacation category, it is a promise to yourself. It is also an affirmation that you are worth a decent vacation and you *will* take one.

The more you plan your money, the more money seems to flow to you. At the very least, you are not frittering it away. You are spreading the wealth to all parts of your life.

Start with where you are. Use your present income level. If you don't have an income of any sort, start the do-things mentioned in Chapter 4, *Claim Your Income.*

For most months, you will have two Spending Plans, one for each two-week period. Alternatively, if you prefer, you can create a monthly Spending Plan. In either case, your Spending Plan covers three sections:

1. Bills
2. Savings
3. Debt Repayment

Bills

Though everyone's life is a little different, most women need to pay bills for Shelter, Utilities, Transportation, Insurance, Taxes, and Health Care. Chapter 6, *Tame the Bills*, goes into negotiating lower bills and more details on these categories. But for now, here is what the Bills section of your monthly Spending Plan might look like:

Sample MONTHLY SPENDING PLAN: BILLS

FAMILY INCOME: $3200	Partner 1: $1300 Partner 2: $1900
BILLS	**COSTS**
Car Gas	160
Car Insurance	142.50
Cell Phones	75
House Insurance	21.50
House Gas	77.50
Hydro	122.69
Internet	22.03
Life Insurance	19
Mortgage/Rent	1200
Property taxes	146
TV	11.50
Water	36
TOTAL BILLS	2033.72

For most families, this kind of *joint bill paying* is the norm.

1. One checking account.

2. Both paychecks deposited there.

3. All bills deducted from one place.

While it seems neat, organized, and practical, in fact, it is *not* the ideal way to get clarity on your *own* Spending Plan.

PROPORTIONAL BILL PAYING

A preferred way to pay bills is for each partner to have their own checking account. The goal is for you to have control of your own money, being interdependent with your partner.

Therefore, each person's paycheck is deposited into his or her own account. And the bills are divided up according to ability to pay.

Any remainder from your paycheck stays in your own checking account. That balance is then divided into Savings categories which I will discuss shortly. Each partner takes agreed-upon responsibility for bills and certain savings categories up to the amount of money they have available.

1. Two checking accounts

2. One paycheck deposited into each account.

3. Bills paid from each account, proportional to income level.

4. Balance in each checking account pays proportionally for agreed upon savings categories.

Here's an example:

MONTHLY SPENDING PLAN: SEPARATED BILLS

INCOME	$1300 Partner 1	$1900 Partner 2
BILLS	COSTS	COSTS
Car Gas	160.00	
Car Insurance		142.50
Cell Phones	75.00	
House Insurance	21.50	
House Gas	77.50	
Hydro	122.69	
Internet	22.03	
Life Insurance	19.00	
Mortgage/Rent		1200.00
Property taxes	146.00	
TV	11.50	
Water	36.00	
TOTAL	691.22	1342.50

There is a third option, though not as preferred: you each have your own account, but also run a third account for Household Expenses to which you each contribute. The remainder stays in your own checking account for the Savings portion of your income.

The problem with this system is that both people have to be religious about depositing their part of their paycheck, in a timely fashion, into the Household Expenses checking account. Is your partner good at this sort of thing? You are going to be dinged with late payment on bills, or stomach-churning frustration if they are not. It's best to have fewer accounts, and total control of your own money.

You can see after all the bills are paid, the partner who earns $1300 allocated $691.22 for bills and so has $608.78 left. The partner who earns $1900 net a month allocated $1342.50 to Bills, and so has $557.50 left. This money will be divided into various savings categories. That's the fun part! If you have no extra, go back to Chapter 4 and Claim your Income!

Large Bills

For large bills, like the Rent or Mortgage, the person whose responsibility it is can save half from each of their paychecks if they are paid more than once a month. Therefore, if the amount is $1200 a month, they can save $600 from their first paycheck, and $600 from their second paycheck. When the payment is due, they'll have the full amount waiting in their checking account. It means there will be less of a financial hit on the first of the month. Consequently, it will balance out how much money is left from each paycheck for other bills and savings.

Savings

Once you've paid your bills, excluding debt repayment for the moment, it's time to fund what you value in life. How you spend your money reveals how you spend your life. The secret to creating a good Spending Plan is to fund the life you and your family value, while staying within your means.

Savings, as I define it, is really spending forward. You figure out what you want, what it costs, and then put a certain amount of money towards each category, and watch the amount grow. You *will* be spending it. It will not sit in savings jail, turning to dust!

No one knows exactly how it works; all the same *feeling* prosperous attracts prosperity. It may come from giving yourself permission, within your balanced Spending Plan, to buy things that bring you pleasure, like the chair you've been eying, or that DVD you'd love to watch.

The reason that Savings categories work is you save for several items at the same time, in *parallel savings*. This is how it works: while you're saving for that cabinet, which will take a while, you are also saving for the DVD. In a short time, you'll be able to buy the DVD while still saving for the chair. Then you continue saving in the DVD category which will fill up again. Eventually, you'll have money for the chair. In the meantime, you may have purchased several DVDs. You can get everything you really want. Time is the variable.

Some categories of spending for which you have to save are not exactly pleasures: car maintenance and repairs, for example. Cars need servicing, and repair, so you might as well accept that as an unpleasant fact of life and begin a savings category now. Then, when the dreadful event occurs, you'll have the money. That money sits there and hopefully gathers dust for a long time. Nevertheless, when you do need to, you'll pay it. No credit cards, no drama, simply a sigh and a check. And you'll go on with your pleasant life.

EMERGENCY FUND

An Emergency Fund is critical to any Spending Plan, and I have discussed it previously. But, a caution here: emergencies are urgent situations, a crisis, or a blow. Contained in all these words is the concept of the *unexpected*. When there is an ice storm and you're involved in a car accident, the insurance deductible is an unexpected blow to the budget. Or, when your aging mother needs help in her hometown because of sudden illness, that airfare is an unexpected, crisis expense.

Nothing in that definition includes needing to go out for dinner because you've had a terrible day, and your Restaurants category has run out. What would you do instead? If you had a bad day at work, you'd go home and maybe have to eat leftovers, but you will also take a hot bath, listen to good music, phone a friend, and say a prayer:

God, I've had a terrible day. I feel bad. Anyone going through the same thing would feel as I do. But, please, transform these negative feelings into peace of mind. Thank you.

Your Emergency Fund is not for a last-minute invitation for a weekend trip, and it is not for impulse buys, such as the great jacket or shoes on such an amazing sale. If you spend your

Emergency Fund on these things, when a real emergency comes up, you won't have the money and will have to resort to debt.

Saying No to yourself builds your impulse control muscles. Since your Spending Plan has been well thought out, it will meet your needs and your dreams. You don't want to let spending whims throw off your potentially beautiful life.

DEBT REPAYMENT

The secret to creating prosperity is the Savings part of the Spending Plan. Without this, you will debt again. You are in debt now because you have not been funding your real needs. Wild splurges, or drastic deprivations have burdened your spirit to the breaking point.

You are now in the grips of a financial obsession which leads you to believe your debts are more important to pay for than your life. Sure, you will repay what you owe, but first, you need to repair your life. Once you have funded a reasonable life which addresses your dreams, you will use what is leftover to pay down Debt. You will repay every renegotiated cent, in time. Your needs and wants must come first. Trust me on this, please.

Until your Spending Plan is up and working to pay for a balanced life, Debt Repayment has to pause. I know that's blasphemy, and I know your creditors will not be happy about this. But, think about it: if you do not get your living expenses in order, you will either be late with your debt payments, or worse, debt more.

Once you know how much money you have, and need, you will be in a position, for the first time in your adult life, to repay all the money you owe, in a timely fashion. That will be worth the waiting, for both you and your creditors.

There is more on Debt Repayment in Chapter 9, *Make Things Right*.

WHO PAYS FOR WHAT?

If you're single, or there is only one wage coming into the home, your Spending Plan will be relatively simple. One paycheck pays for everything. However, if you have two incomes in the family, there are special issues to be resolved. There are five main problems couples face when trying to match expenses to income:

1. How to handle expenses when one partner earns significantly more than the other.

2. How to handle the situation when the total family income isn't very high.

3. What to do if one partner does the earning while the other cares for the household and/or children.

4. How to decide who gets their way.

5. One partner won't play nicely.

1. Different Salary Levels

One couple had a huge discrepancy in their salaries. He was moving up in the ranks, and because of his many years of experience, was making a good salary. She worked for a small chain of newspapers. Though she was a valuable employee, her salary was half of her husband's.

The obvious solution would seem to be for them to pay a portion of every bill in proportion to their income. They would divide all bills with the higher income paying proportionately higher, that is, two-thirds, and the lower income paying one-third. While this system seems neat mathematically, it is hell on wheels in reality. It means they must divide each household purchase, and then one of them must collect the right amount from the other partner, and make the payment. For example, a light bulb from Canadian Tire which costs $2.19, divides into

$1.47 for him, and 73 cents for her. Whoever bought the item would need to collect that amount from the other person. Happy days. This method can drive couples crazy. It can feel like nickel and diming each other to death. And, if the person owing doesn't have the money at the moment, the other partner becomes a debt collector. After all, they might need the money owed to pay their share of other bills. The bookkeeping can be daunting.

My preference is to give full responsibility for different expenses over to one partner or the other, proportionately. She takes categories which cost one-third of the overall monthly expenses. These might include clothes, school expenses, hygiene, and vacation. He takes on the rest of the categories, which total two-thirds of their expenses. They might be the rent or mortgage, car expenses, house maintenance, food. Now each partner handles all the purchases and payments for their categories, alone. Of course, they confer with each other over major financial decisions, such as renegotiating the mortgage, or vacation choices.

The problem with this system is each partner needs to be responsible. If you do not trust your partner will hold up their end, pay the bills they are responsible for, and save the money they said they would, you have therapy issues. That's right. If you cannot get your partner to take on their share of the money management, you have deeper issues than finances. Make an appointment with a therapist. Talk to someone, even if you have to go alone, initially. Both partners have to be adult about this system, and seek outside support if needed.

The advantages of this system is it allows more personal freedom in decision-making, and less nitpicking over small amounts of money. You share the responsibility and the load, so it is far less exhausting for each partner.

If you happen to be in the situation of a few couples where you make about the same income as your partner, then evenly divide the categories, picking which ones you want to pay, and take care of your half.

2. Low Family Income

If you are a single-income household and that income isn't very high, or you and your partner are working at low-paying jobs, there really is only one solution: Surrender your situation to God.

God, please remove every obstacle that stands in the way of my usefulness to You and to the world, and bring Your abundance into my life.

Now, beat the bushes for more money from *all* sources. Re-read and read again Chapter 4, *Claim your Income*. Be receptive to ideas which come out of the blue, different from ones you usually have. As long as it is legal, and won't hurt anyone, take the money.

In the meantime, create a Spending Plan. This is the blueprint out of poverty and into abundance.

3. House Job

If you're living with a partner who is contributing to the household not with wages but with services, most families find an Allowance works well. The wage earner might get the allowance, or the homemaker. The allowance needs to be large enough to cover their own bills and savings categories. The other partner manages the rest of the income. In consultation, of course.

The problem with this system is that one partner can be cheap, insisting the household live on less than it really costs. Or, one partner may splurge on things which do not meet the needs of the family.

Once again, financial maturity is called for. And not easy to come by. Ask for Help.

4. Who Gets Their Way?

When there is money allocated to dreams, which person's dreams count? Everyone's! No family member is more important than the other, though adults do take precedence. Sometimes, people think one partner's dreams need to be funded while the other waits, and then the reverse. Or, they should give more to one person in the family than the others. But, those are not the best ideas.

It works well if you split whatever money is available to fund dreams between the family members, including the kids. In this way, each is motivated to fulfill their potential. Fund everyone's dreams.

When a category involves other people in the family, like the Vacation, while you may be the one saving for it, does it mean you get to decide where it will be? Hardly. You are saving the money on behalf of the family, so consider everyone's wishes, and in an age appropriate way. Mom and Dad get veto power. This applies to household purchases, too, like new appliances, or cars. Make a joint decision both partners can feel good about.

5. My Partner Won't Play Nicely in the Sandbox

Just because you've seen the light at the end of the financial tunnel doesn't mean your partner has. According to a 2004 study by *Smart Money Magazine*, the top six money arguments that couples have are about merging their money, dealing with debts, budgeting, how to best invest, money secrets and planning for emergencies. Statistics vary widely, saying anywhere from 20-90 percent of Canadian marriages break up primarily over money. That's, at best, one in five. Don't go there. Solve the problem.

If your partner has a *don't-worry-about-it* attitude, or strong views which differ from yours, it is harder, but not impossible, to get out of and stay out of financial chaos. Now, the bad news: you cannot change your partner. No amount of nagging, lecturing, logic, or manipulating will work. Fortunately, you can get your partner on your side.

Ask them about their dreams, what will make them happy. Tell them what dreams you have which will make you happy. Read Chapter 3 together, *Splurge on Dreams*. Using the tools you're learning for financial management, focus on the mutual pursuit of happiness, whatever that means for each of you. Then plan your finances so you can reach those goals.

Once you have this vision, divide the bills. Ask your partner to take responsibility for a few big bills, like the mortgage or rent, car payments and maintenance. It will ease your workload and free up the rest of the family money . You divide the balance into spending and savings categories. You're so good at that! You'll be surprised at how giving each other autonomy with money will ease tensions.

Still, if your partner is hard-core, and won't play nicely in the money sandbox, you have to protect yourself. Some women believe that a marriage of two souls translate to a marriage of the money; in other words, one checking account for the family, one savings account. However, if you're arguing about your finances, can you take each dispute to your clergyman? Isn't it better get this calmed down before it permanently erodes the quality of your family life?

Why not give this a temporary trial? Set up a personal checking account to which your partner has no access. Deposit your paycheck and your other funds here. This will prevent their raiding the account. Set up automatic deductions for all the bills you can, like your rent or mortgage, utilities, car payments, so that the bill paying is less work. If you don't have enough money to cover all the bills and family expenses, including your own, ask for a monthly household allowance check from your partner. Your partner will use their remaining funds to pay for their own expenses, like coffees, lunches, clothes, toys, and other personal choices.

If your partner is credit card happy, in Canada, marriage alone does not make you responsible for your spouse's debts. You can contact the credit card institutions and request, in writing, to be removed from the accounts. You must get confirmation in writing from the financial institution or you won't have a guarantee they have removed you from their records. Now, you are no longer responsible for *future* debt. Your partner can use the cards, but you are not liable for any new charges. However, you will no longer be able to use those credit cards yourself.

If you want access to credit, get a new credit card in your name only, and do not allow a secondary card to be sent to your partner. Make this one a secured credit card. Put a set amount of money on it, and use it like a debit card.

However, no matter what you do, begin today to pray for your partner. Money issues may only be the tip of the iceberg. With God's help, you might find underlying relationship problems resolving with little effort on your part.

No matter what the cause of the money issues with your partner, which are likely complex and deep-seated, the only lasting solution is spiritual support. Every night for the next two weeks, (or longer) ask God for help:

God, please help me forgive (partner's name), and guide them and myself to right thinking and right action around our money.

P.S. One financial advisor suggests you both get into the bathtub, naked, and have a money talk. Let me know how that goes.

SPIRITUAL SOLUTION:
Harms Done

Y our battle for financial survival is taking all your energy. Even though you may agree with the *Man's Prayer* from the Red Green TV Show: "I can change... if I have to... I guess." changing how you think and act is not easy. Spiritual Help, alone, can restore you to permanent financial and emotional strength. Healthy behavior can be yours every day when you see the world through this marvelous filter. You will make different financial decisions; you will get out of living in chaos and into living a calm, happy, abundant life. Take the leap; give it a shot. You have nothing to lose but your misery.

After a lifetime of self-sufficiency, haven't you found there are limits to what you have been able to achieve? For example, you have tried budgets but you couldn't keep to them. That's o.k. Accept your limitations; then, ask for and accept Help from a source more able than you. This brings hope.

You can now have hope for a balanced life. Believe your problems will start to disappear by asking God for help, and listening. Watch for small, positive shifts in yourself. Maybe this time, you won't do that unproductive thing you always do in a given situation. Or, maybe this time, you'll leave the room instead of getting into it with them. Or, maybe this time, you will have the money in hand, not a credit card.

HARMS I'VE DONE

In order to live the life of your visions, first you have to admit that in the past, you have done things which you would not want made public. They may be bad, or just feel bad. In spite of this, once you write them down, in black and white, you will see they are not worse. Keeping shameful memories in your head gives them room to swell up, causing pressure, which explodes at awkward times. That is, you act like a wild woman over a trifle. Or, you spend the rent on an outfit.

Admitting to ourselves where we've messed up in different ways with different people can have a calming effect on our emotions. We are less likely to react so strongly, which includes spending unwisely, once rid of lingering guilt, shame and resentment. Most women can point to how others harmed them, and it's likely true.

On the other hand, most women have done harms to others, too. It may be nothing more than putting themselves in harm's way. They start the ball rolling, and things get worse from there. Or, maybe the harm they are doing is holding onto a grudge long after they could have let it go. Or, it may be real, painful harms done to others.

You will need courage to face yourself this way. Call for Help. Fill in this self-analysis. A blank form is on my website. Once you have filled in the last two columns, wait. You do not have to do anything right now. Simply record what happened, and what might have been done differently. That's all for now.

Sample HARMS I'VE DONE

The Harm	Who I Hurt	Is It a Secret?	What I Might Have Done Instead?	How Do I Make It Right?
Had an affair	Husband, lover	yes	Gone for marriage counseling	Speak to a counselor now
Stole $ from work	Company	yes	Asked for a raise	Speak to a lawyer first about the consequences, if any. Then decide how to proceed.
Yell at the kids too much	The kids	no!	Speak to them one-on-one, calmly	Learn to meditate
Refuse to talk to my sister-in-law	Husband, kids, her	no	Ask her to stop lying to me.	Pray for the right words.

No part of you wanted to hurt anyone else. You were trying to survive your own life. God will now do for you what you have not been able to do for yourself: give you a break. Try this prayer:

God, relieve me of the habit of self sabotage, and restore me to the hopeful, healthy, and abundant life You want for me.

There is no need to deprive yourself of small things while you're taking the time to get the big things you want. The first time you buy a CD you really wanted, at the regular price, the feeling will be totally out of proportion to the purchase. You'll think you bought a diamond necklace.

The first time you spend some of your Entertainment money on a planned outing, like a movie for you and the family, and have enough for snacks, without sweating it, you'll enjoy the evening in a completely new way, and glow the day after—no recriminations for *wasting* money. Money used from planned spending *feels* like money well spent.

There is a difference between control and discipline. While a Spending Plan might feel like restriction or penny pinching, it really is mature acceptance that healthy limits bring security. While some of your spending might be less than before, you will now fund pleasures long ignored, important categories for an enjoyable, balanced life. Your Spiritual Guide wants you to live an abundant life, full of all that is healthy and nurturing. With this perspective in mind, become willing to do the next right thing. What awaits you is a wonderful change in your finances, and in your life.

6

TAME THOSE BILLS

Power Up!

O nce you are receptive to spiritual help, and are willing to follow these next suggestions, you will find your worries about bills diminishing, and your confidence in yourself as a money manager improving.

ALL THOSE BILLS!

This may be the first time in awhile you actually looked at what things are costing you. Don't hyperventilate. Reality sucks sometimes, but it's still there. Might as well face it. Soon you will get your service providers to give you a better deal. For the moment, become aware of your bills. Here's a list to stimulate your memory. Make a list of your own:

BILL CATEGORIES

alimony	health insurance	storage
banking fees	heat	subscriptions
cable TV	house gas	telephone
car gas	house insurance	therapy
car insurance	internet	transportation
car payment	legal fees	water
car registration	life insurance	
cell phone	long term care insurance	Other
child care	maid/contract labour	
condo fees	mortgage	
daycare	pager	
dental insurance	parking	
disability insurance	phone long distance	
electricity/hydro	property taxes	
garbage pickup	public transit	
gym membership	rent	

Your job today and for the next few days is to reduce the cost of your bills. Every one of them is a target. While not all bills are negotiable, like government fees, reducing those you can is one of the fastest ways to gain income.

Start with these quick fixes:

QUICK BILL REDUCTIONS

Addictions: Alcohol, cigarettes, recreational drugs, and food binges are expensive. Maybe it's time to address these issues in your life. There's a 12-step program for every vice. Or, you can call a free counselor at Canadian Addiction and Mental Health (CAMH), or ask your doctor for help. You will save money, and you may save something far more important, your mental health.

Barter Online: Barter sites are usually free and shipping is cheap.

Cash or Debit: Statistics support the idea that people spend up to 20% more when using a credit card than when using cash. Buy only with cash or debit cards.

Clothes: Thrift store shopping is all the rage. Maybe it isn't something you want to keep up, but as a temporary measure, you will find what you need and want, and at rock-bottom prices.

Credit Card 0% Interest: Shred all incoming credit card offers, even those 0% interest. They are sneaky. Once the initial promotion period has ended, they charge you a significantly higher interest rate.

Credit Report: Obtain your credit report and score. It is free if you ask for it by snail mail. It only takes a few days. Clear up any problems which might be on your report. A better credit score will save you money on major purchases by getting you lower interest rates.

Discount Websites: Red Flag Deals and the like offer rebates, discounts and coupons for items other than food. They can be great resources for saving money on everything from clothing to electronics. Make sure they take PayPal, not only credit cards.

Free Banking: Compare banks and their fees. If necessary, switch to a different bank that offers free checking and ATM use or pays higher interest on checking and savings accounts. This could save you $30-80 dollars a month!

Libraries: Libraries have books, music and movies free. Use them instead of retail stores. Once you're in the habit, you won't forget the due dates. They remind you electronically anyway.

PRACTICAL SOLUTION:
Negotiate All Bills

M ake a complete and accurate list of your bills, then call each provider and negotiate a better deal. If you don't want the trouble of changing your provider, remember there is so much competition in the marketplace right now, they are inclined to give you more service and better prices if you mention their competition and can quote a deal you can get elsewhere.

Go after your phone company first. Want free long distance in North America? Free call answer or call waiting? An overall discount if you use their internet service? Know what the other phone companies are offering by giving them a quick call, then contact your own company, and bargain hard!

It is worth the effort. All these negotiations will add up, and put money back into your pocket, where it loves to be!

Simply speaking to her phone company's Loyalty Department netted this woman a reduction of $25 a month, yet more services! She mentioned that she was talking to the competition. That $25 a month totaled $300 a year. That's a weekend away, or the kids' ballet lessons, or fresh fruit more often.

Then, go after each of your utility providers, and any other bills you have. If you can't get the bills lowered, make better payment arrangements.

For example, this couple called their gas and electric companies to arrange Budget Billing. This meant that they'd pay the same amount each month, no matter how much they used. If, at the end of the year, they were over or under, they would make that up, but the providers checked in a couple of times a year to be sure they were on track. This meant no huge heating bills in winter and no huge electric bills for air conditioning in summer.

Therefore, though they still paid the same over the year, it was more manageable to budget.

Alimony

Are you paying alimony? Typically, women are on the receiving end; then again, if the courts ordered you to pay alimony, view it as a bill like other bills. Once you see it this way, you remove the emotional baggage.

You can negotiate the terms and conditions if your partner is willing to listen. If not, it's time to consult a lawyer, or legal aid, if the circumstances of either party have changed.

If you're behind in the payments, this is a debt. See the section on *Debt Repayment* in Chapter 9 before taking any action.

Banking Fees

These fees are unnecessary in today's banking world. You have a choice of banks which have no banking fees, like ING or President's Choice. While they may be less convenient, or simply require you to make a change which is uncomfortable, you could be saving more than $200 a year with free banking services. That money could go a long way towards a plane ticket to a sunny clime in winter, a theatre subscription, or Christmas gifts.

Cash System

Of course, there is the old school way of avoiding banking fees: it's called Cash. You take out a set amount of money each week, based on how much you usually spend, and avoid bank machines entirely.

Some women divide the large sum into smaller amounts. They divide the money into different change purses or envelopes, and write the name of the expense on the outside. It is amazingly effective. And no fees.

Cable TV

If your family enjoys TV, cable is a fine expenditure. All the same, can you get a cheaper rate for the channels you most frequently watch? If only one person in the family watches a station, but regularly does so, let them have it. We try to honour even the smallest members of the family, especially the one who is the most different. We guard each person's uniqueness, even in TV preferences. However, if one family member is dominating the bill, subscribing to more channels than the rest, redo it fairly. This will probably cut down on the bill.

Also, there are other cable providers. Check out the competition, then, negotiate a better deal with your present provider. And do this exercise yearly. Providers are always offering promotions. Or, how about Netflicks. For around $9 a month, you can access slightly older movies, TV shows and documentaries. This may only net a 5-10% savings, but hey, even $10 a month means $120 at the end of the year. Put that on a fancy Valentine's Day dinner, a new bicycle, or family night at a bowling alley!

Speaking of TV, studies have shown watching TV lowers the heart rate below what it would be looking out a window. In other words, watchers are in a trance. TV really does create couch potatoes. Is this how you want your family to spend time?

How about experimenting with allowing kids to have only one hour of TV a night, or only one show a week. Revolutionary! And probably rebellion making depending on your TV habits. You are role modeling. Limiting TV can be an interesting exercise if you replace it with interesting activities. Some women try board games (you can buy them used at thrift shops), cards, giant puzzles, or even talking to each other. Some kids use vacant TV time to start hobbies, or read.

Therefore, while the goal of inspecting your cable bill is to reduce the cost without removing the pleasure, it can also be a chance for some members of your family to get their homework done!

Car Gas

To reduce your gas use, you can do several things:

1. Car-pool, especially for kids' activities.

2. Map out your errand routes to hit more stores each time, instead of making several trips.

3. Shop closer to home.

4. If it's convenient, experiment with public transit.

5. Fill up when it's cheaper, often Monday or Thursday evenings.

6. Bike to work. It's healthy and cheap. But, keep safe!

7. Get frequent-buyer points that can be cashed in for free gas.

You'll find it a small thrill to have beaten the gasoline giants at their own game!

Car Payments

Leasing a car is cheaper in the short run, but you will never own a leased car unless you buy it out at the end of the contract, a very expensive way to buy a car. If you have a leased car which you no longer can afford, or no longer choose to afford, sign up for Lease Busters, and get rid of it. You can buy a better car later.

However, instead of leasing, buy new, and drive the thing into the ground, that is, ten years or more. You need to read books like Lemon-Aid to find the best value in new cars, and pick one which is highly recommended.

Negotiate this way: know what the going rate is for the car of your choice. You can check sites, like blue book prices which the banks and insurance companies use. Know the names of other dealers you plan to visit before you walk in the door of the first place. Make sure the salesperson knows you plan to visit other showrooms. And do not pay a price higher than the one recommended in your research. Know your market.

Should you take the dealer's financing when you purchase? Avoid it, no matter what pressure they put on you. It's likely at a higher interest rate than a credit union or a bank. If they offer zero percent financing, it is legit, although they will penalize you if you're late even one day on a payment by retroactively charging you a high interest rate on the entire loan, even on the payments you have already made. If you already have a loan with the dealer's financing, and it's too expensive, see if you can buy it out, and switch to a lower interest loan at a credit union.

Taking out a car loan at a floating interest rate is a gamble, yet it might pay off. You will pay out the loan faster, if the interest rates stay low or go lower, which in recent times has been the case. Of course, if the rates go up, you're stuck paying those.

How about no car at all? You can simply rent a car when you need wheels. There are car-sharing services, like Zip Car, if you live in a downtown area. You pay a booking fee, around $300 a year, and get the use of an automobile for the few hours of the day you need it. If you stop owning a car and use public transportation, or rental cars, you will save money on car payments, insurance, and maybe monthly parking.

You may wonder how buying a car is different from going into debt which I've been decrying. This kind of debt is Secured Debt. If you were unable to continue paying for the car, you could sell it and repay the loan. The same goes for a mortgage or any debt which is backed up by collateral. It is unsecured debt, like credit cards, lines of credit and loans from friends, which get you into trouble.

Car Registration

Once a year, on your birthday, you have to register your car by paying a fee, often about $75. You also have to renew your driver's license once every 3-5 years. Also about $75. Though this bill isn't negotiable, it doesn't have to break the bank when it pops up unexpectedly.

How do you save for these cyclical things? Simple. Set up a savings category. Though these are bills, you don't spend what you have saved until a certain amount of money has accumulated, and the bill is due.

The beauty of handling a bill this way is when you get the demand for payment, which you may have forgotten about, the money will be there because you have been saving all year long. To save $75, you have to put aside $6 each month for the registration, and another $2 to save up for your driver's license renewal. That's $8 saved each month. Though the amount is small, and that's a good thing, when these bills come due, that $75 won't throw off the rest of your Spending Plan.

Child Care

Before and after school care, daycare, homecare, babysitting, these fees can be astronomical. Negotiating them may scare you. You think if you don't pay the going rate, your kids may suffer consequences when you're not there. Still, there are ways you can reduce these costs and feel confident there will be no ill effects.

- Can you work at night?

- Can you ask your company for flextime?

- Can you look for a new job which allows flextime, so you can avoid putting your kids in childcare?

One woman took a school bus driver job which meant her kids had to go with her on the bus, but there was no childcare expense as a result.

- Can your partner work at night thus be home during the day for the kids?

- Is there a relative who might benefit from living with you and providing childcare?

- Are you comfortable asking a relative to do the babysitting?

- Is there a neighbor who stays home and who might be interested in taking in your kids, maybe on a babysitting barter system—she does certain hours for you, and you do certain hours for her?

- Or, is there a neighbourhood person who might be less expensive than where your kids are now?

- Any chance of working from home?

- Would working part-time and saving the childcare expenses equal full-time pay?

- How about moving to a smaller home, smaller city, or anywhere which would reduce your living costs, and allow you to stay home to avoid childcare expenses?

Keep your love for your kids in the forefront, and the money on the back burner when you make these decisions. Try this wise question and see if it nets you an answer:

If it were free and I weren't afraid, what would be my decision?

Once you have that answer, see if you can make the idea work. And know, no matter what you decide, you will wonder if you did your best for your kids. It goes with mother territory. Consider all these options, and pray. Keep your eyes and ears open for the answer to your prayers.

Clothes

You can dress fashionably by using consignment stores. They take only the most modern clothes because they want them to sell. You get expensive clothes, lightly used, at steal deals. As well, you can sell your own clothes there, for income.

Consider restyling what you already have. Find an alterationist, and see what can be done. You'll be amazed with how good it can look, and how much less it will cost than buying new.

Credit Cards

Try these steps to reduce your credit card bills now.

- Ask to transfer your balances from all your cards to one with a lower interest, either in your bank, or at another, competing bank. Tell them you will switch banks if they don't cooperate with you. Be pleasant but firm.

- Consolidate all credit card debts on a line of credit if the rate is lower.

- Call any credit union for which you might qualify for membership, such as government, police, or teachers, and switch your credit cards to them. Their interest rates are lower.

- Investigate programs like Manulife One which consolidates debts and makes use of income interest to reduce indebtedness.

- However, do *not* put your debt on your mortgage or take out a home equity loan. You will go further into debt for much longer. Do you really want to be repaying Visa on your mortgage for the next 25 years?

Condo Fees

These can be expensive. Before you choose to buy a condo, know that the maintenance fees never go down! You can't negotiate these fees, but you can keep them lower if you buy in a new building and stay only a few years. However, watch out for those Special Assessments levied for unforeseen expenses. Can be thousands of dollars.

Debt Repayment

Debt Repayment has a whole chapter of its own, Chapter 9, *Make Things Right*. You will learn how to negotiate a manageable repayment plan with each creditor. Moreover, you will be amazed not only at how fast the debt disappears, but also how you can live an enjoyable life at the same time.

Gym Membership

Hard as it may be to accept, paying daily for gym use might save you money in the end. If you only go once or twice a month, your costs will be under $400 a year. And the fact is, most women's enthusiasm wanes, and the gym happens less and less often as the months roll by. On average, over the year, you probably only attend 24 times: three times a week the first month= 12; twice a week the second month= 8; twice a month the third month, and maybe once here and there for the rest of the year. That's about 24 times at $15 per day use = $360 a year.

Believe me, I'm not trying to talk you out of exercising. It's the best stress reliever there is. Yet, be realistic. A gym membership is a bill, and if you contract to pay for a year, they will force you to pay in full, even going to court to make sure you do. These people can't let anyone get away with non-payment in case the word spreads. Consider paying the daily rate, and see how often you really go. Face reality and save money.

Housing

Whether you rent or pay a mortgage, the real question about your living accommodations is, are you living in a safe place which you enjoy? Compromising safety and aesthetics speaks about your self-esteem. Keep searching until you find a wonderful place to live which fits your finances. More on that in the *Mortgage and Rent* section below.

Heating

There are programmable thermostats you can buy for around $75, often from your utility provider, which will automatically raise and lower the house temperature at specific times. These devices pay for themselves in one year. Lowering the heat at night when you sleep from 71 to 61 will save 10% off your heating bill. People sleep better in cooler temperatures anyway. Doing the same while everyone is out of the house during the day can save another 10%.

If you can stand it, or wear a sweater, lower your heat by one degree during the day when rates are higher and save another 3% on your heating bill. With all the money you save, you can fly to Florida for a warm winter vacation!

Hydro

Governments are getting antsy over the brownouts happening during summer months. All those air conditioners. Their attempts to fix the problem have resulted in consumer rates going way up. And it will continue this way for the near future. What to do?

There are many ways to save electricity. The utility companies have brochures telling you about it. However, what they won't tell you is this: the biggest electricity users in your home are the stand-alone freezer and the clothes dryer. Fight back.

o Unplug your freezer. Plug it back in those few times a year when you need it. Alternatively, sell it on Craig's List or Kijiji.

o Reduce clothes dryer use. How? Wash your clothes less often. *Gasp.* What a concept! How often do you do laundry? Every few days? Weekly? Every time your teenager needs a shirt for a date?

If you really want to save money on electricity, start doing laundry every two weeks. If everyone in the family has 14 pairs of unders and socks, and they wear outer clothing at least twice (unless you're dealing with infants, or raunchy items), you can do laundry once every two weeks. Then dryer loads will be full, not half-empty and used half as often.

Or, you can air dry on a backyard line. It's coming ba-a-ack. Or, set clothes on a rack over the bathtub. Expect your electricity bill to go down. And oh dear, what will you do with all that extra money? Perhaps something will come to mind.

o Turn Off computers and all peripherals every night.

o Turn Off TVs or radios if no one is listening.

o Turn out lights when no one is in the room.

Not rocket science, just being alert.

Internet

Libraries have computers to use if you don't own one. Nevertheless, if you want internet at home, and life is very difficult without it these days, how can you afford it? First, internet providers have different levels of service. While the cheapest may not remotely meet your needs, how do you know? Start at the bottom. Unless you need large amounts of data delivered to you daily, word processing and internet searches work fine at the basic level. However, you can work your way up the food chain until you find the level which meets both your needs and your budget. Likely, the second level from the bottom will work best.

Believe me, your provider will be happy to increase your level of service anytime you want to experiment. In addition, don't let the teenager whine you into buying the fastest speed. Patience is a virtue they need to learn. Not that they want to. Remember that joke?

Dear God, last night I prayed for patience. Well?

On the other hand, if high-speed internet is something your family really wants, what other expenses can you reduce to make room for it?

This man decided to buy high-speed internet, but get rid of the newspaper delivery. He reads the newspaper online now, and still enjoys the benefits of the high-speed internet for other things.

No added expense overall, yet wish granted.

Insurance

You may be over insured. Do you know the details of all your insurance? How much life insurance coverage do you have? How much do you need? Get the facts from your insurance company; write down the information in one place. That will help clarify if you need to de-clutter your insurance.

MASTER INSURANCE RECORD

Insurance Company Type	Policy #	Coverage	Cost/mo	Payment Date	Address	Phone	Contact
Torst *Car*	R2334	various	$345	1st of month	1026 Yonge St	555-3142	Cherie
Manulife *Life*	7952	$175,000	$70	1st of month	123 Bloor	555-1213	Ned
Manulife *Health Dental*	A010-09	various	$105	15th of month	123 Bloor	555-1213	Ned
Greens *House*	T7768	various	$50	1st of month	34 Daville	555-9078	Sylvia
Meloche *Travel*	890	various	$20	10th of month	19 Queen	555-7846	Nahem
Total			$595				

Car Insurance

Car insurance is mandatory and expensive though there are many ways to reduce the cost:

1. Raise the deductible. This will definitely lower your rate. Insurance is a game of chance. You take the chance you

won't have an accident. With a higher deductible, you will pay more out of your own pocket if you have an accident, which you're betting you won't. The insurance company lowers your rate because if you do have an accident, the higher deductible reduces how much they have to pay you.

2. Another idea is to look at the various insurance sites online. Make a note of lower rates from at least three different companies. Your present insurer will often match or beat the lowest rate since they want to keep your business.

This woman was astounded to hear her present insurer keep saying, "We can beat that." The agent bent over backwards to lower her rate in every category to beat the competition. At the start of the call, her rate was supposed to go up $400 a year, but by the end of the call, it had dropped by $600. Research and negotiation work so well in our free market system.

3. If you're planning to buy another car, buy an older one. A two-year-old car is 30% cheaper than a new one, and will give you many years of service. The lower the cost of the car, the lower the car insurance. Many women have had good luck buying used rental cars

4. In addition, if you insure your house contents with the same company that holds your car insurance, there is often a 5-10% reduction for multiple policies.

5. Likewise, if you do not drive your car to work, live in a less congested area of the city, or have a good driving record, your insurance will lower your rates. Be sure to mention these to your insurance agent to get the most discounts.

6. If you have a child in university or college, get their insurance reduced to an occasional driver, and if they took driver's training, ask for that discount. Oh, and try to have only girl children. They're so much cheaper to insure.

7. Another discount idea is to pay your whole insurance bill at once. This takes quite a chunk of money, but if you have it, you can save on the interest the insurance company is charging on the balance. However, in order to do it again next year, you'll need to save the monthly payments in a category anyway. Still, overall, the cost will be lower each year.

8. Be willing to change insurance companies. Switch to the one with the lowest quote, always checking it has a good reputation.

9. Winter tires will also reduce your insurance rate, and add safety during that scary season. Of course, they are expensive to purchase, about $800, but remember that you will use your regular tires that much less.

Contents Insurance

Contents Insurance is far cheaper than car insurance. This insurance covers both the building and the contents of your home. If you live in an apartment, and you buy Contents Insurance, it covers not only major calamities like fire or water damage, but also loss or theft under a certain amount. If you have jewelry, like an engagement ring, or valuable items, like cameras or laptops, this policy can pay for itself if you experience a loss.

If you have expensive electronic equipment, or jewelry, (don't you wish!) some insurers will want you to put it on a separate schedule, while others will insure it for fair replacement value without that extra cost.

While camping, this woman left a gold necklace in the washroom. She remembered, but when she went back, it was gone. Because she had a no-deductible rider detailing her jewelry, the insurance company paid in full.

This woman lost the diamond in her engagement ring, and never found it, but the insurance company paid for a new one!

Ways to reduce this bill are similar to car insurance: raise the deductible, place this policy with the same company as your other insurance for multiple line discounts, and pay the whole thing once a year to avoid the interest charges.

To keep things simple, arrange for automatic monthly deductions especially for this bill so you will never be late. You don't want the insurance company to say you were uninsured when you make a claim. Would they do that? Some will!

It is an adult decision to forego something more amusing to pay for something rather boring. This is how you navigate in the real world. Once you accept, and you plan to be a good shepherd of your valuables, you will feel more secure. This will have the bonus of calming your mind for future financial decisions.

Disability Insurance

Why would you want disability insurance? It covers you for work stoppage in cases of medical or emotional crisis. Though the length of coverage of the policies might only be two years, this can be an enormous financial aid if you cannot work.

To make it affordable, join an association, like your university alumni group, or profession. It will be cheaper than buying it on your own. If you cannot afford it at all, there are government disability payouts for those unable to work.

Health and Dental Insurance

Health and Dental Insurance is a benefit you want to negotiate with your employer, if they won't give you a raise. If you cannot get coverage, contact your alumni group or union or professional association to get in on their group rates. Much cheaper.

Life Insurance

Life Insurance is most necessary to cover your mortgage, especially if you have young children. Then again, don't act too fast. Many workplaces provide adequate life insurance coverage. Do you need to pay privately for more?

This man with no children had been paying $70 a month for a private life insurance policy for ten years. When I suggested he research his benefits at work, he saw his company already covered him for as much life insurance as he needed. He had wasted over $8,000 in premiums, money he could have used to upgrade his boat. Instead, an insurance company enjoyed it.

Analyze your master insurance record to see exactly how much life insurance you're carrying, how much you're paying, and if this is really what you need. Without children in the picture, most women want a policy which will cover the cost of their funeral. That is about $20,000 at today's rates. If you want a cremation, the cost will be around $10,000 for the cremation and funeral with a service and visitation. The cremation and the urn alone cost about $4,000.

Legal Fees

If you're in the middle of a divorce or custody battle, or if you're in a dispute with your landlord or another creditor, you already know legal fees can be as high as $600 an hour.

To reduce these costs, start with the free half hour initial consultation where you can ask questions and become aware of your options. Then, consider Legal Aid which helps those who have an income low enough to qualify. Paralegals are another option. They can help with filing legal papers and can give certain legal advice. You will pay far less for their help. As for divorce settlements, mediators train specifically in this area and charge far less, with less acrimony for the divorcing partners. As an example, a mediator will not pose this wording: "Who will be awarded custody?" Instead, the issue is stated: "What future parenting arrangements can each of you agree to so you can continue to be involved, loving parents?" Nice.

Mortgage Insurance

Some lenders will require mortgage insurance equal to the value of your mortgage. If so, there is a cost to this, about one to three percent of the value of the mortgage. While it is not legally required to take this insurance in certain cases, your lender may charge you a lower interest rate if you do.

Legal Obligations

You may have long-term contracts like gym memberships, or subscriptions. As soon as you can, get out of the contracts. Month to month payments add a flexibility which leaves you nimble during tough financial times. Though it is often a better deal to buy a year's worth of a product or service, how often do you really use it? It is cheaper, in the end, to use some things on an as-needed basis, even gym memberships, than pay in advance. This same logic works for tanning salons, classes, music lessons, and internet movie services.

Paying attention like this falls into the category of being a good shepherd of your resources. It is taking time out of your busy day to say your home is important, your money is important, and you will pay attention. This is not exciting. And that's the good part. Regular attention calms the background noise of worrying about high bills.

Maid Service

Should you have cleaning help? After all, it's your home, your family. Shouldn't *you* be the one changing the beds, and loving your home by dusting and washing the much-loved kitchen floor?

I don't care if you have no kids and a small apartment, or a big house and many kids, if it overwhelms or depresses you to clean your place, save those pennies and hire help. Even if you're not working, but have a partner who is, you do not need to clean the toilet. Unless you want to.

A word to the woman who does enjoy cleaning her house: good. The only people who need cleaning assistance are those who want it.

If you think having someone come in once a week is too expensive, try every other week. A lot of cleaning people make this arrangement, and have another client on your off week. Some women have help every third week or once a month. At once a month, you may not feel your house is getting that clean feeling while once every third week can be a boon to your spirits.

If you're a neat person, have few kids, and have a smaller house, you'll be one of the lucky ones who pays less. If you estimate $75-100 for the cleaning session, you can now see how often you can afford to have someone in. For many women, this is not a luxury. With the time saved, you might make more money at your job. Money well spent!

Mortgage

Consider the idea that you might one day live mortgage-free. Allow that thought to percolate into your deepest brain for a few minutes. Get there sooner by cutting mortgage costs.

The first way to reduce mortgage expenses is to repay the loan every two weeks instead of once a month, especially if you are paid every two weeks. That's 26 mortgage payments instead of 24 each year. It means you pay a whole extra month of mortgage which can reduce your payout by six years, and save thousands in interest. It's easy to set up mortgage payments every payday. Your bank mortgage holder will be delighted to help you.

Another way to become mortgage-free faster is to rent out part of your house, like the basement. With no investment, or a small investment, you might have a basement apartment. Always check with your insurer before you rent. You don't want them to void your policy. Though some municipalities have it on the books that renting basements is illegal, they turn a blind eye because of affordable housing shortages. However, be sure to check the facts in your area. Still, this is a painless way to get extra income, and apply it to your mortgage; then, you're on your way to being mortgage-free.

You can even take in boarders, such as foreign students who have come to learn English. They need a room, and meals. It can be an interesting experience in many ways, as well as a way to pay off the mortgage faster.

If you simply want to reduce your payments, request an extension on the original repayment period, that is, the amortization. If you go from 20 years to 25 years, you will lower your monthly mortgage payments. Or, request a temporary, lower payment amount; however be prepared to explain how this will be temporary. You can also ask for an 'interest-only' payment for a while.

When it comes time to renew your mortgage, be proactive in negotiating. Do the footwork: consult at least three mortgage lenders and compare interest rates. Don't forget those discount banks, or credit unions. Then take the best rate and show it to your present lender. They will usually try to match the competition, and you will have a lower interest rate.

Even if your mortgage isn't up for renewal, investigate what it would cost to get out of the present one if you find a lower-interest contract.

House Poor

It used to be the banks set limits on how high a mortgage you could get, and the limits were low, so few people were house poor. You couldn't get a mortgage if your debt-to-income ratio was over 40 percent.

Now, your bank may be happy to loan you more than you can reasonably afford to pay in order to collect fines and penalties. This is the new reality.

Fight back for your solvency. Do not spend more than your income will handle on housing, about 30% of your net.

Or, if you can't find an acceptable single-family, detached house you can afford, be willing to look at

- A townhouse: some of them are gorgeous. Less land, more house, lower mortgage payments.

- A good area of town which you have never considered.

- A condo

- A home in the country

- A home in a smaller city or town

- A house with a rentable basement or room for boarders

Your prayer can be:

God, I want to live in a safe and lovely place within my means, and I know this is Your will for me. Please guide me.

Parking

If you have to pay for monthly parking, would you consider moving to avoid it?

This woman paid $300 a month to park downtown near her office. She moved where she could take public transit, and ended up several hundred dollars a year richer.

If you go to an event, parking can be anywhere from $5 to $20. Check for municipal parking lots near your event. They are cheaper.

Phones

Elementary school kids have cell phones; teenagers have cell phones-- the world has shifted to such a degree there are barely any pay phones left. However, how much phone service does everyone need?

If you have a computer, you don't need an email data package on your cell phone. Data plans are expensive. Are you thinking $70 a month, and more? Don't all your other electronics do the job already? Your landline phone, your computer, your car GPS? Forget about phone fads and keep your costs down.

This applies especially to teenagers who will hound you for the next, newest phone. But, with the money you save by stripping down your services, you can go on a nicer family vacation. Stay strong!

Teenagers and Phones: text messaging has become more common than phone calls with this segment of society. Accordingly, get them to find you the cheapest text package for the most texts sent and received. As for their cell phone use, it is up to you to set a limit. If you pay for their monthly use, make them pay for any charges over that. It may mean your teenager will have to get a part-time job, use all their allowance, or monitor their own cell phone use, but hey, they are practicing adult life skills. If they overbill and don't or can't pay you, maybe they have to lose the use of their cell phone for a bit. One month without a cell phone will be a lesson in agony.

Landline: If you have a landline, consider if you really need it. Can you get along with your cell phone alone? If not, check what the competition is offering, then ask your provider for similar promotions. Imply you might sign up with a competitor, and see how creative the customer service rep can be. Here are some things you can ask for: free long distance; a cheap bundle which includes call waiting, call answer, three-way calling if you want those; multiple line discounts if you have your cable service or cell phone account with the same company.

Long Distance: Do you know much much you're paying for long distance on your phones?

Skype and VoIP can offer vastly reduced long distance rates. You can even make free long distance calls through Google. Moreover, what about the newest gadget, Magic Jack, where you can call from anywhere around the world using your high-speed internet connection? So, if your phone company is charging you seven cents a minute for long distance, make a better deal with them, or with someone else.

Once again, this is an opportunity to have the bill automatically withdrawn from your checking account every month to save late charges and stress.

Reduce Your Phone Bills

If you have been with your provider for some time:

- Speak to the Loyalty Department, or a manager, no one less important, someone who has the power to cut back the amount of your bill, if you can give a good reason for the request, of course. Have you lost your job, been ill, or another crisis?

- When you speak to the Loyalty Department, say you will take your business to a competitor. They hate that. However, if they cannot accommodate you, switch!

- Change your phone plan to meet your income and your needs. That will lower future bills.

- If the phone company cut off your service, get a prepaid phone. You'll be more efficient in your communication, that's for sure, as it costs more per minute to talk!

Public Transit

A bus or subway pass is about $100 a month. If you take a commuter train to work, it is between $200 -400 a month. If you agree to buy for a year, though, there is a discount. If you choose not to buy for the year, consider this: unless you will use your pass more than 10 times that month, it is wiser to buy daily tickets. Think about December. With all the holidays, will you be using a pass more than 10 times? Additionally, what about the month you take your vacation?

If you're disabled, or of a certain age, like a student, or a senior citizen, you may qualify for a discounted rate. Student Services at some colleges and universities arrange for their students to get transit discounts. Ask for this.

Rent

Lower rent. Wouldn't that make life easier? Consider these options for getting a decent apartment within your means:

- A bachelor apartment
- A basement apartment in a house
- Off the bus route
- In the country
- In a smaller city or town

Re-Negotiate With Your Landlord

Yes, it can be done! Here's how: Set up an appointment, whether or not you are current in your rent. Tell them the following:

We enjoy living in the building, and we want to stay. But with our new budget, we need to pay a little less rent. We will be paying on time every month, but is there anything you can do to help us out?

If they won't reduce the rent on the first request, offer one, or all of these:

1. you will help rent other apartments.

2. you will do some small clean up or fix up jobs.

3. you will let them use your apartment as the show home of the building. That'll keep you clutter-free!

4. you will take package deliveries, freeing up the superintendent.

If they *still* won't lower the rent, ask them to

1. Lower your share of the utility payments.

2. Provide new appliances.

3. Re- paint.

4. Do snow removal.

5. Do other small repairs.

Also, make sure the landlord is complying with the law around how much they can raise the rent. As well, be sure you are getting interest on your last month's rent which your property owner is holding. It's the law. Once your lease is up, ask for month-to-month rent, so you have the flexibility to move quickly if something better comes up.

Sanitation

Garbage collection is free in most neighbourhoods, but only for a certain number of bags. If you put out a lot of garbage, and drive around the neighbourhood dumping bags of your garbage on your neighbour's driveway, it will probably cost more in gas than the $2 extra-garbage tags. Consider a trash compactor, a device which compacts garbage into much smaller packages. Based on the size of your family, the investment could pay for itself quickly.

Storage

Self-storage facilities now number 45,000 nationwide, representing slightly less than 2 billion square feet of rentable space. Even though a quarter of homeowners have two-car garages, and use them exclusively for storage. If you are paying for storage, how long have you been paying? How much is the total you have paid during the life of this storage? Though it's emotionally charged, is the stuff in that storage compartment still worth as much as you have paid in storage bills so far?

One woman stored her furniture from her lovely home while she lived with her ailing mother. Now she herself is sick. The stuff in storage has been there for three years. She could have bought new, modern furniture instead of paying all that money to storage.

Frankly, you may need the help of a professional organizer or therapist to let go of some of this stuff. Failing that, you can read join 12-step support groups such as Clutterers Anonymous or Messies Anonymous, which will address the underlying issues which drive you to hoard. Research has shown a link between hoarding and emotional deprivation and the level of warmth expressed in the family during adolescence.

Whatever the case, if you have stored things without an end date, and it's been over three months, ask God for the help you need to release them.

Subscriptions

Many subscriptions save you money over buying the item or tickets occasionally. Still, how many subscriptions do you have? What's more, do you have the time for everything you're paying for? Some clever women swap, so that they only pay for one subscription, yet get to use several. Keep only what you actively use and put the money saved into your visions categories.

Taxes

There are many reasons to track expenses, and taxes are a big one.

Income Taxes

Check the Revenue Canada website for allowable expenses for your income. Then start trackin'!

Or else, hire a bookkeeper to help you get them done. Their fees are tax deductible.

Property Taxes

Some mortgagors will tack the property taxes onto your mortgage payment, so if you're nervous about paying your taxes on time, ask the mortgage holder to take this on. Check if there is a fee for this, and factor that in against late fees.

Property taxes make up about 10 percent of your overall taxes. Do you know what your property taxes pay for? Here is a comprehensive list of how municipal governments use your money:

airports
ambulance
animal control and by-law enforcement
arts and culture
childcare
economic development
electric utilities
fire services
garbage collection and recycling
library services
long-term care and senior housing

maintenance of the local road network, including snow removal

parks and recreation

planning new community developments and enhancing existing neighbourhoods

police services
property assessment
provincial offences administration
public health
public transit
sidewalks
social housing
social services

storm sewers
tax collection
water and sewage

Eye opening, isn't it? If you live in a newer area of town, your property taxes may be higher than women who live in established areas. It makes sense. Your area still needs parks, sidewalks, and fire stations.

To save money, you can move to an area of your city which has a user fee system. This means people pay more for the services they use, but less for the ones they don't.

If you think your property taxes are too high, apply for a rate reduction. Here are some reasons municipal governments might reduce your property taxes:

Do you live on a busy street? Ask for a reduction of your taxes for loss of enjoyment of the quiet. If the city has a post or some obstruction on your land, ask for a reduction.

For example, we had a hill in our backyard which reduced its usability. We took a picture of it, asked for a rate reduction and we got one. Amazing.

Alternatively, if the tax office assessed *your* house higher than your neighbour's, ask for a re-evaluation.

Therapy

Though your health insurance or the government insurance pays for psychiatrists, perhaps you have someone you love who is not covered in this way. If you can't let go of your present therapist, can you try fewer appointments, like twice a month? Alternatively, what about shorter sessions?

You can get help within your means. Join a group, like school alumni, or credit unions which have reduced-rate health and dental insurance plans. Research this.

Tithing

While tithing may be a monthly obligation you have willingly taken on, it is not a bill. Why not ask God if the amount you're tithing meets His wishes, considering your family's needs?

Also, get clear on your real motive for this type of donation. I know someone who believes he'll get back tenfold for every dollar he tithes. That sounds more like gambling than tithing.

Within a balanced Spending Plan, charity or tithing has its place. The key concept is balance.

Water

We are lucky in North America to have enough water, but we can also ascribe to the philosophy of being good shepherds of our resources. You can find shower timers which are common in Australia, a country which is very conservationist about water. These small, waterproof devices give you three minutes to complete your shower. Not that it turns off the water, but it alerts you to water wastage. Mind you, if you have a teenage daughter, you're doomed. Well, even here it is possible to get low flow showerheads. There are fewer openings in the head so they use less water each time. It is a gentler shower, too. This will save about 25 % of your water usage.

You can also reduce the temperature on your hot water heater and still enjoy your showers. Most water heaters are factory-set to 140 degrees, although if you reduce that to 120 degrees, you won't feel any difference. Lowering the temperatures by 20 degrees could mean a savings of about 6 percent in your water heating costs.

If you have an older water heater that lacks built-in insulation, consider buying a jacket or blanket for the heater – especially if it's located in a cold area of the house. Such jackets cost between $10 and $20 while they might save you 4 to 9% on water heating costs. The cover will pay for itself in about a year. Lastly, some town councils are so eager for you to use less water, they subsidize low-flow toilets. Enquire at your city hall.

It's ideal to pay less for bills as part of your balanced spending. All the same, you do not want to reduce your family comforts unnecessarily. By lowering your present bills, you may even be able to afford more than before. Being a good shepherd is rewarding.

EASY BILL PAYING

With your busy life, do you pay bills late, often getting late penalties? Alternatively, do you have to re-budget when you get an unexpected, large bill? Why fight it? Try these techniques and rid yourself of this stress.

Automatic Withdrawals

To create bill-paying peace, arrange automatic bill payments with your service providers. The provider will deduct the bill from your checking account on a set date. That is, you will not be paying online, at the bank, or mailing in a check. Your supplier will automatically deduct the bill, and you will never pay a late fee again! Contact each company you deal with. Most will be happy to direct you to the simple application form.

What you're *not* doing is having the charges placed automatically on your credit card. You want to stay away from constant use of credit cards.

Equal Billing

Equal Billing, sometimes called Budget Billing, is the best! It allows women to have the same payment from month-to-month to keep their Spending Plans calm. You pay the same amount for 11 months and then your provider reconciles the account in the 12th month.

These plans do not change your total annual gas or electricity cost, they help even it out through the year. No ugly $400 bills in February, and $10 ones in August. While the bonus of paying less in summer sounds great, in fact, it makes for very tense financial times during the winter. In other words, having a set amount to pay each month allows you to balance your budget by having the money ready. This brings calm to the home.

Despite all of that, you say, what if the money isn't in the account on the due date? Aha! It will be. You will know the amount to set aside each month and have balanced it with your other expenses. This is peace of mind.

Bill Scheduling

If you have your rent, and the hydro and the phone, cable, and internet payable out of one paycheck, you're in a world of hurt.

INCOME MATCHED TO BILLS

In this example, the Rent is $700, and once you add in the Bills of $212.68, it totals $912.68. Since this woman's income is only $878.41 twice a month, she is short $34.27 on the first of every month. Not to mention, there's no money left for anything else, like transportation or food, until her next paycheck. This would make for a tense first of the month.

INCOME MATCHED TO BILLS

1st of the month	15th of the month
INCOME: $878.41	INCOME: $878.41
Rent $700	
Cable $30	
Hydro $96.49	
Cell Phone $ 35	
Internet $51.19	
Total Bills+ Rent: $912.68	Total Bills: $0
Short: - $34.27	Balance: $878.41

One way to avoid this problem is to arrange for some of the bills to be due in the middle of the month.

BILL SCHEDULE

1st of the month	15th of the month
INCOME: $878.41	INCOME: $878.41
Rent $700	Cable $30
	Hydro $96.49
	Cell Phone $ 35
	Internet $51.19
	Total: $212.68
Balance: $178.41	Balance: $665.73

However, this method only leaves $178.41 on the first of the month, likely enough for groceries, but not much else, like transportation, entertainment or clothes. It would be better for her to save off part of her rent from each check, and pay some bills from each check. Then, she will have more money left from each paycheck. Here's an example:

Preferred BILL SCHEDULE

1st of the month	15th of the month
INCOME: $878.41	INCOME: $878.41
Hydro $96.49	Cable $30
Cell Phone $ 35	Internet: $51.19
Rent: Save off $350 [half of $700 total]	Rent: Save off $350 [the rest of $700 total]
TOTAL: $481.49	TOTAL: $431.19
Balance: $396.92	Balance: $447.22

To arrange your bill due dates, call your providers. Most are happy to make the due date whichever date works for you.

Bill Calendar

However, if you work on contract, commission, or for tips, your income will not be wholly predictable from month to month. What should you do to get your bills paid more easily? You need an early warning system. You need clarity about bill due dates compared to your income dates.

You do this with a Bill Calendar. You can go low tech and use a regular wall calendar with lots of space around the dates. On the other hand, you can go high tech, and use a computer calendar. Either way, you will finally be able to see everything, bills and income, in one place. A Bill Calendar gives you advance notice you might be short of money for bills that week. Knowing this, you can beat the bushes for more work.

On the paper calendar, draw a green box around dates you expect checks, or circle the date. Then write in the amount and the name of payer in the square. Write small. If you're doing this on the computer, bold the income. You can change the font colour to green. It does help to have the visual.

Total your expected income for the month, and write that at the left top of the calendar page. Total your expected bills for the month, and write that at the left top of the calendar page. Is there a match, a surplus or a shortfall? There's your first bit of clarity. If there is a shortfall, review Chapter 4 on *Increasing your Income*. If there's a match, or heaven sent, a surplus, take the next step.

In red, box in or circle the dates you have bills due. Write in the name of the supplier and the amount due. If you're doing this on the computer, italicize the bills.

BILL CALENDAR Month: January, 2xxx

BILL CALENDAR					Month: January, 2xxx			
Mon	Tues	Wed	Thurs	Fri	Sat	Sun	Income Balance	
Total Monthly Income: $1375	*Total Bills: $1150.19*	Surplus: $224.81						
1	2	3	4 √The Star- $600	5	6	7	$600	
8	9	10 *Ontario Hydro $90*	11	12	13	14	$510	
15 *Bell Cell $105*	16	17 √*Sharon's Place $375*	18	19	20 *Roger's Internet $45.19*	21	$734.81	
22	23 *Tor Inc $300*	24	25	26 √*Tor Inc $275*	27	28	$1034.81 $1009.81	
29	30	31 √*Transport Tor. $125*	Feb. 1 *Rent $910*				$224.81 $199.81	

Put a checkmark next to income you have received. If you were not paid as much as you expected, or on time, cross out the amount, and write in the revised amount. Then note which date it actually arrived.

Create a column in the right-hand margin of the calendar page, and keep a running tally of income minus the expenses at the end of the week. Update it as the week progresses. If you see your income will be below expenses, and you think this is a permanent pattern, change your bill due date by calling your provider right away. When you can *see* all is well with your income compared to your bills, you will feel peace of mind.

SPIRITUAL SOLUTION: Courage

Hard as it is to believe right now, one day soon you will experience money as a simple means of exchange, no emotions attached. You will shrug when it comes to paying bills, paying them in full, and on time. In the meantime, stoke up your courage to negotiate them.

QUOTES TO HELP YOUR COURAGE

Courage is fear that has said its prayers.
- Dorothy Bernard

Courage is the price that life exacts for granting peace.
- Amelia Earhart

Courage is very important. Like a muscle, it is strengthened by use.
- Ruth Gordon

Act and God will act.
- Joan of Arc

Leap and the net will appear.
- Julie Cameron

I discovered I always have choices and sometimes it's only a choice of attitude.
- Judith M. Knowlton

What one has to do usually can be done.
- Eleanor Roosevelt

Risk! Risk anything! ... Do the hardest thing on earth for you. Act for yourself. Face the truth.
- Katherine Mansfield

It takes great courage to break with one's history and stand alone.
- Marion Woodman

You can ask God for the courage to negotiate. Here is a prayer which might help you:

God, please give me the courage to negotiate with this service provider, and please give me the words.

7

SAVE YOUR LIFE

Power Up!

While some people have so little, other people have so much. Clearly, there is no lack of abundance in the world; despite that fact, you don't have it. We've spent time looking at your Needs, now we are going to address your Wants. Don't you deserve prosperity? Don't you deserve to enjoy the little pleasures of life?

GUILTY PLEASURES

Though a life of all indulgences may seem a happy one, you know it feels empty and empties your bank account. Conversely, a life of all obligations is no healthier.

For you, maybe going to a movie is not an indulgence, but a pleasure in life. If it's part of a balanced spending plan, then it's not a problem. No guilt necessary. Likewise, buying a fancy coffee is not a waste of money if it is part of a balanced spending plan, and makes you feel special, or is social.

Savings categories keep your attention on what matters to you, and provide the funds. You never debt. You stay within your income, and save for all these categories in parallel savings: a little to every category, every pay. You top up your favorite categories when unexpected windfalls drop into your lap. And they will, they will.

God wants you to enjoy the abundance of this beautiful world. If you do your part, paying attention, you will get your enduring wants, in time, and you won't have to go into debt to do it.

Umbrella Saving Headings

Remember the chart with savings category ideas in Chapter 5, *Spend the Proceeds*. You can group them under umbrella headings for easier use.

- **Business Personals**: computer, postage, supplies, trade magazines

- **Clothes:** accessories, alterations, dry cleaning, garments, jewelry/repairs, laundry, shoes/repair

- **Dependents:** allowance, classes, clothing, elder care, family events, food, pet care, school, sitters, special foods, sports, parties/outings, transportation, veterinarian

- **Education:** books, parking, supplies, travel, workshops

- **Emergency Fund**

- **Entertainment**: books, CDs, clubs, concerts, dates, DVDs, hobbies, houseguests, magazines, newspapers, sightseeing, theatre

- **Food**: coffee/tea, restaurants, fast food, groceries, hosting, snacks, pop

- **Gifts**: anniversaries, babies, birthdays, cards, holidays, weddings, work

- **Health**: chiropractor, doctor/specialist, glasses/contacts, prescriptions, therapy

- **Housing:** TV, maid/contract labour, decor, furniture, gardening, maintenance, moving, storage

- **Investments:** contributions, RRSPs, TFSAs

- **Self Care:** cosmetics, gym, hair, manicure, massage, pedicure, toiletries

- **Transportation:** airfare, gas, maintenance, repairs, taxis, trains

- **Spiritual Growth:** books, CDs, classes, donations, meetings, tithing

- **Vacation:** air, boat, bus, hotels, meals, sightseeing, souvenirs, cell phone fees, taxis, tips, train, Mini-Emergency fund

Here's a question: in the Food category, are Groceries a bill or part of Savings? Well, an outside provider doesn't invoice them. You control how much you spend each month. That would make groceries part of Savings. On the other hand, the money doesn't stay around for long. So, if you feel more comfortable making the Grocery category a Bill, do that.

Once you have noted which Saving categories are appropriate for your family, divide the overall amount you have available for Savings into the various categories.

You can save once a month, or each time you get income. If you are paid sporadically, there is a way to manage this calmly. It was discussed in Chapter 5, *Spend the Proceeds*

PRACTICAL SOLUTION:
Fund Your Wants

A fter you have subtracted your bills from your net income, what is left is divided into your savings categories. In the example below, Partner 1 has $608.78 available from net income after paying bills. That $608.78 is divided into the various savings categories for which she is responsible.

How will she determine how much goes into which category? This is where you go back to Chapter 3, *Splurge on Dreams*, and look at your One-Day-Soon Spending Plan. It will give you an idea of how to divide things. Remember to stay within your total available amount, $608.78.

Once you have divided your savings amount into the big umbrella categories, to the best of your ability, *in pencil*, you can subdivide each into the subcategories, if you want. You don't have to.

For example, look at the *Clothes* category of the following Spending Plan. The overall amount saved is $75 a month. Then, subdivide into the subcategories of *accessories, garments, laundry/dry cleaning, and shoes.* Though, for simplicity's sake, you can leave it at Clothes, $75.

Sample SAVINGS SPENDING PLAN

Savings Income: Every two weeks	$608.78 Partner 1	$557.50 Partner 2
Savings Category	Amount	Amount
BUSINESS PERSONALS		25
computer		10
paper		5
postage		1
supplies		4
trade magazines		5
CLOTHES-FAMILY	*75*	
accessories	*5*	
garments	*50*	
laundry/dry cleaning	*10*	
shoes/repairs	*10*	
DEBT REPAYMENT	--	--
DEPENDENTS		130
allowance		10
classes		15
elder care		---
family events		10
pet care/vet		15
school		15
sitters		20
sports		30
parties/outings		15
transportation		---
EDUCATION		----
books		
parking		
supplies		
tuition		
workshops		
ENTERTAINMENT		100
books		10
CDs		10
clubs		10
concerts		30
dates		10
DVDs		---
hobbies		5
houseguests		5
magazines		---
newspaper		5
sightseeing		5
theatre		10
FOOD	450	
coffees/teas/drinks	15	
groceries	400	
restaurants	30	
snacks	5	

GIFTS		72
anniversaries		5
baby		5
birthday		10
cards		2
celebrations		10
father's/mother's day		5
holidays		20
weddings		10
work		5
HEALTH	25	
chiropractor	10	
glasses/contacts	5	
remedies	10	
HOUSING		45
decor		10
furniture		10
gardening		5
maid/contract labour		10
maintenance		10
moving		---
INVESTMENTS		42.50
contributions		---
RRSPs		42.50
TFSAs		---
TRANSPORTATION		43
maintenance		10
parking		28
repairs		15
SELF CARE	45	
cosmetics	10	
hair	20	
manicures	5	
massage	5	
pedicure	5	
SPIRITUAL GROWTH	13.78	
Books/CDs	2	
classes	3	
donations	8.78	
VACATION: Goal $1800		100
TOTAL	608.78	557.50

Adapted from *The Numbers: One Approach*, Debtors Anonymous

Initially, the amount you save in each subcategory doesn't matter: it can be 50 cents or $50. In time, more money will come into your life through raises, better jobs, and windfalls. Then, you can increase the amounts you put into your savings categories. In the meantime, put something into every category from every check.

You are declaring to the universe, and more importantly to yourself that your savings matter as much as your bills. You handle your financial responsibilities *in order to* fulfill your life wishes.

Being realistic, you can increase the amount of money you have for savings *today*. For example,

An older client was buying expensive fruit because she liked the taste. However, because she lived alone, the fruit often rotted before she could finish it. With an adjustment to her ego, she began to buy frozen or canned fruit. She had to admit the fruit tasted almost as good. In addition, the money she saved allowed her to lower her grocery bill, and use the extra for Savings, in her case, Vacations. She also gave up her large car. Though she felt it befitted a person of her age and status, she came to realize no one was watching her as closely as she thought. She traded it in on a smaller car, saving money on gas, insurance and car payments. Then she had even more money for Vacations.

PAYING YOURSELF FORWARD

Based on past spending behavior, with numbers gleaned from your spending record and your One-Day-Soon Spending Plan, you can predict what you need to save for each category. Guesstimate a reasonable number if you have not spent in a category which you want in your life now.

Some Savings categories will grow over time as you deposit money and leave it there, like vacations. On the other hand, you may spend all the money in some categories, like food during the month. Once a category is empty, stop spending. Not easy. Ask God for help.

God, please remind me more income is on the way, and help me wait to buy more.

Remember, you will deposit more money into all the savings categories in a few days, the next time you are paid. God wants you to live an abundant life full of prosperity and peace of mind. Your time and effort used to calculate how much to save in each of the following categories, considering your present income and your comfort level will help bring that about sooner than you ever thought possible.

Watch out for category Lumping. The Clothes category is a favorite. If you are putting aside $25 each pay for your clothes, you should be able to buy a nice shirt or new unders each month. However, you can't if you get your winter coat dry-cleaned and your boots repaired from the same category. Clothes are not dry cleaning or repair. It's easier to be clear, even if you have to have a million categories. Get this: men only have seven categories, but then, that's their strength.

Allowances

What are the reasons an allowance might be good for the little and the big members of your family? This reliable amount of money gives a child a stable sense of income. Maybe you never had that, and you continue to replay your childhood experiences of feast or famine. A regular allowance, always paid, can establish a different set of life expectations for your kids. If you hand out allowances you can afford on your payday, the kids see income is cyclical, and reliable. They will also learn very quickly that it does not come on demand, that is, whenever they want it. Plus, once it's gone, that's it until the next, scheduled time, like in the real world.

This teaches them that money has to stay around if they want to have some a few days after they were paid. If they divide their money into present spending, and future savings, like for bigger items, gifts, or donations, it is a great money lesson to teach your kids, and it is one best introduced early.

Here's the best part: Allowances stop the requests for more and more money throughout the week. (Although, school expenses are not a part of their allowance.)

How Much?

Kid Allowance: While some experts suggest you give each kid an allowance equivalent to their age, I think that is too much. It would mean a 10-year-old would get $10 a week. That's $40 a month of disposable income for a kid. Do you have $40 a month to do with whatever you please? I think not! What if you have more children? You could be shelling out $100 a month for the little ones to buy gum and video games.

No. While allowances have their merits, the amount has to fit into the overall family Spending Plan. Even $1 of independent income can be a wonderful learning tool for a child. Depending on your income, $1 up to $10 every two weeks might be right for kids under 13.

Another way that involves no guesswork is to calculate how much the child's expenses are bi-weekly, and give them that amount of money. For example, if your child pays dues for a club, gives a charitable donation, and buys snacks or small toys, calculate how much you *already* pay out bi-weekly. You'll give one lump sum each payday.

You'll need to explain to the kids about putting aside their dues money and donation money. In addition, if they save a little in their piggybank for maybe six allowances, they'll be able to buy a big item. That's a life lesson right there.

The rest of the money is theirs to spend as they wish, when they wish, given your health and safety guidelines. However, when it's gone, it's gone. If they can't buy something they want because they have spent all their allowance, they will have to wait, as you or I. That's the way life is. You cannot spend what you do not have. No credit! We know all too much about that pain.

Teenager Allowance: As for teenagers, this system is invaluable. These little men and women are money-demand machines when it comes to hair, activities, and mostly, clothes.

Calculate how much you're already spending on these categories, break it down into the bi-weekly allowance, and give them the lump sum twice a month. This way, when they want some designer jeans, they have to use their allowance to buy them. You will no longer have to mention buying things on sale, believe me. They will be scouring stores for good deals, so they can buy more with the amount of money you've given them. Good training for adult shopping.

Furthermore, they will have to balance the new outfit against going to a concert. These are all choices adults make. It's not too early to give your kids a taste of real life decisions where money is concerned.

A word of caution here: if you go shopping with your kid, don't wimp out and pay the little extra they don't have. It will be hard not to, yet this is the lesson, isn't it? They have the amount of money they have. If the item is too expensive, they can choose something different, or, wait and save for it. In the same way, if your son buys a video game with his lunch money, guess who will be bringing lunch to school, or going hungry for a day? That's one lesson a young boy will not soon forget. Conversely, if you bail him out this time, giving him more money for lunches while he also gets to enjoy his game, that is also a lesson he will not soon forget.

Child rearing books talk about the ideal backbone parents, versus iron parents or noodle parents. When it comes to money, I think many of us are in the extreme, either too cheap or too extravagant. The use of an allowance, carefully calculated, and reliably given will solve myriad money problems with your kids, and teach them how to handle money for life, lessons you probably wish you'd been taught.

Adult Allowance: This idea creates a way to allocate and contain personal monthly expenses. If you go out for lunches, give a couple of dollars to colleague charity requests, and buy coffees, that adds up. Perhaps you don't want to be spending so much on these little things, and would rather put some of that money into a more interesting category, like a hobby.

Give yourself a set amount a month, and stay within it. This may mean bringing coffee from home, or drinking the brew the office offers, but you'll know the money is going to a better place!

Appliances

When major appliances need replacement, they are such big-ticket items, they need their own savings category. If it looks like your stove, refrigerator, washing machine, dryer, or dishwasher is aging ungracefully, start a little fund. Name it by the appliance, or in a group category, like Appliances.

Research the cost of the model you *really* want by checking at least three sources. Include tax and delivery, and divide that total by 24 paychecks. This way, you only have to save $15-20 every two weeks for a few months instead of shelling out $500 all at once, and unexpectedly.

If it breaks down unexpectedly, ideally, you will have saved enough to buy the item you really want. However, if the full amount is not there, you can buy *used* on websites, or buy a less expensive model. This category reflects the inevitable: everything in the kitchen with a plug will need replacement eventually. This fund will keep your spending plan in balance.

How Much?

Try $10 a month. This adds up to $120 a year, enough to get a new coffee maker and a toaster, and have money left over.

Birthdays, Anniversaries, Mother's Day and Father's Day

They come up every year. And every year, they seem more expensive than you expected. Not only is there the gift, but there is also the special food, the decorations, and maybe a party. Figuring the costs of a birthday party may take some guesswork if you don't have a spending record from a recent one. Remember the party favours, the food and cake, drinks, games or room rental, and the gift including tax. Hiding your head in the sand will not fund it. Set a limit for each celebration, and start saving.

Of course, the first year you do this, you may not have much in the Birthday category. You may have to scale back *temporarily*. If your kid is more interested in a gift than a party, try just a cake and drinks at home for an hour. Alternatively, if your kid is getting a bunch of presents from other kids or family, then you can spend less on your present; for *this* year, honey, don't fret. You'll have lots more money next year.

If you're dealing with adult birthday gifts, or anniversary gifts, the kids can use part of their allowance at the dollar store. As for you, try IOU's for services. You know the drill: one bed-making coupon, one back rub coupon, one *wink-wink* coupon. Be prepared, though. They will want to collect!

When the children are young, Mother and Father's Day can be no more than making a special, possibly burned breakfast. Be sure to let the kids do some part of the celebration themselves, even if it's only to put a flower in a glass of water for the tray. These horrible breakfasts will be the sweetest memories.

Gift Requests: If your birthday person declares what they want as a gift, is it really a gift, or them shopping through you? A gift is supposed to be something the giver has noticed the person yearning for by paying attention to them. Isn't it ideal if the giver has spent time thinking about, and analyzing the receiver's likes and dislikes?

It isn't that hard to figure out a gift your kids want; your spouse is another matter. As their birthday approaches, listen for dropped hints. *Ask* them to drop a few hints if you're desperate.

How Much?

Keep this category for your immediate family. Start another category for Gifts for Others which will handle friends and extended family.

Saving $10 a month for each family member adds up to $120 a year. That is a whopping gift. That may be enough money to pay for the party, too. However, $4 per month also adds up nicely to $48, and saving $2 per pay gets you $24 which is a very acceptable amount with which to buy a present.

This category will bring you peace of mind around gift shopping because you will have a boundary of money. You spend what you have saved, no more.

Here's a last word about gifts. Remember you're setting a tone for the family. No matter what your budget, children or adults may want something that costs next to nothing that brings a feeling of closeness, like a walk at night with the family, an evening of playing board games, or a picnic in a park. Sometimes an experience is the best gift.

Books, CDs, DVDs, Flowers, Magazines, Newspapers

What do you define as a luxury in your life? Music CDs are luxuries to some women, yet necessities to others. Magazines are time-wasters to some women, and an enjoyable hour to others. Into this category, you can also put things like novels, DVDs and flowers. These are the butter on the bread of life. Little delights. This money, laying in wait for these items, gives you a feeling of self-care, and permission to live a life you enjoy.

If you are afraid of making a mistake, and wasting your hard-earned money, remember, you're saving more money every pay. Over time, there will be enough money to make even an imperfect purchase, and not suffer self-recriminations.

You'll enjoy your purchase more using this deliberate method of saving for the item and planning the shopping trip to get it. You will feel the quiet satisfaction of having the money to indulge a passion.

How Much?

How many of these items do you buy now? Check your Spending Record. If you want to buy more or cut back and use the money in different categories, pick a number, say one item every other month or every three months, and calculate the cost.

If you buy one every other month at $15 including tax, that would cost about $90 a year. In order to save that much, you'd need to save about $7.50 each month. Subtract that amount of money from your disposable income after the bills are paid, and in a few weeks, you're going shopping for flowers, from you to you!

Car Roadside Assistance & Car Registrations

Have car, have car trouble. Canadian Automobile Association, CAA, is weather insurance, towing insurance, flat tire insurance, run-out-of-gas insurance and who knows what other evil tricks your car will play. These roadside assistance programs are brilliant solutions.

Unfortunately, the cost gets up there by the time you have more than one person in the family. Therefore, CAA needs its own category to be sure the funds are there when the bill comes due. Some of these clubs also provide free maps and other discount services.

Car Registration happens once a year. Saving for it will ensure you have the money when the bill comes due, often on your birthday. Some gift! In addition to that, there is your driver's license. Though you renew it only every three to five years, an unexpected bill is always a blow to the bankbook. Better to save a little over time.

How Much?

You will likely have to save about $7 a month to have about $80 for a family CAA membership. It's approximately $75 for car registration yearly, which is another $6 each month. Then, add another dollar in savings for every driver's license you have to renew. Therefore, you're in the $15 amount each month.

Now, when the bills come, you can shrug and pay them. No big deal. How good is that!

Car Gas

Being short of gas money is not an option for most people if you need your car for work. On the other hand, if you drive when you could reasonably walk or take the bus, or if you're driving one of your kids when they don't really need it, or if you go out for one item at a time instead of figuring out stops enroute, it is a waste of gas and money. Gas is expensive enough without wasting it. Buck up, and get disciplined! If you're a good shepherd of your gas money resources, you'll have extra cash left for the fun stuff, like vacations.

Speaking of cash, sad to say, credit and debit cards have a history of problems at gas stations. Store cash in a separate change purse. That way you won't inadvertently spend money meant for gas purchases on something else.

How Much?

Look at your Spending Record to know how much money you *have* been spending, and then figure it forward for the next two-four weeks. If the price of gas has gone up in the last month, which is too often the case, or you will be driving more in the next two weeks than the previous ones, face the truth, and put extra money into your Gas category.

Extra Money: Where does the extra money come from if you have allocated every cent to your various needs and wants? The easiest way is to take a little out of two or three other categories. Don't remove the whole amount from any one category, like Vacations. This hurts too much, and makes it feel impossible to get ahead. If this is a one-off occurrence, you'll go back to the old amounts next pay. However, if you have to take out a higher amount of gas money again in the next month, it's probably time to raise your gas category permanently, lowering a few others. The system has only so much money in it, the amount you net each pay period, and you need to keep all spending and saving within that boundary.

Planning for your gas purchases means never having to resort to plastic to fill up the tank. Those debting days are over, thankfully. The feeling of having the money in your wallet to pay for gas will make you feel like a high roller for a while. Then, you'll settle down to feeling competent.

Car Maintenance

Is there a human being who has not used a credit card to pay for emergency car repairs? Doubtful. However, since your goal is to stop digging your debt hole bigger, you want to avoid using credit cards. Then realistically, how do you pay for unexpected car problems?

If you're excellent about taking your vehicle in for general maintenance, you probably won't be surprised by unexpected breakdowns. Nevertheless, there will always be big repair bills if you own a car. If you fall into the wishful thinking camp and believe you won't have any repairs, or if you are willing to drive an unsafe car, you are living in a temporary paradise. Neither of these approaches is long term. The only way to manage this unfortunate fact of life is to save money in advance in a Car Maintenance category.

How Much?

Any amount will be better than nothing. However, since, sad to say, most car repairs come in at about $400 a pop, if you're lucky, save $35 each month and be covered.

Think how calm you're going to be when you hand the money to the mechanic without sweating over how you're going to pay off more credit card debt.

Celebrations

Gratefully away from car woes and onto happier topics, planning for celebrations before they occur is a balm to the soul every time you put money into this category. What celebrations might these be? How about the day a member of the family gets a new job, a raise, an excellent report card, or a learner's permit? You know you'll want ice cream cake.

How Much?

How much does it cost to get an ice cream cake? That sucker can be $30-40 bucks! Almost cheaper to go out for dinner. Well, anyway, saving $4 a month will net you $48 in a year. Even $1 saved per month adds up to $12 in a year, and that buys a celebratory chocolate cake!

Having this category, however small, gives rise to the hope you will have good things to celebrate in life. Each time you deposit money, it will lift your spirits.

Charity/Tithing

As we prosper, we share more. Research says we get happiness from sharing our abundance. Except for now, you need a boundary on your sharing. Some women go overboard in this way.

One woman was donating to so many places she truly valued, it was depriving her of her retirement income. Her financial advisor insisted she invest some of those donations for her old age. Then, save a set amount for all charitable giving, and once a year, write checks to her favorites. It wasn't as grand, but it was in balance with her other life goals.

If you're one of those sweeties who loves to give money to various street people, get a small change purse and fund it with $1-5 in change. Distribute this until it's gone. On your next pay, fill up the purse again. You'll feel great but be within a safe financial boundary.

If you must give more often, send a small check to the charity of your choice once a month. If you send $10 or over, you can claim it on your taxes and you can use part of your refund for more charitable giving! Sure, it's not much; still it's money the charity didn't have before.

Tithing is an obligation you place on yourself. You can decide what works best in your spending plan. If your peer group all give a certain percent of their income, you may be tempted to match them. However, we never *really* know what people are doing with their money, how much they owe, and what sources of income they have. Other people need not affect your financial decisions.

Anyway, what is your real motive? If you have been told you will receive 100 fold back on your tithing, and that is why you're doing it, sounds like a deal with the devil.

Once you're on your financial feet, tithing is great if that's what you want to do.

How Much?

Tithing is a choice, not a bill. Some people give 10% of their gross income, while others give 10% of their net income. It may be to a church or charity, something in the name of God. The amount is less important than the spirit in which you're giving. Remember the story of the widow's mite.

Some rich men came to a house of worship and ostentatiously donated large sums of money; then, a poor widow came in and gave half of all her money which she carried in her purse. It was a tiny sum. The Holy man declared that she actually gave more than the rich men.

Many say 10% is how much people should tithe. Let's work out those numbers: If you earn $100,000 gross, you'd donate $10,000 and that is a lot of money. Of course, it still leaves you with $90,000 to scrape by on. However, if you earn $20,000, while 10% of that is much less, it only leaves $18,000 for the necessities of life. That is a much bigger hit.

Forget any set percent mandated by who knows who. Instead, as part of your balanced spending plan, earmark some funds for charity and be guided by generous motives. An easy way to donate is through using automatic deductions at your office, or the charity itself, like the United Way. The United Way is an umbrella organization funding a variety of charities. You can state which charities you'd like your money to go to, or suggest one.

Another way to donate is to save a little with every pay in your Charity category. When you have the sum you want, donate it. Even $2 saved per month will net $24 in a year, and any charity will be pleased to get that donation. If you want to save more, $5 a month is $60 a year. That is a sizeable donation.

However much you donate, you're thinking about someone outside of your immediate family, and role modeling that for your children. Whether you give to Ducks International or tithe, the act of sharing your wealth is a reminder you have enough, and the world is an abundant place.

Cleaner

This service can create harmony in your home like nothing else. Mind you, it is not easy to give yourself permission to hire such a person, never mind relegating some of your money to it. First, let's talk about permission. If you work outside your home, someone has to clean up the house. If you and your partner are doing it, how is it working out? Maybe you divide the chores and get it done quickly, early Saturday morning, and then go out and do the other chores and have a little fun. More likely, you do one of these:

- One person ends up with the main cleaning jobs, and resents it.

- A few people help, but with tantrums and tears.

- The cleaning doesn't get done to your standards,

- No one does the cleaning.

- The cleaning takes precedence over more important things, like family fun time.

Women reject hiring help because of guilt: aren't they the ones who are supposed to do it? In addition, they declare it is too expensive. But, is it? If cleaning is interfering with the quality of your life, think again. Even stay-at-home moms may need someone to help with the cleaning. It will free up your time to play with the children, refresh yourself so you're a more enjoyable partner, and give yourself time to catch up on things you'd like to do.

Give yourself permission to consider the idea. Your money is there for you, and you get to make the choice of how to spend it.

How Much?

If you look for a local person, not a cleaning service, they may be willing to clean for you every other week, or every third week. Don't hire someone for less than once every three weeks. Your house will look so bad the last few days, it will depress you. Every second or third week works.

An experienced cleaning person can scrub two bathrooms, change three beds, vacuum the house, and wash floors in about 3-5 hours. Therefore, though it may cost $100 a month which seems like a lot, if this is a mental health issue for you, it is non-negotiable. You'll have to shave a little from a few other categories until you have that amount to put aside under Cleaner. That is, take $2 from one category, and $5 from another, and $3 from another. Do not leave any category at zero, but you can put in less for now while you're testing out the cleaning person idea.

Remember, more money will start coming in as you begin to take good care of your money.

Clothes

Clothes make the man. Naked women have little or no influence in society. Mark Twain.

Women definitely use clothes to create an impression. If we overdo it or under do it, we are making a statement. For centuries, clothes have controlled people's perceptions of each other. In fact, in England during Shakespeare's time, the law allowed only certain people to dress in certain ways, to maintain class distinctions. Nowadays, some women wear clothes with labels clearly visible, Prada, Versace, or Gucci to imply wealth, and therefore social status. For these women, times have not changed that much.

Back in 1975, John Malloy coined the phrase *dress for success*. As a social scientist, he interviewed 100 executives in Fortune 500 companies. Without exception, they revealed they rated dress as Very Important, and stated they would hold back the promotion of a person who did not dress appropriately. Of course, *appropriate* does not mean *designer*, in most companies.

Except in work situations where the right outfit can make a difference, who is this invisible audience you think is judging you through your clothes? Are you really dressing to impress strangers on the sidewalk? Where is your self-approval? Looking to society for approval means you're missing one far more important: your own.

How Much?

What is the appropriate amount of money to spend on your clothes? You can use many yardsticks: for example, the average Canadian woman spends $1700-2000 a year on clothes, shoes and accessories. On the other hand, some fashion advisors suggest you spend a yearly total equivalent to one month's salary. While that seems better adjusted to income, it's still 8% of your income on clothes. Where are you on this spectrum?

Are you happy with the amount of money you spend on your clothes? Are there other areas of your life underfunded because of your clothes costs? On the other hand, are you stinting on appropriate clothes, adversely affecting your appearance?

Try this: Look at your Spending Record to see how much is going on clothes. Are you over or under the 8% of your income average? As an experiment, if you're over, cut the dollar amount in half. If you're under, double it. How do you feel? I bet you're very uncomfortable. That's self-esteem rearing its head. Either you need more clothes to buy self-approval, or you don't want to spend that much because you don't feel worthy.

Why not start by saving about 2% of your net income for clothes for you, an equal amount for other adults in the family, and probably twice that amount for kids. They do keep growing! Then again, if you're so low on clothes that 2% won't touch it, there is a temporary way for you to build your wardrobe up to an appropriate level: consignment and thrift shops.

A homemaker had a financial crisis when her husband was unemployed due to a car accident. There was a wedding in the family, and she needed a fancy outfit. She got a silk pantsuit that seemed made for her for $7 from the Salvation Army Thrift shop. She looked and felt great.

If you're squeamish about wearing used clothes, some retailers do donate new items to places like the Salvation Army. You can tell new clothes by the crisp, fresh-looking label. Moreover, if you need further inducement to shop thrift, remember these shops have to sell these clothes to someone to make enough money to run their charitable programs. Your money is helping others. Thrift shopping is all the rage these days, saving you quite a bit of money you can use for other important categories. Don't let pride get in the way of a good outfit.

However, if you *have* been shopping at thrift or consignment stores for years, your goal is to *stop*. Save until you have enough money to buy something *new* in a retail store. It will do wonders for your prosperity feelings. And always use the Help available:

God, please guide and protect me as I buy clothes.

Some months, you will buy nothing and just save. For example, if you need to buy a coat, you will save for a few pay periods until you have the right amount, including tax. Give this a six-month trial and then revisit to adjust the amount up or down, to meet reality.

Computer/Office

Internet information may be free; however owning a computer is not. There is always a need for paper. And those ink cartridges! They almost need a bank account of their own. Then there are those office accessories which make your desk a workable space.

If you have kids, office expenses may spill over into School Expenses what with construction paper, special pens, presentation boards and photocopying. If you have a home office, this expense belongs in your separate Business Spending Plan since you can deduct it from your taxes.

You can start to save money in this category by trying these ideas:

o Buy refillable ink cartridges once your printer warranty is up, and get them refilled at specialty stores.

o Print out rough copies of documents at 50% ink or draft mode.

o Use the backside of scrap paper for rough copies. Saves paper.

o If you need a computer, don't buy new. There are used computer stores with very knowledgeable staff. Plus, used computers often come with the major software you need, and so you save a lot of money there.

How Much?

Refer to your Spending Record. It is invaluable if you have made purchases recently for your office. If you have no figures, use these:

Assume about $75 for ink cartridge kits, $6 for a ream of 500 sheets of paper. You probably use two or three of those a year. Are there other office expenses around holidays, or work items you pay out of your own pocket? Divide that total by 24 pays, or 12 months, and you now have a realistic figure to save so you can fund your computer/office category.

Cosmetics

Raised on advertising as we all have been, cosmetics make everyone think appearance and smell attract partners. Women want attention from men. Men are visual. Cosmetics help us look pretty. Even men now think lotions and scents attract partners.

Yet how much of that is true? Sexual pheromones have a scent, the scent of a woman. The perfumes in cosmetics mask those scents. Are you attracting the right man for your pheromones? Think about using unscented products for a 3-6 month trial, and see who comes into your life. Maybe the right man with the right nose is sniffing around for you!

As the Baby Boomers age, the cosmetics industry is aiming to help them stay younger-looking. Many Boomers think looking younger will overcome ageism in the workplace. Research also shows society perceives women wearing cosmetics as more successful.

Cosmetics are clearly here to stay, but they can be very expensive, in many ways. Lately, reports have been surfacing about cosmetics firms using unhealthy ingredients in their products. Before you allow chemicals onto your skin, read *Slow Death by Rubber Duck* by Rick Smith and Bruce Lourie, or Paula Begoun's first and most famous book, Don't Go to the Cosmetics Counter without Me. It lists every conceivable product, and what ingredients are in it. Did you know Biore Cleansing Strips once contained a hairspray chemical?

On the flip side, the industry has done a good job of putting SPF in moisturizers to help protect us from skin cancer.

Manicure, Pedicure, Facial: Under the heading of Cosmetics, and within the amount you save, indulge in facials, manicures and pedicures if you enjoy them. Keeping within your financial boundary will stop overindulgence in this area without cutting it out altogether. You can handle a few luxuries, can't you?

How Much?

Body wash, perfumes, bronzers, lipstick all add up. The cosmetics category is no small line item. At $5 from 24 paychecks, you will have $120 for cosmetics in a year. Since lipstick alone can be $30 a tube, is that a realistic amount for your family? Alternatively, is $10 per pay, $240 a year, enough for your wants and needs? You decide, based on the reality of what you actually spend on each family member now, and keeping balance in your Spending Plan.

Unless, you have teenagers. They consume vats of cosmetics. To avoid conflict, whining, and begging, let them pay for it themselves. Remember Allowances? Alternatively, within reason, considering homework time, let them get a part-time job. In either case, their available cash will form a boundary on how much they and you spend on their cosmetics.

At $5 or $10 a pay, it does not take huge sums of money to indulge in a little perking up if that is what you want to do with your money. Guilt-free.

Emergency Fund

I've already mentioned the Emergency Fund many times, maybe too many, but you need to acknowledge that unexpected expenses will put pressure on your income. Once you have saved up to the number you think you need in your Emergency Fund, you will feel more secure. No need for an emergency credit card. You've got it covered.

Where to Store Emergency Funds?

You need to be able to get at your Emergency Fund money quickly. In other words, it has to be liquid enough to pay for the emergency at the time. Therefore, real estate, or term investments do not work. While stocks are cashable, their value is unstable. Keep your Emergency Fund in an interest-bearing savings account or savings bonds which are liquid. If you're really in an expensive emergency, use any balances in your discretionary categories, such as birthdays, clothes, or vacation. Use the money in those categories for the Basics of food, rent, gas, and utilities. You'll re-save once the emergency is over.

This Emergency Fund is the road to financial peace of mind. It is your guarantee against debt. With this cushion against the vicissitudes of life, that is, the leak in the roof, the car repair, the broken window, you will have cash on hand to pay for it. No financial chaos. You will not have to pull out the plastic. Just imagine!

Furthermore, having cash to pay for an emergency means you will make a better decision on what to buy because you will be thinking with a calmer brain. You will know you can pay for it comfortably. You may not want or like the situation, though as for the money, it won't be a problem. Imagine the freedom.

Financial Crisis Response Drill!

If you anticipate a financial crisis, or are in one now, act quickly. Do not wait until you get laid off or the bank repossesses your house. Take evasive action *now* to ward off sudden financial disaster before it strikes. However, if you are in crisis right now, do the following:

1. Don't panic. You always have choices. You are in charge of making them, no one else.

2. Cut back on the discretionary categories. Fund them in the same amounts, but reduce your spending. Now.

3. Beef up your Emergency Fund. That is going to not only help you by providing a cushion if the money gets short, but it will also give you peace of mind to weather this turmoil.

4. Stop funding retirement savings, extra payments on the mortgage, or investing. Use those funds for your Emergency Fund top up.

5. If you will be late with your bills, call your suppliers and explain what is going on. They'll more likely be able to help you if you give them advance notice. Check the banks for any mortgage help. If you explain your crisis, and are up-to-date on payments, they may allow you to miss up to two mortgage payments by tacking them on to the end of your term. If you're renting, ask for a better deal. Review the script on Negotiating Rent under Spending Plan.

6. Immediately go after lowering the interest rates on your loans, especially credit cards. If you haven't already done it, transfer your credit card balances to lower interest loans.

7. Postpone vacations, Christmas gifts, or decorating.

8. Pay for shelter, utilities, food, and transportation to get to work. Those are your Basics. *If* there is money leftover, fund the categories which matter to you most.

9. Downgrade your cell phone, TV, subscriptions.

10. Reduce Housing costs: get a roommate or tenant; move in with your parents -- until you get back on your feet; rent out your house and move into an apartment; rent out a room in your house to a foreign student; ask a family member to move in, a single aunt or grandparent, to help with the bills.

11. Move to some place more affordable, maybe just for a year;

12. Cut Transportation costs: Sell your car and buy a cheaper one; or have no car and take the bus for awhile

13. Re-shop childcare—ask at churches, synagogues, YMCAs, places where the care is good while the rates are lower. Check daycare costs one mile on either side of your neighborhood. Ask about discounts: two kids, church affiliation, and your willingness to work to lower the fees. You could team up with other families and share a caregiver. Look for Play Groups which may also be day cares. Pull the kids out of activities for a while.

14. Lower your insurance costs. Most women overpay for insurance of all kinds. Shop again if it's been two years. Get five quotes on car, house, life and health insurance. Raise your deductible to at least $1,000.

15. Take a loan as long as it's *secured* with collateral equal in value to the amount you want to borrow. Your guitar, your laptop, or a good piece of jewelry is exchanged for money. You promise, in writing, to repay the loan by a certain date. Borrowing this way is more mature money handling. If you cannot repay the loan in time, the item goes to the lender, no getting out of that, *but* you do not have to repay the loan. You'll see how different this feels from begging.

How Much?

Some financial advisors suggest an Emergency Fund of $1,000. That's a good start, definitely. Some advisors suggest you have enough to pay for three months of bills, and if you're self-employed, six months. That is a *lot* of money to have sitting around. My experience is you need $2500 in an Emergency Fund.

Start where you are even if it's $1. Make it a priority. Put at least one-third of any windfall money, government rebates, overtime, or cash gifts into the Emergency Fund until it is at the right level.

If you withdraw money to cover an emergency, replace it as a savings priority so you have financial protection in place again. Your Emergency Fund is the best part of your Spending Plan. It will bring peace of mind, and justifiable pride in how you manage your money.

Entertaining

Is your house a fort or a castle? When was the last time you had someone over for dinner, or even dessert and coffee? Everyone loves these invitations, so what is holding you back? If it's the cost of entertaining that's stopping you, money should not be allowed to stop the pleasure you will get from enjoying a meal with a friend. You may not do it often, yet at least you can do it once in awhile by saving up for it. That's what the Entertainment category encourages.

Then again, maybe it isn't only money which stops you from entertaining. Do you feel too shy to ask someone over, or don't think you have anyone to invite? Beer commercials can make anyone feel socially inadequate. Here is the solution: Pray about who to invite into your home. Someone you know will appreciate it, and will be good company for you. Ask for courage to ask.

God, please guide me to right thinking about who to invite into our home, and give me the courage to do it.

Make a list of three different people to invite. Ask them one at a time. This way, a refusal will not ruin your plan. God knows which of the three best fits your lovely invitation, so keep asking until you get a *Yes, I'd love to come.*

My Chinese friend regularly hosts an Orphans' Christmas. This is for people who have no one to celebrate with for a variety of reasons. Everyone is thrilled to be invited somewhere and to be with company on that day. Sometimes, Saturday night is as important.

Recognize God is a steadfast friend, and loves you exactly the way you are. Imagine one of the empty chairs in your house for God. Be sure to extend an invitation.

How Much?

As always, you base numbers in savings categories on reality. Unfortunately! Reality in this case means you estimate how much special food and drinks cost for the number of people you're inviting. A bottle of wine can be about $10. If you want to have them over for dinner, research the costs of the menu you'd like to serve. Then again, snacks, and drinks, or coffee and cake are also fine with people. They are coming to be social.

Take a typical dinner: an appetizer like cheese and crackers, a salad, a main course of roast chicken, and a dessert of cake and coffee. Though this isn't a gourmet meal, remember people are coming over for the company not the menu. This dinner might cost $45. If you divide that by 24 paychecks, you'd need to save about $2 a pay to invite a couple of people over for dinner once a year. Saving $4 per paycheck will net $96 a year. This is enough to have people over twice, with money leftover.

It may not sound like much, still if it increases the home entertaining you do, it's opening up your life in the right direction.

Entertainment

Sports, theatre, movies, concerts, clubbing—any of these appeal to you? In the large scheme of things, these planned pleasures give you something to look forward to in life. Your Entertainment category is saving for that.

You can count on it and look forward to it. Sometimes, we get as much enjoyment out of anticipating the event as we do from the actual event. You get a bigger bang for the buck if you plan the treat. In addition, if you know you're going to see your favorite band, playwright, or team in a few weeks, it will make you a happier person. A happier person is easier to live with. Try this on your family: I'm not *really* going to the concert for *my* sake; it's for *your* sake. Heh.

In addition to the enjoyment of the event itself, the pleasant memory will feed your spirit for weeks afterwards. Thus, an investment in Entertainment is money well spent.

It may take you two or three months to save up enough to go to the movies or a club with your partner, still you will eventually go somewhere you like. This means you have to figure out what you like to do. When was the last time you did some concentrating on that?

By saving a bit every pay, you'll be able to do this a few times a year. And why not! Now that you're taking care of yourself in a responsible way, you fund your bills, and you fund your pleasures.

On the other hand, overindulging in nightlife puts your progress on hold. If you need permission to enjoy your life, that's one thing; however if you're a party person, spending all available cash on these types of things risks your very life. You know now you have Enduring Dreams, and they need capital to make them happen. It is easier to make the decision to resist yet another club night when you remember you're saving to start your own business, go back to school, or travel to Europe.

If you feel pushed by friends to join them in yet another extravagance, or hounded by your own droning sense of entitlement, that is, thinking *something is owed to you by life in general; or because you are who you are,* turn to your Spiritual Source for help. You do not have to resist alone. In fact, resistance certainly can be futile. Yet, when God filters your thoughts, you'll clearly see where your life priorities are, and become willing to forego excessive indulgences to realize your dreams.

Repeatedly, you can see the theme for an enjoyable life is balance. No play makes Jill a dull girl; nevertheless, all play means Jill is unrealistic.

How Much?

Tickets cost what they cost, and they aren't cheap. That is reality. Since these are special events, you'll only want to do something major maybe twice a year with minor ones, like movie tickets, thrown in a few times, say three times. This way, you'll have something to look forward to every other month or so.

Events can range in price, but let's say the big ones will cost $75 a person, and the minor ones about $20. That totals $210 for the year. Divide that by 24 pays, and you need to save about $9 every two weeks.

Fit this amount into your overall category set up. It's important. You want to live *within* your means, but also live *well.*

Exercise

Gym memberships are hardly free. All the same, certainly there are places to lift weights where you can spend more or less. The gold-plated gym will not build your muscles or reduce your fat any sooner than the city-run facility. Your comfort level is a factor, though we are trainable apes. We can adapt to new surroundings. The status of your gym need no longer be a factor because now you're aware of how quickly money can drain out of your Spending Plan and your life.

There are also other options for exercise outside of a gym membership The Parks and Recreation programs in all cities offer classes. Schoolyards often have free tennis courts. Moreover, the sidewalk outside your home is made for walking.

In fact, experts report a 30-minute walk three times a week or three ten-minute walks a day will give you these benefits:

1. Help prevent Type 2 diabetes

2. Strengthen your heart

3. Improve brain function. Yay.

4. Strengthen your bones.

5. Alleviate symptoms of depression

6. Reduce the risk of breast and colon cancer.

7. Improve your cardio-respiratory fitness.

8. Improve physical disability in older women.

Therefore, whether you're exercising for weight loss, increased vitality, or thinking power, walking will do it for you free, and as an added bonus, you'll get to know your neighbourhood!

Clear thinking and reduced stress are important when you're trying to change your financial life. Nevertheless, what if you cannot get yourself to exercise? This is an act of self-sabotage, undermining yourself. Your emotions are incapacitating you. Your positive self-talk hasn't worked, but prayer will.

God, please help me take loving care of my body with the exercise best for me.

Ask for Help to take a step in the right direction. This is how God will break the back of self-defiance.

How Much?

Gym memberships range all over the place, but you can always get a deal. They are famous for having you pay in advance for a year, serene in the knowledge most women stop coming after three months. You can likely get a membership for $40 a month at a pleasant place. You can take a Parks and Recreation program for about $70 for nine weeks. That's about $35 a month. Alternatively, you can ride your bike, walk the block, or dance to the rhythms of your favorite tunes in your bedroom free, no new shoes or clothes required.

Multiply any monthly cost by 12 months, and divide by 24 paychecks. Now, you know what you need to put aside every two weeks or monthly to fund your exercise program. In addition, with Help, you might actually do it!

Garden

If you plant it, it will grow. Maybe. Garden nurseries are devilishly seductive if you're addicted to plants. Like any hobby, enough is never enough. Still, having some money in the category will give you both permission to spend guilt-free, and a boundary to keep your spending in balance.

To stay within your category for this year, use the phrase, *This is enough*. Say it over as many times as it takes. You can vary it with *My garden is lovely enough"* and I've *done enough*. And if you're really in the mood to contradict that scratchy inner voice which is criticizing you, say, *I am enough*. That should shut it down.

If you want a bigger garden than you have money for this year, stage it in. Plan a two-year garden. This year, buy to your limit, and plan to buy the rest next year. This kind of patience is a virtue though it is not easy. Ask God for help to feel peaceful around your garden efforts.

God, please help me enjoy my garden and accept it as it is.

How Much?

Since gardeners love to go all out, look less at how much you spent last year than how much you want to spend this year, within a balanced Spending Plan. If you save $5 or $10 a pay, you will have $120-240 a year to aerate your lawn, fertilize your tomato plants, and buy flowers or fruit trees. Go for perennials if you have the talent. Less cost and less work over time. Then, watch your garden grow peacefully.

Gifts

Sometimes your heart is so full of love, you want to give people a present out of the blue! So, set up a category to give you the money to spend this way, and the joy of knowing you have it.

For Family Members

A special gift category for each member of the family, outside of the normal birthday and holiday gifts, also sets a boundary on how much you spend on the little darlings, and the big darlings, too.

What kinds of gifts are we talking about here? It's not a bicycle or an iPad. Those are big-ticket items and if given at all, are worthy of the big holidays. We're talking about a set of baseball cards, underwear with the names of the week on them, a movie ticket, or maybe earrings. A surprise gift for your partner cannot be underestimated. A bouquet of flowers, a specialty beverage, or a coveted DVD all come with a small price tag and a big wow factor because it is a surprise. They realize you have been thinking about them.

The bonuses for you are many. First, boundaries around spending on kids are one of the hardest to maintain. The pressure the kids feel to keep up with their friends, and subsequently the pressure you feel to keep up with the other families is enormous. Children also know which buttons to push to get you to fork it over. This may not be pretty. They press on bruises you have, like feelings of inadequacy, incompetence, or fear of being unloved.

There is no need to go in that direction if you have set aside a little fund to address spontaneous gift giving, within reason. And the *within reason* sets limits. The limit is the amount of money in the category.

Secondly, buying a gift, or going on an outing, just the two of you, is a reminder each person in your family is unique, and you want to have a special relationship with each one. Good quality relationships are the best guarantee of a satisfying life.

For Others

This is a tricky category for most women. The tug on your pride, your love for the recipient, and your own family's needs may be at odds. Unfortunately, this kind of people-pleasing has contributed to your debt in the past.

It's time to review different gift-giving guidelines. This thought-provoking paraphrase to the gift-giving dilemma comes from a 20-something on an internet site. What do you think of his advice?

An Alternate View to Giving Gifts:

- No money gifts. It says nothing about your relationship, and kids will grow up materialistic.

- No gifts people Need. It's like giving money, but you've taken away the "hard job" of them shopping.

- No very expensive gifts, either, like diamond rings or hi-tech hardware. You are trying to impress them, or at least they will think so. And it will imply you are insecure.

- Don't be concerned about what they like or want. You're still trying to impress them. A present is about giving them a part of you. You have to like the gift, then think if the receiver will, too. It's the enjoyment of making the connection between the gift and you that is the real present.

- Buy something cheap and fun. Something like a cool toy or device that does something interesting is great for teenagers. Adults like something a bit more sophisticated, like an advanced corkscrew.

- Try to buy something unique, but still cool.

- Go for symbolism if you're giving flowers, or one great flower. It can make a big point.

- How about hand-made gifts? Try using art to express your personality. Write notes by hand, build something, create sculptures.

- Presentation. Wrap the gift yourself, and pay attention to all of the details. Maybe stick a note inside somewhere which they will find as they unwrap it. Or, those nesting boxes are always a hit. But, keep the real present in your hand, so when they get to the littlest box, you come forward with the real gift.

Are you charmed, or disgusted? One woman I know *hated* these ideas. She is the type to give her family a complete, detailed shopping list of gifts she wants. Moreover, if she doesn't get them, gets angry.

However, before you experiment with changing your gift-giving habits, you might want to explain what you're trying to do so your family members will expect less, and support your efforts. Nevertheless, will they applaud you for it? Not likely! Presents bring out greed. Maybe you have spoiled them in the past. Of course, once they understand that some restraint in this category translates to *them* also giving less extravagant gifts, they may like this new reality.

My husband and I received a gift recently that met many of the alternate view criteria. It was several, old fashioned, used records. Somehow, it seemed so thoughtful for the gift giver to have gone to the trouble of searching out such a store, and picking through all the options, and finding those he knew related to our interests. And you know it wasn't that expensive.

How Much?

This category is for presents for your children's friends, teacher gifts, coach gifts, your friends and family's weddings, bar mitzvahs or confirmations, colleague special events, and all the other gifts that crop up in the year.

As for gifts to your kids' friends for birthday parties, you can set a dollar limit, then go to a discount store and let your child help choose the gift. Figure out how many kids' birthday parties they might attend this year, and multiply out the yearly cost. If the total is too high, lower the amount you plan to spend per gift. One good gift is always movie passes which are popular and under $10 each.

As for weddings, the going rate is something to consider, though it is not your job to pay for someone else's party. Your Spending Plan will determine how generous you can be, balancing all the other needs and desires of your family. The amount will change as you become more prosperous.

If a big event is coming up in the near future, you will have to generate extra income in the next few weeks. Review Chapter 4, *Claim your Income* for ideas on how to get an infusion of cash quickly, but avoid going into even one cent of debt.

If you save $10 per pay, you'll have $240 a year to spend on gifts for other people. Won't that feel good?

Groceries

This woman was so health conscious, she spent over $400 every two weeks on food items from a health food co-op. Though this was a cheaper way to shop for health food, still her total grocery costs were too much of her net income. She felt she couldn't compromise her family's health since there were allergies, so she was in a bind. Also, she felt they lived in a poorer part of town, not where she and her husband thought they should be, so to *separate herself from the neighbours, she used special food to make her feel special.*

Food satisfies more than physical hunger for many women. There are emotional components that have little to do with the actual food item. If you're overweight, or obsessing about food, consider bringing those issues to a therapist or food support group like Overeaters Anonymous. This will save you grocery money in the end.

If you have special food needs, or shop organic, your grocery bill may be higher; however, that is your choice. You get to choose how you want to spend your money within a balanced spending plan.

Then again, there may be hidden reasons why your grocery bill is so high. Look at what you buy at the grocery store: is everything going into your mouth?

Groceries which You Do Not Eat are not Groceries.

The dictionary defines Groceries as *products you get from a grocer.* Therefore, this could be cat food, laundry detergent, and celery. Despite that, the money you put aside for weekly groceries needs to reflect the things you are buying to put in your mouth. If you have a pet, wouldn't a Pet category give you a clearer picture on how much you are spending on Fur-person? In addition, wouldn't a category called House Supplies give you a more exact read on how much you spend on laundry, like maybe too much, or too little?

When you lump all these things under Groceries, it gives the impression this is food. Therefore, when you look at your category and see you are spending about $50 a person a week on groceries, you immediately think there should be enough food in the darn house, so why is dinner always such a problem? While the truth is, you are spending about $5 a week on Furry-face, $10 a week on laundry, and that leaves only $35 on food.

How to Save Grocery Money

You like to think you're making rational choices in grocery stores; however, research shows that retailers lay out the route they want you to take, like department stores. Watch out for these tricks which try to manipulate you into buying more groceries.

- **Sales on the End Aisle**: Most women assume if products are located on an aisle end-cap, then it's a bargain and sometimes, it is. More often, the items are old, stale, or poor sellers. It's like a clearance section of a department store. Other times, items are on the end-cap of an aisle because a manufacturer has 'rented' this space. That area gets a lot of attention from shoppers as they round the corner. It rents for a higher price, making it a good profit center for the grocery store. To make their own profit, the manufacturers have to sell high profit items in that location. So, though it may look like a sale, it ain't. Don't expect to find good products at sale prices on an end-cap.

- **Slow Music and Low Temperature**: According to research, music in a major chord with a slower beat sells more groceries. I am not kidding. The music makes you relax, and so spend more time in the store. The longer you spend in the store, the more you buy. Also, research shows when the weather is colder, women tend to eat more. Therefore, the grocery store cranks up the air conditioning in the summer and lowers the heat in the winter. And you thought they were trying to save on their gas bill.

- **The Bakery and Free Samples**: Research also reveals women buy more when they smell baking bread. It's a comfort smell. While free samples induce a sense of indebtedness to buy. They feed you, and you return the favour by buying something. Aren't humans polite?

- **Coupons:** According to experts, when women use a coupon, they automatically assume they're getting a good deal. However, that's not always the case. Stores offer coupons on higher priced items where a lower-priced item would do as well. As in, when was the last time you got a coupon for your regular bread, milk or coffee?

- **Crowded Aisles**: Ever wonder why the horizontal aisles at the front of the store are so crowded? It's because by the time you have lined up, and gotten tired, anxious to get out, you're more likely to buy a little something to perk up.

- **Sales not Bargains**: Many advertised sales are anything but. Often times the list price shown in comparison to the "sale" price is not the original list price, rather a much-inflated one. Surely not! 'Fraid so.

- **Scan Errors and Grocery Carts**: Whether it's placement, computer updating, or sloppy signage, scanning errors can cause major differences in your expected price and your actual receipt. If you check over your bill before you leave the store, many times you will find an error. Also, look at the size of your grocery cart next time you shop. It has expanded enormously during the past 50 years. Bigger cart, more room for you to purchase more things.

- **Product Placement**: Grocery stores place sale items near high profit items, often when they go together, like salsa and chips. Salsa on sale; expensive fancy chips. Also, the store places a staple item next to a luxury item: apples near caramel dipping sauce, or the cereal opposite the candy shelf. Research shows healthy produce placed at the front of a store will make shoppers feel less guilty about not-so-healthy purchases elsewhere in the store. Grocery stores also like to place items like cookies and high sugar fruit juices close to the cash register, so even if you pop in for one or two items, you can't miss them. In addition, grocery retailers put the more expensive, often name brands at eye level. You see them first. Along with that, they place children's products on lower shelves at the kids' eye level. Devilish!

- **Prices on Larger Packages**: Not all 'family-size' items are cheaper than two of the smaller ones. Sad to say, some grocery stores trade on the common expectation that less packaging equals lower price. Yet, when you double the price of the smaller can, you may find two of those equal the volume of the bigger can, yet are cheaper. That's so sneaky.

- **Store Route**: Supermarkets place the dairy and other food essentials at the back of the store, so you have to walk through the entire place and pass every other product. They also regularly move items around, so shoppers may be enticed by new products.

More Grocery Savings Tricks: Depending on eating habits, you can save money if you

- Shop at no frills grocery stores. Though the fancy stores have wider aisles and more variety, are they worth the sticker shock at the checkout?

- Buy store brands. Often they are good quality.

- Consider *frozen* fruits and vegetables. You may like to buy fresh; however how much of it rots uneaten? Frozen items are very high quality these days, and there's far less waste.

- Menu plan dinners for two weeks to buy in bulk and shop from a list. Lists reduce impulse buying, and as a bonus, menus reduce meal preparation stress.

- Shop only once a week. Don't go into the store for that one item. You can probably do without whatever it is for a couple of days. Even if it's a staple, you can eat something else. A good opportunity to reduce refrigerator clutter!

- Do not shop when you're hungry. Who put those cookies in the basket?

- If you purchase organic foods, many chain grocery stores stock organic and health food items, now. And remember the Dirty Dozen: these items are the ones which you are wise to buy organic because they are the most contaminated by chemical pesticides: peaches, apples, sweet bell peppers, celery, nectarines, strawberries, cherries, pears, imported grapes, spinach, lettuce, potatoes. If funds are tight, don't worry about the rest.

Out of Balance Spending on Food

If you already know all this, what is stopping you from following best practices around food shopping?

Are you overspending because you are competing with other women in your circle, or are you buying food that makes you feel prosperous and competent? Do you feel food is a treat, your one indulgence in life? On the other hand, are you under spending, so tight for cash you deprive yourself and your family of sufficient, healthy food?

You will solve many of these problems with a proper Spending Plan which has money being set aside for your Dreams. You will find yourself willing to spend less on food luxuries. Now that you have set amounts for all the things in your life, you can fund your groceries properly.

Before you enter the store, with your list, ask God to go with you. If you're tempted to buy things you've decided against, ask God for Help! Rely on your Spiritual Source to give you the peace and neutrality around food shopping that you feel around turning on the TV.

God, please guide and protect me in this store. Help me to choose healthy, affordable foods in appropriate amounts.

How Much?

Government figures say basic food groceries for a single person should be about $200 a month. For a family of four, about $715. That's not steaks, or pop, or chocolate bars. It's also not laundry detergent or toothpaste. It is basic food your family puts in their mouths. If you can do it for less and still eat nutritionally, great. Most women can't. If you're spending more, look to see if you're buying convenience foods, or letting foods like produce go to waste.

This makes how much you're paying for food much clearer, and you want to be very clear about where your money is really going.

Hair

Hair products are so vast in range, it's hard to know what's best for your family's hair, and good value, too. There is hope, though. Paula Begouin, author of Don't *Go Shopping for Hair Products Without Me*, has done extensive research on all hair products, and prices, and can help you through the quagmire. When it comes to shampoos, conditioners, hair colours, hair growth products, and all the rest, there is no requirement to spend a lot of money because many products don't do what they say they will, especially hair growth products.

Begouin likes almost all L'Oreal shampoos and conditioners, including those for kids, Johnson and Johnson shampoos for kids, and Clairol conditioners, while not most of their shampoos. These products are easy to find, and to find on sale. For shampoo, you're looking in the range of $7 for 13 ounces. If you use the recommended amount of product, which is a dollop in your palm about as big as a Looney and not much thicker, a bottle of shampoo will last a long time. Experts also say washing hair once or twice a week is enough for most women to have clean, healthy hair and scalp. That will cut down on your costs.

Your hair makes a big difference in how you look. Carving money from your income for regular, appropriate hair care is a Must not a Want. Make colour, whether you do your own or go to the hairdresser, styling, and haircuts for the family part of your balanced Spending Plan.

How Much?

If you ask around, you can find women who do hair in their homes and who are talented, and cheaper than salons. Some franchises offer less expensive services. Barbers, in particular, are less expensive for women.

These days, everyone seems to use hair colour. At-home products are easy, excellent, and far cheaper than hairdressers. In spite of this, if you're experiencing hair loss, go to a hairdresser from now on or risk further hair loss. If your hair is growing normally, before you pay that $80 to your hairdresser for a colour, ask yourself if you're spending more on your hair than on your dreams.

If you need a haircut every two months, and your partner needs one every month, total the amount it will cost for one year of services. Divide that number by 24 pays, and you'll know how much to save in the Hair category. For example, a woman's haircut can be $50, a man's $30. Six woman's cuts a year would be $300. Twelve men's cuts would be $360. Shampoo and conditioner each at $7 a bottle, four times a year, totals $56, and hair colour, if you buy it at the store, is about $15 every three months totaling $60 a year. That's $680 a year, divided by 24 pays. You need to deposit $28 a pay into the Hair category. If there are kids, add them in and adjust the saving amount.

You will experience a sense of well-being and peace when someone in the family needs a haircut, and you look in the category and see the money is there.

Health and Dental

There are vitamins, band-aids, cough medicine, and prescriptions not covered by health insurance, and numerous other health-related expenses in a year. It is reality.

Your teeth are another matter. If you don't like going to the dentist, you may hope you never have enough money in this category. Minor work like fillings and cleanings are costly enough, never mind major work like crowns and root canals. While you may prefer to stick your head in the sand about these, it doesn't mean you won't need the money to pay for them.

However, there is more to the Health and Dental category than money, as I think you're coming to see is true for all your categories. Ask yourself if you are taking good care of your health? For example, when was the last time you had a complete physical? When was the last time you had your teeth cleaned? This is Self Care. Do you care for yourself?

Do you feel important enough to take the time, the energy and the money to fill your own needs? If not, you're short changing everyone in your life. As you need to put the oxygen mask on yourself first in an airplane emergency, you also need to put your self-care before your kids or anyone else. *Really*.

If you've mistakenly learned you are not important enough to get positive attention, you have to challenge those thoughts. Accept God cares about you, and wants you to be healthy. Imagine God as the good parent you wish you'd had, making sure you see the doctor for the pills, or the dentist for tooth care. Be a good parent to yourself, now, taking care of your neglected health and dental needs.

How Much?

You can set up two categories, one for Health and one for Dentist, or leave them combined. Getting a dental check up and cleaning twice a year is about $300 a person. Divided by 24 pays, it's about $13 for each person. Health supports like vitamins, over the counter drugs, and chiropractor sessions might average

$20 a month per person, or $240 a year. If you divide that by 24 paychecks, you will need to save about $10 per pay for each person in the house.

Care about yourself, first, with God's help, and you'll actually care better for the ones you love.

Hobbies

Encarta defines hobby as *an activity engaged in for pleasure and relaxation during spare time.* You do this to relax and enjoy yourself. You schedule some time each week for nothing except your hobby. It will enrich your life. Whether you like woodworking, knitting, ballet, reading or guitar playing, you deserve an interesting life.

If you swear you don't have spare time for such frivolities, track your time for a week. You'll find spare time. Once you have found the time to pursue a hobby, what will it be? If you already know, you're ahead of the game. If you have forgotten how to play, think back to your childhood. What did you enjoy then? Skating? Dancing? Playing ball? Those are places to start to see if the old spark is still there. Check Google for Hobby Lists to get other ideas.

If nothing clicks, think about what you enjoy on TV. Sports? Singing shows? Then join an amateur group. If you have always wanted to play the violin, there is even a place for that. Google the RTO, the Really Terrible Orchestra. It is for people who love music, but don't play instruments well. They get together, hurt each other's ears, and love it.

You can do hobbies alone or with someone of like mind. It's a way to meet new people. How about Geocaching? It's a free, real world, outdoor treasure hunt. Players try to locate hidden containers, called geocaches, using a smart phone or GPS and then share their experiences online.

How Much?

Remember, $5 a month is $60 a year. That's a good start on ceramics. And, you will no longer feel like a drone, a drudge, or a house slave. You'll feel interesting!

House Maintenance

If you own a house, it is likely your most valuable asset. This category puts money aside for home repair. If you don't own your home, this category is for household needs, from light bulbs to new bowls.

Here is another opportunity to be a good shepherd of your resources. While cleaning supplies come from a House Supplies category, doing the cleaning might mean getting tools to make it easier. It might mean taking the time to look around your house and see what is in need of repair.

You do not have to live with broken appliances, worn out items, or insufficient dishes. While you're getting your financial house in order, you can get yourself down to a thrift shop and stock up on household items for pennies on the dollar. You need not deprive yourself as you work towards prosperity.

Initially, there are things you can do to improve the condition of your home that take very little money, like neatening up the garden, or de-cluttering the closets. In fact, cleaning out the basement or garage could net you cash by selling some of the items online or at a garage sale. You might get a tax deduction if you donate larger items, or do someone good by donating them.

Donating Items

Danger! Some people treat their things with a *binge and purge* mentality. They buy too much, and give away valuable things to get rid of them. Being a good shepherd of your resources means you try to sell things before you give them away. Yes, it takes some effort to clean up an item, list it online, or hold a garage sale; then again, if it's in reasonable condition, it has cash value.

Purging your house by throwing out a bunch of things or donating them is not prudent resource management. Think of what you could do with the money you earn from selling a bike, or kids' furniture. You could buy new items you want for your home, like curtains, dishes, or a power washer!

How Much?

Refer to your Spending Record to see how much you have spent in the last few months replacing light bulbs, kitchen utensils, and tools. You can use those figures as a basis for working out how much to save in this category. Although, if you have been ignoring these needs, it'll have to be a guesstimate.

If you need a lawn mower, the number will be different than if you need to buy a new mop. As always, $5 a pay totals $120 a year. A lawn mower will be three times that and a mop substantially less. Though $5 may not sound like much, in two pays, you'll have $10, and that can buy a mixing bowl.

House Supplies

When you're trying to see clearly as to where your money is actually going, it is vital you separate out your cleaning supplies, shampoo, and other non-food items from your food at the grocery store. It's not that you shouldn't buy those items there, though they are cheaper at the dollar stores, it's that you want an accurate read on how much each category costs. If you add House Supplies into your food total because you buy them at the grocery store, it might seem like you're spending too much on food. It might mask you're spending too much on House Supplies.

Look at where you are purchasing things and how much you are buying. Then, make a small change. If you sense you are unwilling to change, pray for the willingness.

God, please release me from defiance and fear, and help me create healthy financial behavior.

How Much?

Look at your Spending Record. You'll get accurate figures for how much you usually spend on household items in a month. You can see why the Spending Record is so crucial. Whatever your numbers, they are neither right nor wrong. If you find them high, change to store brands, or shop at discount stores.

If you find the number realistic, you will likely spend about the same amount every month. If one month you buy very little, let the money ride, because another month you'll need to purchase a lot.

If you do not have a spending record, yet, start by saving $3 a pay times the number of people in the house. You will probably be in the ballpark.

Maintenance

This category refers to keeping your assets in good condition. Once you have a valuable item like a car, a house, or electronics, it takes money to keep them in shape. If you do not have a maintenance category, part of the item may wear out or break, and not get repaired. That lowers resale value, or can cost a lot more if you have to replace it. Experts suggest, for example, that you set aside 1-2% of the value of your house for upkeep. Big bucks! All the same, how much are you setting aside now? Somewhere between zero and nothing? Therefore, $1 would be an improvement.

How about your car? How often do you change the oil? Moreover, is your wood furniture being waxed, occasionally? This is really a Good Shepherd category. You're a good shepherd of your resources.

Do You Really Like It?

This brings up another important concept. Why would you want to take care of something you don't really like? Look around. Did you buy your stuff because it was cheap? Or, did you buy things you loved and could afford? That's a twin train track: *loved* and *could afford*.

Learn to buy what you really want by saving a bit longer to get it. Then, you will feel so pleased every time you look at it and will want to take care of it.

However, what if you do not have the time or the energy to keep on top of your toys? Well, if you have enough money to hire someone to keep them in shape for you, then you can do that. If you don't, give this job to a family member. Some women give everyone chores, even the youngest child. Let them dust the TV. It teaches them care concepts, teamwork, and creates a one-for-all and all-for-one family atmosphere. Determine to take care of your stuff or get rid of it.

How Much?

What is the reality here? Sure, you can wait until something breaks and then pay to repair it. However, some other category will be depleted. An item breaking from lack of maintenance is not a surprise. Even $1 per pay will total $24 in a year which can buy a number of cleaning or repair kits.

Meals Out

Some people call this category Restaurants. No matter. With either name, these are meals you do not cook yourself. Yay!

Of course, women often think of this as a luxury category, and sometimes it is. But, what is wrong with luxury? Luxuries are enjoyable. You need to believe you're worthy of living a life where little luxuries occur. So, do not remove eating out from your Spending Plan!

Then again, by its very description, luxury means a special treat, not regular fare. Even lunch out everyday is overdoing it.

Reasons You May Eat Out Too Much

Loneliness: Some women eat out often because they live alone and want the socializing. Eating in a familiar place with a familiar server can bring a sense of community. Therefore, it's not the food as much as relief from loneliness. Instead of spending the money on restaurants, fund other activities, like a class, a hobby, or participation in a house of worship. These are far better supports for a satisfying social life than routine eating out.

Once you get to know a few women in the new activity, you may find a community where you make a plan to eat out with each other occasionally. A planned meal out with company is a happy occasion. You get to imagine the pleasant evening before it happens, and look forward to it during frustrating moments in the day. You also get to live it on the evening, having a wonderful meal with good conversation around you, and then you get the warm glow of reliving it afterwards.

Keep in mind, loneliness is a common feeling in the human race. Happily, God is always there as a Friend. Call out when you're feeling lonely, and you'll see the interesting ideas that come to you.

God, please join me. Help me to feel your love and friendship. Guide me to the next right step.

Home Conflict: Perhaps you eat out so much because you'd rather not get into an argument with someone at home. Or else there is another reason you like to escape as often as possible. Address this problem with expert help. Any cleric, social worker, or doctor will be able to start you on the road to getting that help. Eating out is simply delaying the solution rather than solving it.

Special Us: If you watch much TV or go to movies, it seems like everyone is rich, well dressed, and eating at glamorous restaurants. And why is it they never finish the food on their plates? Anyway, it's easy to see why you might want to identify.

Then again, these are not real people. Furthermore, this is not their real lives. You know this, though at some level, the fantasy is so appealing, you have convinced yourself you too should live a life like that, even though you can't afford it.

It may also be your circle of friends. If they have the budgets to eat out often, good for them. You have other plans for your money which include your dreams. You're worth luxuries, too, as many as you can afford in your balanced spending plan. Your dreams fuel real happiness. Redirecting money from restaurant food to your dreams will net lasting satisfaction. This is the best insurance against overuse of restaurants.

How Much?

Track what you spend on take out and restaurant food. Is this really how much you want to spend each month, considering the other categories you now want to fund? If you're happy with the amount, you can use that number. Save ahead.

If you don't know how much you spend, assume you plan to go out once a month or so. Saving $20 per pay per person equals $40 a month per person. If you're a drinker, add $10 per person for a bottle of wine or a cocktail. Plan it. Anticipate it. Enjoy it. You're worth it.

Parking

If you have to pay for parking, is it once or twice or twenty times a month? Whether this is a daily expense or an occasional one, having the right change for parking will prevent you from using a credit card. Are you not worth the few minutes it will take to get coins from the bank? Of course you are! Face reality, acknowledge parking fees, and prepare for them.

But wait, can you reduce them?

o Would taking public transit, even part of the way, be cheaper, less stressful, and even convenient?

o Would car pooling work, and as a bonus, help you get to know a few women better?

o Is there a cheaper parking spot a bit farther away from work? If so, think of the walk as free exercise which is always a good thing.

o Can you work from home part of the week?

o Would you consider looking for a job closer to home?

o How about making a daily commuter deal with a taxi company, even one way?

Depending on how far from home you work, think of your present monthly parking costs, car payments, insurance, gas, and upkeep, and do the math. Even if you don't find you can reduce this expense after crunching the numbers, you're creating a good, new habit: periodically checking to see how much you can reduce your expenses. Every time you reduce the cost of a bill, you get a raise!

How Much?

If you need to pay monthly, save off half the amount you need from each pay period. If you only occasionally need to pay for parking, $3 a pay will add up nicely for when you do. Some women have a parking fund they always keep handy, either in the car or in a separate pouch in their purse. It has coins in it.

Pets

If you have one, or are thinking of getting one, read this, otherwise, skip to the next category. Pets are expensive. No more the philosophy of bygone eras when a pet got sick, it died. Now, society treats pets like children. If this is you, be prepared to pay for your pleasure.

If you have goldfish, only some of this will apply, while if you have a dog, or cat, you're in for it. It is not only their food, walk accessories, and pet sitting, but also those vet bills. Ignoring serious diseases, shots, spaying and grooming cost a lot. Do not think for a moment I'm discouraging you from owning a pet which can be source of comfort, love, and lessons for the whole family. All the same, if you want an animal, be prepared to set up a category to fund its expenses realistically. Decide now before something hurts Fluffy, how much can you actually afford to shell out for the vet.

There is pet insurance, though read the fine print carefully. Sometimes the policies are invalid once a pet reaches a certain age, often the one at which ill health begins. Also, some policies have a cap on how much they will pay for any one accident or a lifetime total. This also has a monthly cost from $15 to much higher.

You will need a Pet category for regular expenses, and a Pet Emergency Fund, too, for extraordinary, one-time costs.

How Much?

Assuming you have a dog or a cat, and barring having your own figures, if you put aside less than $30 a pay, you're being unrealistic. This amount includes the regular vet visits. For emergency care, think $1,000 in a fund.

Note this is $780 a year plus the emergency fund of $1,000. That is a lot of money. It is your choice to use your money this way. Also, for most families it's worth it!

Photography

This is one of those optional categories. Although, think about this: when you consider what you'd save if your house caught on fire, wouldn't it be the pictures of your past? Pictures are a lasting record of your family's young life, vacations, and holidays.

So, if you like to frame pictures, that costs money. If you like to have some printed off, it also is an expense. Albums to house the photos you want to have within reach cost something. There are also photo book sites where you can have books made of your pictures. For the best option, check online regularly as things change fast in the digital world. Some women create a photo book every year to send to grandparents who do not see their grandchildren often. Maybe you want this category to save for a good camera.

How Much?

You start with $5 a pay (x 24 pays a year). You'll have $120 a year to frame or print pix, or begin a fund to buy that next digital camera.

Reverse Osmosis Water Filter, Anyone?

I doubt you have one of these water filters; nevertheless, the category is here to make a point. The filters cost about $100 each, and while you only change them once a year, $100 is quite a hit to the budget. You have to save it up. Look around your house. Is there some item similar in nature to a water filter which needs a little category of its own? Hot tub, bike?

How Much?

Find out how much your item costs, don't forget to add in the tax. Divide that amount by 24 pays. That is how much you need to save in this category.

Religion

Other than Christmas, Eid, Chanukah, or other major gift-giving holidays which should have their own category, most religions have several times a year when special food and special ceremonies are going to cost you money. For example, Easter usually involves Easter egg hunts if you have small children. Easter baskets for the Easter egg hunt are not free. The special family dinner with the traditional Easter ham for the extended family is going to cost more than your normal dinner. If you go to church, there is the donation basket there, too.

If you celebrate Passover, it might mean a huge group of people coming to your house for the Seder. Even if you do it potluck, the host will be expected to buy a few extras, like the cream for the coffee, the pickles, the candles, and who knows what all else.

Even the secular holiday of Halloween brings unusual costs. In some neighbourhoods, there are scads of kids, and unless you're willing to turn out your lights, go out for the evening, and miss all the fun of seeing these little kids dressed up, you're going to have to buy several bags of candy.

Your grocery category is not set up for more than the normal two-week groceries. Face this reality: there are extra expenses around holidays. If you have funds set aside, you won't be penny-pinching and resenting everyone. You'll feel like the gracious host you want to be. You will also feel more confident in asking others to pay their fair share. Your attitude will be more open and positive and so the evening will go differently. You will enjoy yourself more. Imagine that around family get-togethers!

How Much?

If you don't have any figures, you'll have to guesstimate, and add 10%. It will cost more than your wishful thinking! How many times a year do you celebrate these types of events with or without your extended family?

It's rare to get out of these things without each costing $50. Say a total of $150 to cover a year. Therefore if you put aside $7 each pay, you will have enough money and feel like a financially mature member of your family.

Snacks

Admit it, you love to have a bag of chips, or a coffee and a muffin now and then. But, it's not really groceries, is it? Groceries are for the whole family, and are part of meals. These little munchies are wherever, whenever. And there's nothing wrong with that. Be aware this is one of your little pleasures, and be willing to allow yourself to indulge it by putting money into a category.

On the other hand, if you're unhappy about what you're snacking on or how much, more reason to put a financial boundary around the Snack category.

Snacks for Fatigue

If you're drinking too much caffeinated coffee, or pop, or eating too much chocolate which contains caffeine, you're probably overtired. Unfortunately, it's a vicious cycle: caffeine punches up your adrenaline, giving you a spurt of energy, but it can end up exhausting your adrenal glands, so you need more caffeine. Eventually, the adrenals give out, and then you'll know what tired really is!

Deal with fatigue in healthier ways. Certainly, you can get to bed earlier. If you're the creative type, you need, get ready for this, ten hours of sleep a night. And that's sleep, not lying in bed reading, or snacking! Honestly now, what time do you go to bed, and what time do you get up? Track yourself for a couple of weeks, and you may find part of the reason for your low energy.

Our society seriously undervalues the catnap. Thomas Edison used to take one-minute power naps. This may not be enough time for your depleted body, although it is better than another cup of tea with its wallop of stimulating theobromine, as well as caffeine. Now you know why nannies always want a cup of good British tea when faced with obstacles.

If you ask God to help you take a 30-minute break, where you close your eyes, you'll get a second wind for the rest of the day. Ask God to help you give yourself *permission* to rest, my dear. You deserve it.

Snacks for Love

If you're unhappy about the amount or types of snacks you're buying, why do you keep doing it? For example, if you're eating too much sugary stuff, is it because there is not enough sweetness in your life? Many women have relationship issues which they cannot cope with, and do not know how to change. So they use snacks to get comfort, pushing their emotions down with the food, or hiding from reality by using food to numb themselves.

Ask yourself this: *who loves me?* Did you have trouble finding someone? There are two sources of love always available to you:

the first is yourself. This may be the root of your problem. You do not love yourself. If you have not had good parenting, or are not in a positive love relationship, you may not know *how* to love yourself. How you fix that is by asking for Help from the second source of love: ask God to help you feel Love while you learn to love yourself.

If there is a noticeable weight issue because of this, try a 12-step program. Overeaters Anonymous provides a great deal of support, and it's a pay-what-you-can system of donations. If you genuinely want to reach out, but cannot, pray to your God for the strength. If you have a close friend or family member, you can ask for their help and support around this. If you don't, you can call the OA phone number and tell them you need someone to help you get to a meeting. You'll be surprised at people's willingness to be of service to you. You don't have to tell anyone what you're doing if you don't want to.

How Much?

If you want to snack a few times a week, acknowledge your little indulgence, and fund it. If you don't know how much you're presently spending, you can start by giving yourself $10-$15 every two weeks for this category. Spend it all. This is not a category where you store money. Buy what you enjoy over the next few days, and stop when you have used up all the money.

Don't take money from other categories to get your fix! This is where you may need to ask for Patience. Because, in a few more days, your pay is coming, and then you will deposit more into your Snack category, starting the glorious process all over again.

SAVINGS MANAGEMENT

There is more than one way to set up your savings. It depends on your family's income stream.

SET AMOUNT SAVINGS

If your paychecks are pretty much the same each pay period, you can deposit the same amount of money into each savings category every time you are paid. If you want to save a total of $80 a month for the Vacation category, you allocate $40 from each paycheck for a total of $80 at the end of the month. Alternatively, you can save once a month at $80.

However, if one paycheck is significantly higher than the other, save a higher amount from the higher paycheck, and less from the lower paycheck. For example, if you want to save $80 a month for a vacation, deposit $60 into Vacations from the higher paycheck, and $20 from the lower one, for a total of $80 a month.

DIFFERENT PAYCHECKS, DIFFERENT AMOUNTS SAVED

Net Salary Monthly: $1300 – $691.22 for bills = $608.78 for Savings			
Date	Savings Category	$408.78 Pay 1	$200 Pay 2
June 2	Vacation	60	
June 16	Vacation		20

PERCENT SAVINGS

However if your income is variable, coming in all over the month, and different from month to month, try percent allocations. Once your bills are paid, you will divide the rest of your income into your savings categories by percent.

1. First, you need to decide what percent you want to deposit into each category. Referring to your Spending Plan savings categories, allocate a percent to each until you have allocated 100%. Double-check your arithmetic to be sure all the percents add up to no more than 100%.

Sample PERCENT of INCOME SAVED from EVERY CHECK

Savings Income: Every two weeks	$Variable Partner 1	$Variable Partner 2
Savings Category	% of Saving	% of Saving
BUSINESS PERSONALS		3%
computer		1
paper		.5
postage		.5
supplies		.5
trade magazines		.5
CLOTHES-FAMILY	25%	
accessories	2	
garments	15	
laundry/dry cleaning	3	
shoes/repairs	5	
DEBT REPAYMENT	--	--
DEPENDENTS		30%
allowance		2
classes		4
elder care		---
family events		4
pet care/vet		3
school		4
sitters		5
sports		5
parties/outings		3
transportation		---
EDUCATION		----
books		
parking		
supplies		
tuition		
workshops		
ENTERTAINMENT		20%
books		1
CDs		1
clubs		2
concerts		3
dates		3
DVDs		---
hobbies		2
houseguests		2
magazines		---
newspaper		1
sightseeing		2
theatre		3
FOOD	40%	
coffees/teas/drinks	3	
groceries	25	
restaurants	10	
snacks	2	

GIFTS		17%
anniversaries		1
baby		.5
birthday		2
cards		.5
celebrations		2
father's/mother's day		1
Holidays eg. Christmas		8
weddings		1
work		1
HEALTH	15%	
chiropractor	4	
glasses/contacts	10	
remedies	1	
HOUSING		10%
decor		.5
furniture		1
gardening		1.5
maid/contract labour		5
maintenance		2
moving		---
INVESTMENTS		5%
contributions		---
RRSPs		5
TFSAs		---
TRANSPORTATION		5%
maintenance		2
parking		1
repairs		2
SELF CARE	10%	
cosmetics	2	
flowers	1	
hair	4	
manicures	1	
massage	1	
pedicure	1	
SPIRITUAL GROWTH	10%	
Books/CDs	3	
classes	2	
donations	5	
VACATION: Goal $1800		10%
TOTAL	100%	100%

2. Change the percent into a dollar figure by multiplying the percent times the income set aside for savings. For example, if you earned $1000 net after taxes for the month, paid bills with $700, then the amount left for savings is $300. Vacation would get 10% of that. Multiply 10% times $300 and that equals $30 saved this month in Vacations. If happily you earn $2000 next month, your bills will be about the same, $700. That will leave $1300 next month for savings. If you multiple that by 10% for Vacation, you will save $130 next month. Add $130 to the previous savings of $30, and you now have $160 earmarked for a Vacation. Things are lookin' up!

3. Once you have figured out the percents for each category, multiply that amount by your net pay minus the bills, every month. Add the new savings amount to the previous balance.

New Savings Amount

VACATION 10 % per pay			
Date	Action	Deposits/Expenses	Balance
5/1	Starting Balance		$0
5/1	Savings Funds: $300		
5/1	Deposit from pay	$30	$30
6/1	Savings Funds: $1300		
6/1	Deposit from pay	$130	$160
7/1			

SAVINGS TRACKING

It isn't possible to remember how much you have in what category at any given moment with any accuracy. And you have better things to do with your brainpower than waste it on trying to remember hundreds of numbers. So, track what you have in each category in a simple notebook using paper and pencil or on the computer using spreadsheets. Low tech or high tech doesn't matter. What matters is when you want to spend in one of your categories, you can quickly find out exactly, to the penny, how much you have available.

If there is enough, off you go and make the purchase. If there isn't enough yet, you ask God to help you wait a few more days until your next pay. Sometimes, in the waiting, the item goes on sale. No kidding. Sometimes a better idea crops up. Patience, that elusive virtue, can be priceless when it comes to shopping.

Then again, if you don't track your numbers, you won't know if you have the money to buy the thing, in balance with your other spending. Being vague makes fools of everyone. Vagueness gives a murky permission to buy anything you want when you want it. The problem is you may not have the right amount of money to buy that item and pay the rent which is due in a few days. Tracking how much money is available for different areas of your life begins to bring calm to your money life.

TRACKING TOOLS

You can create a paper booklet or a computer spreadsheet to track your numbers. A paper system is easier to start with. You may graduate to spreadsheets, or stay with good old paper and pencil. Your choice.

Paper System

If you're using the paper and pencil method, begin by creating a category page for each of your Savings categories. You can use a blank checkbook register, or buy a small lined notebook, often three for a dollar at dollar stores, or even a *small* business planner with refillable loose-leaf pages, and snap-open rings.

SAVINGS PAGE

CLOTHES $20

1. Write the category name at the top of a page, for example, Clothes.

2. Write in the set dollar amount or percent beside the title.

3. Leave one or two blank pages in the booklet after the first one, depending on how many clothes you buy over a couple of months.

4. If this were the Food category, you'd leave three or four blank pages. If it were the Business category, you'd stick with one page because you have so few transactions in that category in a month.

5. Do a page or more for every category, in *alphabetical order*, so you will be able to thumb through your little book quickly to find the category you want.

Computer Spreadsheet

Some women prefer to use a computer spreadsheet. They update it with their deposits, and subtract their expenses at the end of the day. If you watch any beginner you-Tube tutorial, you will see the power of computer spreadsheets. One caution: if you don't have your numbers on paper first, using the computer might be a frustrating experience. Unless you are very experienced with spreadsheets, it's safer to create a paper record first with all the categories and amounts, and then take a flyer at creating your computer spreadsheet.

Here is a sample of a few of the headers you might use. You can list them across the top. If you have many categories, and who doesn't, you will need two or three sheets in your document.

SPREADSHEET TRACKING

Emerg $60	Home $100	Prop Taxes $328	Car $217	Mortgag e $789	Vacation $65	Healt h $80	Clothes $88	Action: $1777 Net Available
$4,940	$940	$566	$837	$1,981	$597	578	$0	
$4,940	$940	$566	$837	$1,981	$597	$398	$0	Therapist $180
$4,060	$1,040	$894	$1,054	$2,438	$662	$478	$88	Monthly Pay $1777
$4,060	$1,040	$894	$1,054	$2,438	$662	$588	$88	Insurance Repay $110
$4,060	$898	$894	$1,054	$2,438	$662	$408	$88	Washer Pump, $142, Therapist $180

In this sample, the Bills and Savings categories are combined on one sheet. This woman saves $60 monthly to her Emergency Fund, $100 to Home Repair or Improvement, $328 to Property Taxes, $217 to Car payment, $839 to Mortgage, $65 to Vacation, $80 to Health, and $88 to Clothes. This totals $1777 a month. She has been saving for a while, so she has built up funds in each category. Every time she spends something, she deducts it from the balance of the appropriate category.

For example, on 7/31, she had to pay her therapist $180. She took the money from her Health Fund. Also, she had to pay her mortgage. And so took money from her Mortgage Fund. She made a note of what she did in the Action column. When she made the change, she bolded the number which changed. The bolding makes the action easier to spot at another time.

On 8/01, she was paid, and so she used a previously setup excel formula to add money to each of her categories, at the pre-determined amount listed at the top of the spreadsheet. She noted Monthly Pay in the Action column. She bolded each new amount.

On 8/06, her health insurance partially reimbursed her for her therapist expense, so she added $110 back into the Health category, and bolded the new number.

On 8/12, she had to buy a new washer pump for the dishwasher. She subtracted the cost, $142, from Home, leaving a balance of $898, and she made a note of the expense in the Action column.

Also on 8/12, she saw the therapist again. Another $180 subtracted from Health, leaving a balance of $408.

Using a spreadsheet to track your income and expenses means you will have to update it every time you get income, make a purchase, or pay a bill. That way, your balances will be accurate, reflecting how much money you have left to spend in every category. Complete clarity.

Some women use a combination of spreadsheet, and paper and pencil. They print off their spreadsheet once a week, and carry it with them, making notations, subtracting and adding where appropriate. This keeps them up-to-date on the exact amounts in each of their categories as they go through their shopping day. Then, once a week, or once every two weeks, they update the spreadsheet. Of course, this may seem to defeat the purpose of having a spreadsheet, but actually, the spreadsheet does so many calculations easily, it's still an efficient tracking device.

Caution here: KISS. Keep it simple, sweetie. Using Excel, Quicken and envelopes is too much to track. Confusing. Go as *simple* as you can to start. And, even after that!

Many important categories are missing from this sample, like Entertainment, Gifts, Charity, and various regular bills, like utilities. So you can see how you might need several sheets to reflect your Spending Plan. Once your spreadsheet is set up, it's easy to make changes, though, and it's very easy to keep the arithmetic accurate, as long as you keep your numbers up-to-date.

Here's a reminder of the beauty of Parallel Savings: Look at the **Vacation** category. Though this woman had to pay for her therapist twice, and replace the washer pump in her dishwasher this month, the family vacation plans were *not* disrupted! What stability.

Nevertheless, what if she had not had enough money for the unexpected dishwasher repair in Home Maintenance? Then, she would have either washed dishes by hand until she *had* saved enough, or used money from her Emergency Fund as this was certainly an unexpected, urgent expense.

If more home repairs happened, and the Home Maintenance category was always too low, she would face reality and increase how much she saved in Home Maintenance. Of course, that means she would have to reduce one or more other categories, so that the total saved each month matched her income.

SHOPPING GUIDELINES

Some types of shopping encourage impulse purchases. The adrenaline rush of getting what seems like a bargain, especially online, the promise of quick delivery, and the excitement of

242

receiving the package hook you. The lower prices of online shopping make everything seem like a good deal. But, if you're using credit to buy things, you're digging your financial hole deeper.

No matter what the item, especially on the internet, careful shopping is the watchword. Before you buy anything, here are things you can do to keep yourself calm and make for an enjoyable shopping experience.

1. First, **ask for Help** from your God to reign in your impatience and impulsiveness. The benefits are abundant in so many ways.

God, please guide and protect me today as I shop for

_____.

2. **Wait a couple of days** before making any purchase over a certain dollar amount, the amount to be decided by you. Is it $100 or $10? No matter the number, or the venue, check your impatience and wait.

3. **Talk over the purchase** with someone before you go ahead if it's a big one. Do not rely on yourself alone. The buying of a car or a snow blower or a designer purse can be a big number. It's fine, if you can afford it, and if it fits into your balanced Spending Plan. Ask another person whose feelings are neutral. It will help you feel good about the decision.

4. **Set up a PayPal account** to pay for online items. It's not hard. That way, the money comes from your checking account, not a credit card.

Before Shopping

- Look over your present supply of the item you want to buy before you start to shop. Maybe you already have one, or have enough.

- Make a list. Do it before you start to shop. Even if you have to scrawl something in the car or bus before you get out, you will have exercised logical thought. This will help because once you're in the grips of shopping, it becomes harder to remain calm with all those sensory stimuli: lights, noises, crowds or ads flashing in your peripheral vision, and the fatigue of looking at hundreds of items quickly on various sites. A list also sets a limit on how many of an item you will buy. Not six tops when you only wanted three.

- Have a small calculator nearby. Sometimes, in the heat of the shopping experience, your brain gets tired, overwhelmed or confused, and numbers are the first things to go.

- Next, see how much money you have saved in your category.

- It is easy to forget or mis-remember, so have this number handy. Note it *carefully*. Some women find they get number dyslexic when they are checking the balance in categories. They think they have $84 when the number is really $48. Seldom is the reverse true!

- Before you enter any site or the front door of any store, ask God to be with you on this shopping trip. Having a trusted Companion along will make the experience more peaceful. Try this prayer:

God, please join me as I shop on this site, or *in this store or mall.*

While Shopping

- Keep a running total of the purchases using the calculator, or add them all up at the end.

- Add on the tax at the end, too. It can be sizeable.

- If the amount you're buying fits into the amount you have saved in your category, off you go to cash out.

- If the amount is higher, ask God to help you remove some things from your basket. You won't miss them once you're out of the store or off the site. Really.

God, help me to buy what you would have me own, and leave the rest.

You will be pleased with what you did get, and thrilled you stayed within your category.

Ending Shopping

Have you ever felt stuck in a store, unable to leave until you *finish*, though you want to leave?

- When your emotions are in the driver's seat, your will power alone will not be enough to *get out* of the store. Pray like there is a fire in front of you:

God, please help me get out of this place!

- Subtract what you spent from the balance in your category. Now you know how much you still have left to spend!

- Put the receipt in a file in case the item has a defect and you have to return it. However, if what you bought was consumed, like a muffin, throw out the receipt once the amount has been subtracted.

Overspent?

What happens to your Spending Plan if you spent more than is in your category? If you used credit, you're deeper in debt, that's for sure. And for what—a new blouse?

However, if you used PayPal or a debit card and were carried away or miscalculated, you will need to shift funds from another category to cover the deficit. The problem with this robbing Peter to pay Paul approach is that eventually, you will want the money you were saving in Peter, and it won't be there. Still, if you didn't debt, just overspent, that's a victory!

Get back in the saddle, and ask God to give you the courage to stay *within* your category amounts for the rest of the day. And slowly, daily, this will become a habit, both the prayer and the practice.

Spending Spree

Once you have amassed a tidy sum, say, in Clothes, should you go on a spending spree? After all, you deserve nice things, good things, and items not necessarily on sale. Well, yes, spend your savings in one day if you want to, just be sure to create a purchase plan in advance.

When it comes to Clothes, there are four seasons. Therefore, your plan has to consider all the items you'd like to buy for the year. This way, you'll get everything you really *want*, like the beautiful winter coat, not the one you have to buy on sale because you spent too much on summer sandals.

Buying items you love, staying within your category, is very satisfying. In addition, you'll have a gorgeous wardrobe, or laptop, or whatever you want. Very abundant. Very comfortable.

WHERE TO SAVE YOUR SAVINGS

There are several places you can store your savings. Pick one that seems comfortable, or try them all, one at a time, and see which works best.

Multiple Savings Accounts

You can actually set up different Savings accounts at certain banks for no charge, such as ING or Presidents Choice. You can even name each saving account so you'll know what you're saving for, like Vacations, or Gifts. Depending on how many withdrawals the account allows, you can pay for things using a debit card, online banking, or you can transfer sums of money from the appropriate savings account to your checking account.

I find this system too confusing, frankly, but it works for some women.

One Checking Account

You might prefer to leave all your money in a checking account, bills and savings, and divide it up on paper. To the bank, it will look like one large, lump sum, while you will know the money is for Clothes, Vacations, and all your other categories. Keeping an accurate Spending Plan will help you stay clear about how much you have left to spend in each category. To make sure your arithmetic is accurate, use a calculator or the computer.

Envelopes

Here's another way to both store and track your money. It is a great way to get the concept of *finite* amounts of money:

1. Calculate the total amount of money you need for the next two weeks or the month, based on your Spending Plan.

2. Take that amount of money out of the bank in cash. Ask for lots of small bills and dollar coins which will make things easier, as you'll see in a moment.

3. Write the names of each category on envelopes, one category per envelope.

4. Write the amount that is supposed to go into each category on the envelope.

ENVELOPE

GIFTS category
$ 72

5. Then divide your cash into them until you have nothing left. Now you can see why you need so many fives.

6. When you have to buy something, like gas, take out what you need, and leave the rest in the envelope for the next purchase.

Some women use small jars to store money for each category a la *Til Debt Due Us Part*, the Gail Vaz-Oxlade TV show. They keep the receipts in the jar when they buy something, and record each purchase in a 3-ring binder with a category title at the top of each page. And they subtract each purchase from the money available in each jar.

Feel the strange thrill of paying cash instead of using plastic. It will make the cost all too real. You give yourself permission to spend that money even on things like DVDs. Though, when the money is gone, and you'll know because the envelope will be *empty*, you have to stop spending. Of course, you will put more into the envelope with your next check, so all hope is not lost!

You don't need to carry all the envelopes with you all the time. Most likely, you'll put Transportation, Snacks, and a small sum for an Emergency Fund in your purse. The rest of the envelopes can stay in a cupboard until you decide on a shopping trip. Then, you'll put your Grocery envelope or your Clothing envelope in your purse, and take it to the store.

What if there's money left in some envelopes at the end of the month? It will remain in the envelope. Even though when you next are paid, you'll be putting more money into that envelope, you leave any balance. It adds up. You call that Savings.

When you want to spend it on some big indulgence, you will have the money, and permission from *yourself*, because you're taking care of all of your life needs and wants in a balanced Spending Plan. Once again, this is the glorious parallel savings. Everything is getting a little bit of money with every check. Buying a DVD does not affect how much you have available for a Vacation.

Raid!?

When the desire to spend comes over you, the temptation to borrow money from one envelope to fund another, called Raiding, will be overwhelming. Here is an example of a Raid: Trying to stay within your Spending Plan, you look to see how much you have in House Decor. You want new curtains for the bedroom. You need new curtains as the daylight wakes you up too early on the weekends. You want new curtains because they'll look so pretty in the bedroom. And you know your friends have lovely curtains in their bedrooms. All sorts of triggers to make you want to spend, *right now*.

In your House decor category, you have $26.89. You can look for curtains which will fit into that amount of money. But, you say to yourself, curtains go in the 'house'. You will 'supply' the curtains to the house. Therefore, the amount in House Supplies, $20, can be added to the amount in House Decor, and voila, you have $46.89. Now we're talkin'!

The fly in the ointment is that when you go shopping in a couple of days for toilet paper, there will be no money in House Supplies. I'll skip the bathroom humour. Lesson? Scout out the stores to find the curtains you love, without bringing your cash. Price compare, ideally, with three suppliers. Then if you have to, save more to get the curtains you want. Soon you'll have the curtains you've dreamed of, and toilet paper, too.

In the same way, you cannot have a minus figure in a category. If you think you'll replace the money the next time you are paid, that is using yourself as a credit card. Except, there is no *extra* money. If you have realistically allocated money to each category, there is no fat in them. You need what you're saving in each.

Wait, you say, what about a real emergency? Let's carefully define "emergency": *an unexpected and sudden event that must be dealt with urgently, a crisis: a situation or period in which things are very uncertain, difficult, or painful, especially a time when action must be taken to avoid complete disaster or breakdown.*

Do you see the word *curtains* in that definition? Or, restaurant, or concert? However, what if it is something you truly need, like a bed for the kids? Bringing the kids into any financial equation will add a million pounds of pressure to raid from one category to fund another. What will be the result? Play the tape to the end. It will short the other category, and when you need that money, it won't be there. It starts a vicious cycle.

If you want to improve your money management skills, you will make new choices. The best choice in this case is to practice the spiritual virtue of patience. Say *wait* to yourself. If you wait until you have enough money saved for a discretionary item, sometimes you get a better item, or a better price. Sometimes waiting reveals you no longer want the item. Strange, but true. As for the kids' beds, even they can manage for a short time while you save.

No doubt about it, though, staying within your categories is hard! Without Spiritual Support, you won't be able to keep it up. Ask for Help.

God, please give me the willingness and the ability to stay within my categories.

On the other hand, if something comes up that you truly need but you will have to dip into a foreign category, call a financial friend and discuss it first. Then, you will know if your thinking is clear, and you won't feel guilty about it, nor face self-recrimination down the road.

SPIRITUAL SOLUTION:
Full Bathtub

E xcessive shopping, sometimes jokingly called Retail Therapy, briefly distracts you from emotions you'd rather not feel, or situations you'd rather not face. Shopping brings relief from anxiety, and gives you the illusion of control. This is why you shop till you drop. But, what is enough? How many jeans, dinners out, or books are enough?

There is only one answer for this: *none*. You are a bottomless pit, never feeling you have enough. That's because there is a hole inside you *things* will never fill. Love will fill you as no item ever will. However, until you can love yourself, ask God to love you.

God, please fill me with your light and love.

FULL BATHTUB

Whether or not you think you can draw, try this exercise and be amazed.

1. Draw a bathtub. What does it look like? Is it a Jacuzzi, a claw-foot antique, or simply one you can draw with as few strokes as possible? *This is your life.*

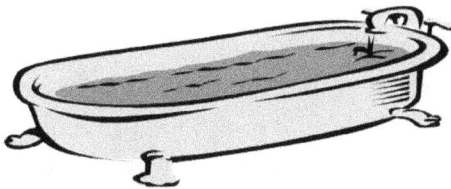

2. Next, at the bottom on the tub, create a drain hole for every person, situation, or item which drains away your energy. Would you have a drain for your partner, a particular child,

a boss, work, tax time, a friend, late nights, money? Name each drain which is robbing you of the energy of your life.

Boss   Money   Work

3. Finally, draw several faucets above the tub. These represent the people, situations or things which pour energy, health, or vitality into your life. Is it your partner, your mother, a boss, work, your church community, your grandchild?

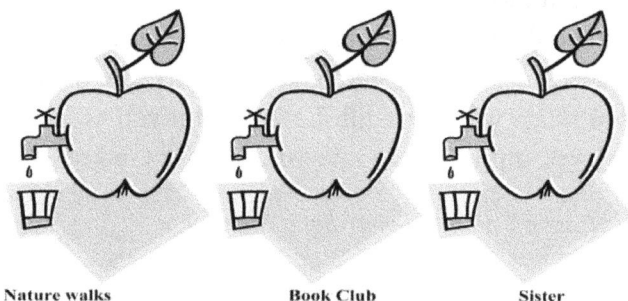

Nature walks   Book Club   Sister

Were you surprised by anything you saw? Simply admitting these things to yourself is a step in the right direction. You'll want to minimize contact with people and situations which drain you, and nurture the people and situations which are support you.

Does *your* God want you to be happy? If not, throw out that fraud, and define a good God. This is Who will help carry you, your new hopes and your new dreams safely over that ditch into which your old hopes and dreams have fallen.

The power to fly you over that ditch has to come from a source stronger than you. Though you may not believe it, yet, you're meant to get to the other side, to the joy of abundance in all areas of your life. It's time to enjoy your life.

8

PREDICT THE PREDICTABLE
Power Up!

B ig, one-time events or big yearly events have unique expenses. Planning for them gives you peace of mind as well as a hefty sum available to pay their costs. If you have a professional fee that comes due once a year, if you know your kid's dance recital has a hefty costume price tag, or if you're pretty sure your child will get married in the next five years, you can start a savings category for each now, and be relaxed and smiling when the bills comes due.

Save for all of the expensive yearly, or future events you can think of, even a small amount. It will ease your mind.

PRACTICAL SOLUTION:
Mini-Spending Plans

T hough expected, women put their head in the sand and pretend big, annual events won't happen because each is so expensive. Christmas, taxes, summer vacation, subscriptions, sports fees, dues. These things repeat themselves year in and year out, yet every time, we wring our hands and gasp, "*How* much for that?" Then out comes the plastic. As well, there are the big, one-time life events, like weddings, babies, and retirement. They aren't free.

If you can face the situation now, and squirrel away small amounts each pay, when the time comes for the big expense, the money will be there. No more drama. That's a good thing.

ANNUAL EVENTS

Christmas

Need I say more? Does this Holiday make you feel excited or despondent? Christmas is the biggest wallet-draining occasion of them all. It is a debt trigger for most of the Christian world.

Though many women don't celebrate Christmas, this problem occurs for any gift-giving holiday like Diwali, and the Chinese New Year. You don't want to be an elder in your family on Chinese New Year, believe me. You give money gifts to each member of your family all down the line!

Some women feel ashamed because they do not have enough to give the level of gifts they think fit. Do you find yourself trying to manage your image, that is, buying big gifts on sale so it looks like you spent a lot, so it looks like you are doing better than you are? Or, buying expensive gifts to please, impress or fawn on someone who doesn't seem to like you. On the other hand, are you buying gifts you can't afford because you feel guilty for how you've treated them? Even if you love everyone on your gift list and treat them well, if you're giving them gifts you can't really afford, what are you saying?

Customize Your Holiday

What parts of Christmas do *you* enjoy? Is it the gifts, the family excursions, the parties, or the spiritual aspect? If you most enjoy giving the gifts, put more of your holiday savings there, and cut back on something you don't enjoy as much, like the family excursions.

One family always took their kids to see the Nutcracker ballet which cost a fortune. One year the kids refused, sick of it. Bonus!

Here are more hints to make the most of the money set aside for gifts:

1. Make a recipient and gift list in advance.

2. Research online to get a general idea of how expensive things are. This will narrow down your gift options to realistic choices.

3. Be sure you have a copy of your Spending Plan on hand so there is no doubt about how much you have allotted.

4. Ask God to guide you to the right gift for each person on your list. Keeping your price point firmly in mind, you'll know which gift is guided because it will fit into your amount. As well, you will feel happy with your purchase. Try this prayer:

God, help me find the perfect gift for So and So that fits within my Spending Plan.

Here are other phrases you can say to feel good about your purchases and to keep from splurging:

This gift is not the last gift I will ever give this person.
Mine isn't the only gift this person will get.
Gifts do not make up for the past, or prove love.

If you most like the family time, cut back on the decorations, and the alcohol. Ask the kids what they'd like to do together as a family, then fund that. You might be pleasantly surprised.

When one father asked his two kids what they wanted to do as a Christmas excursion, the little one wanted to go on a walk in the snow at night with the family. The older one wanted to play Poker with everyone.

Put your money where your heart is. And don't panic thinking your kids will have unhappy Christmas memories if they don't get great gifts.

Here's a classic, but common tale:

This mother bought her two-year old an expensive toy car one Christmas. It came in a huge box. He climbed in and out of that box for three solid days before he noticed the car.

If you most like the spiritual aspect, a trip or two to church, a homeless shelter, or a plan of your own making might leave you with a full heart at the end of the season.

A woman called a minister of the church she sometimes attended, and asked if there were a family who needed special food for Christmas, but who didn't qualify for food banks. He told her of a hard-working African family where the father of two had just lost his job. She and her kids researched the Christmas traditions around food in Ghana. Turns out beef was the treat.

They shopped for the groceries, and then delivered them, saying they were from the church. She got a note back through the minister a couple of weeks later. The mother said she'd been praying for the food they wanted but could not afford: the beef made their Christmas.

Save Now, Avoid Debt Later

Don't kid yourself and say you'll spend less this Christmas. Most women spend a little *more* each year. What did you spend last year, including special foods, new clothes, trips, host gifts, office gifts, family and friend gifts, cards, house decor, and all the rest? If you have records, they are probably pretty accurate. If you don't, guesstimate, then add 10%. Our memories have a way of under remembering money going out.

Once you have figured out what you will spend next Christmas, set up a savings category, and start your own Christmas Savings Club. Deposit money every pay for a year until you reach your goal. You can set up a separate bank account. You can track the amount on paper. Alternatively, some women find it easiest of all to save into an envelope.

Christmas is Waiting in an Envelope

Take a regular white letter envelope. Write the words HOLIDAY CASH on it. Write the total amount you need to save. Let's say $300.

Count the number of paychecks between now and the week of December 1. If it's late, as in Christmas is only two months from today, you'd need to put $150 each month into the envelope. That means by Dec. 1, you'd have $300. No credit card bills in January. Imagine the feeling! By cutting back on your other expenses now, for a few weeks, you will be debt-free from the Holidays.

All the same, if you fear it will be all too easy to *borrow* from the envelope for other things, like pizza nights, ask Santa to help you keep sticky fingers off. If that fails, ask your God.

Energy Resources

Please, please, remember your energy account. You know, where you are not getting sick, but actually enjoying all the festivities. Have you had a season like that lately?

To reduce exhaustion, why not start your holiday on December 1st? The Christmas season is long enough what with the stores decorating in November, and hyper-advertising from then into January. If you decide the decorations and the shopping won't start until December 1, you shorten the season of rushing, and chaos. Instead of feeling exhausted and stressed, you'll feel calm, and enthusiastic.

Christmas mini-Spending Plan

While a mini-Spending Plan seems like a lot of work, it will keep you clear about your spending, give you boundaries, and keep you out of new debt! If you can't save enough to spend the same or more than last year, where will you get the money? A credit card? A line of credit? Run the tape to the end. You spend a lot in December, and then comes January. *What's in the mail, honey?* Christmas bills which you can't afford any better now than you could in December.

It's either save in the present for the future, or pay for the past in the future. If you save in advance, you will enjoy the holiday without money worries. Just imagine that for a moment.

Divide your Christmas savings between all the different expenses:

Charitable Donations if you like to do that

Christmas Tree purchase if you get live trees

Christmas Decorations, gift wrap or those handy gifts bags, Christmas cards if you're one who still sends them, and don't forget the cost of stamps

Company might be family or friends staying with you, coming by, or a party you like to give. You may have to buy household items, or party favours. Consider the extra food costs in the Special Food section, or as part of Company costs.

Family Outings cost money, for things like snacks, transportation, or tickets

Gifts, of course, for your immediate family. Gift for Others, like work colleagues, letter carriers, neighbours, friends, and extended family. If they are out of town, factor in the mailing costs and exchange rates

Mini-Emergency Fund is a crucial part of this mini-Spending Plan. There is bound to be one expense you have forgotten, or some category which will go a little over the allocated amount. Keep in mind, though, the Mini-Emergency Fund is there for miscalculations, or small, forgotten expenses, not buying little Joey an extra gift. You want to avoid the plastic coming out at all costs. That price is too high.

Special/Extra Food is for your traditional holiday treats, the Christmas dinner, and other traditions you have adopted, like snacks during the trimming of the tree.

MINI- SPENDING PLAN for CHRISTMAS

Year: 2xxx	Cost	Running Balance: $500
Charity: (church-$10, donation gifts $10)	$20	$480
Christmas Tree	25	455
Company	15	440
Decor, wrap, gift bags, stamps, cards	10	430
Extended Family Gifts: 5 people: About $20 each	100	330
Family Outing – food, tickets	25	305
Immediate Family Gifts: 3 kids, 2 adults: $35 each	175	130
Other gifts: Letter carrier, paper delivery person, 2 neighbours, 3 work people, 3 friends. About $5 to $10 each.	60	70
Out of town Mailing Costs	15	55
Mini-Emergency Fund	25	30
Special Food	30	0

How Much?

Let me turn that question back to you. How much would you feel comfortable spending on Christmas? Not what you spent last year, or hope to spend this year, but what would feel comfortable? Now, add 10%. Depending on how far away Christmas is, you can have this amount of money if you are willing to earn a little more, cut a little back, sell something, or some other clever income idea. Think this out in advance. Not worrying, but planning.

As soon as this Christmas is over, start saving for next year. It's the Christmas Club mentality without the use of a bank. And you will leave the money you save in that category, not raid it (such a temptation once it begins to pile up!) Then, next Christmas, you'll have such peace on earth as you begin to plan where to spend this abundance.

Other Holidays

Happily, there are other holidays during the year. Unhappily, they too, require money. These might be New Year's Eve, Valentine's Day, Canada Day, Fourth of July, Halloween, March Break, or Reading Week. Each of these means family members are home from work or school, and expect a celebration of the holiday. It could be traditional food, anticipated outings, or holiday materials, like fireworks.

If you do not acknowledge these special days, you and your family will feel left out, or party-poopers. The joy of celebrating is an antidote to a life of drudgery. However, the pressure to conform to community norms is intense, especially if you have children. You may end up spending money you don't have or don't want to spend to avoid a tirade from disappointed kids. Not much opens a reluctant wallet faster than the fear of disappointing a child.

If New Year's Eve, Valentine's Day, Canada Day, Halloween, March Break, and Reading Week are big money users, create separate categories for each. And you may need a mini-Spending Plan.

How Much?
Guesstimate the total cost of each holiday based on what you can remember from last year, and add 10%. Divide that number by the number of paychecks until the first holiday coming up.

This will give you how much you want to start saving now to avoid debt later. The first year you do this, your celebration may have to be smaller than you'd like because you haven't had a full year to save.

What to do? You can get clever:

- New Year's Eve: Search free events. New Year's Eve often has a community get-together, free and fun with the entire crowd celebrating with you.

- Canada Day: Play games, hold tournaments, or contests vs. buying something. Print off a few Canadian flags, and give them as prizes. No need for fireworks. Alternatively, go to a city display. It'll be fabulous.

- Valentine's Day: Make gifts or offer services vs. buying. Valentine's Day can be an I.O.U. for a free back rub, or bed making, or some chore your loved one hates and you don't mind.

- March Break/Reading Week: Search the internet for free ideas.

- Halloween: A bag of 100 suckers goes a long way, and is under $3.

However, keep in mind, you will have saved at least *some* money for each big holiday. Nice change.

Black September

Why does September startup always come as such an unpleasant shock? Is it because it is a black hole where money is concerned? First, there are school clothes and school supplies, like the new backpack which will cause your kid to see a chiropractor for the rest of her life, gym clothes, lockers fees, art supplies, after school daycare, and who knows what-all. The teacher usually spells out even more in a letter if you're unlucky enough to find it.

A few days later come the fees for sports teams, dance, Boy Scouts, and other after school programs. Who can afford all this without pawning the family silver? This year, you. Because there will be no more hiding your head in the sand. You will save for the inevitable and breathe free! Well, not free really. Instead, let's say, you'll breathe easy.

Of course, instead of tearing your hair out because you do not have the money to pay for all of this, you have other choices: you can apply to the Salvation Army for school supplies. You can appeal to the school Principal for relief from paying the school fee. You can take him out of hockey and her out of dance. If you want to lower your costs, these are the decision you can make.

How Much?

Once you have decided an expense is necessary, fun, or a growth experience for your kids, here's how to afford it: In the same way Christmas is a predictable event, September rolls around after August every year.

Look back to see how much last year cost you. If you don't have records because you'd rather not remember, and I'm with you, take a good guess. Put a figure beside each one:

Ballet: $300/year
Boy/Girl Scouts: $45
Hockey: $450/year
September School clothes/shoes: $75 x number of kids
School Supplies/fees: $80/year x number of kids
TOTAL COST: $950
Divide: $950 /24 pays = $40 per pay

If you have a year before September rolls around, putting aside $40 per child from each paycheck will mean you'll be laughing instead of crying come Black September. If you don't have that much time, divide the Total Cost by the number of paychecks you do have left before September. Yes, it will cut into your disposable income. Accept the cold water dousing called reality, and start to put away the money now. And when September rolls around, you will be like the Cheshire cat, smiling and purring, instead of watching your hand shake as you write the checks.

Camp

What other major event during the year costs you a fortune? Overnight summer camp. That's a big hurt. Instead, how about trying church-affiliated camps, or day camps which are more affordable. Yet, even these require certain clothes, snack money, and transportation.

How Much?

Research and pray. Ask God for ideas about the best camp for each of your children. Not every child flowers in every soil. Once you know where you want to send them, get the facts on the costs. Breathe. These babies are expensive!

Nevertheless, the same saving system works for this large expense as for all the others: start a category called Camp. Save a little out of each paycheck towards the total. When the bill comes due, you will have the money to pay it. Simple. It becomes a non-event rather than an embarrassing shuffle of credit cards and more debt.

Conventions/ Tournaments

If your life includes a yearly golf tournament, a once a year, out of town convention, or sports tourneys for you or your kids, while each can be lots of fun, they are also pricey. We're not talking Christmas pricey, still quite a hit if you haven't put money aside.

How Much?

If you acknowledge each event is going to come at the usual time, and create a category for it, it will mean a small amount of savings out of your paycheck, maybe $6 a pay. That gives you $144 at the end of the year. As a result, when that flyer comes around, money will not be a factor in determining whether or not you can go.

Subscriptions

Not everyone likes plays, music, ballet, or internet magazines or newspapers, but do you? If so, are you allowing yourself this pleasure? Saving up in advance for a subscription means each time you put money into that category, you're affirming you deserve enjoyment in your life. Whether it's season hockey tickets, glossy magazines, or internet game sites, you do it for yourself, and that is self- affirming.

Your subscriptions give you topics to talk about at parties! In fact, once you start talking about your passions, you may attract other people who share them. You will be attracting people you may like, and who will find you interesting. Even if you don't gather a crowd at the next party, you will have the satisfaction of taking part in something you enjoy, just for you, special you. If no one ever gave you such a gift, you can now give it to yourself.

Research the various venues and see who has events you might enjoy, and ask if they have any special pricing for your age group, for families, for taking an early or partial subscription. Don't forget matinee performances, and community theatres which have good quality performances, and reasonable subscription prices.

If you cannot find someone to go with, remember God loves what you love. You always have a spiritual companion. With that attitude, you will eventually attract the right people to enjoy what delights you.

How Much?

Subscriptions are cheaper by far than one-time uses, so start saving now for your future pleasure. At $5 per pay, you'll have $120 in a year. Look up prices. You'll be amazed how much enjoyment you can get for that amount of money.

Taxes

If your employer doesn't deduct enough from each paycheck, or you're self-employed, you may end up paying taxes at the end of the year. In any case, regular as clockwork, every year, you have to pay taxes. And hey, we get good services for our taxes. We get roads, education, and healthcare, and we can't expect these as freebies. It's not reality. In reality, taxes need to be paid.

Save and Hide

If you deduct the tax from the gross as soon as you get it, and put the money away in a Tax Category, you won't be tempted to spend it. If you save it as you earn it, you'll have the right amount in your Tax Category so you will pay your tax bill coolly, and go calmly on with your life. Does that sound good?

How Much?

To calculate your tax burden accurately, check your tax bracket from last year's tax form. Or, look it up online. If you are in the 30% tax bracket, ask your company to deduct that much from every check. If for some reason they can't, or won't, or you are self-employed, you'll have to start a little Tax Fund of your own.

Vacations

Had a nice one lately? Bet you haven't, at least, not one you paid for with cash. Saving for a vacation is a promise to yourself. Every time you put money into that category, it brings a thrill of joy to your life. In addition, saving in advance means you get to pre-plan a vacation.

This brings a three-fold pleasure:

o You get to research the vacation. Put pictures on the refrigerator. Daydream about the trip. Anticipation is the reward of planning.

o you get to go on the trip. Camera in hand, savings fund full, a list of events you want to attend, souvenirs you want to purchase, and things you'd love to do, you go and enjoy.

o When you get back, you get to relive it once again, and for as long as memory holds. You have pictures, you can invite people over to try a dish you enjoyed while away, show them your pix, and watch their eyes gleam or fog over. Who cares? Love those memories.

You may need more than one Vacation fund. There are Daytrips, Family visit trips, and then Recreational vacations:

Day Trips

Do you pine for a weekend away, or even simply an outing in the country where you visit wineries, and a good restaurant for the day? When you first start saving, this may be the vacation you can most comfortably afford. It can be a terrific, abundant day away, or a weekend at a bed and breakfast. It's much cheaper than a week in the Caribbean. If this is something you'd love to do, start a category of Vacations called Day Trips.

Family Visits

Many women think a family visit is a cheap way to vacation. On the contrary, it is not a vacation where you get to do what you want to do when you want to do it. Or, eat when and where you desire. No. You are going to be spending time with people you haven't seen in awhile, not touring the sights very much. You'll need to go and do what they want, often. Sometimes, too, there are expectations and strings attached. After all, you're living in someone else's home and eating their food. It can be stressful. Will you have to go to xxx to keep the peace? Will the kids behave according to the host's standards? Will your sister-in-law insult your husband, again? Can't wait, huh?

Generally, you do want to spend time with family. Good things like weddings and family reunions are opportunities to see cousins and reconnect. Sadly, so are funerals. It would be distressing to miss any of these solely because you don't have the money.

Family Visits are usually cheaper than vacations, so deposit about half of what a recreation vacation would cost. If you plan well, you will be able to afford to visit family occasionally, and take a real vacation, too. These miracles do happen.

Family Visit Mini-Spending Plan

Most categories in a family visit are the same as Vacation, except no Tips! Still, there is the addition of Gifts for family members and to the hosts as a Thank You. Family, especially, appreciate good manners.

FAMILY VISIT Mini-SPENDING PLAN

$1,500 Available	Cost
Activities/sightseeing	$20/6 days = $120
Airfare	$625
Food	$350
Gifts	$150
On route Expenses: airplane or airport	$30
Mini-Emergency Fund	$75
Souvenirs	$50
Transportation: taxi to airport & back home,	$50
Trip Preparation: fix suitcase, clothing items, sundries	$50

This Spending Plan shows a total of $1500 for 6 nights. It allows for some meals in restaurants, like lunches, which is realistic, a Thank you gift, and the famous Mini-Emergency Fund for the "I forgot about..." items.

Track your spending and you might be surprised to find money left over. Moreover, no new credit bills will arrive after you get home.

While some of the visit will be a joy, some of it will feel like an obligation, and you will not necessarily be refreshed when you come home. Still, you do want to see family. On the other hand, accept this is *not* a vacation.

Recreation Vacation

Europe? The Rockies? New York City? If the place makes your heart beat faster, you're on the right track.

This couple were thrilled to take their first vacation in years after using the tools in this book. They and their three kids travelled to Ottawa, about 500 miles from their home. They had only had a chance to save a certain amount, but this still gave them choices: They could stay in a fancy, downtown hotel for three nights, or stay in a modest motel on the edge of the city for five nights. They took a family vote, and everyone agreed to the better hotel, which meant a shorter vacation. As it turned out, three nights was long enough. All had done something they loved, and all of them came home feeling refreshed and delighted with themselves as a family.

While this long-awaited vacation was modest, don't be disheartened if your dream vacation needs a *big* number. The more you work this Spending Plan concept with Help from your God, the more money will flow into your home. We've already touched on Windfalls. Now you might notice more of them.

Instead of slapping them onto the debt, or on an impulsive purchase, use the Rule of Thirds: as a reminder, you divide the Windfall into the Past, the Present, and the Future. The Past refers to debts still owed. The Present refers to needs or wants right now, or something you will be buying in less than a year. And the Future refers to long-term savings. Vacations get a share of the money from either the Present or the Future.

Vacation Mini-Spending Plan

Vacations have a way of relaxing more than our tense muscles. Your purse strings relax way too much. Before they disintegrate, create a mini-spending plan.

In this example, a woman saved $3,000, and chose to fly to the Caribbean for a week at a resort. Here is her first attempt at a Vacation Spending Plan:

First Draft VACATION SPENDING PLAN

$3,000 Available	Cost	Balance $3,000
Activities/sightseeing	$40/6 days = $240	2760
Airfare	$425	2335
Evening drinks and entertainment/ 6 evenings at $30	$180	2155
Food	$800	1355
Resort	$1000	355
On route Expenses: airplane or airport	$30	325
Mini-Emergency Fund	$75	250
Souvenirs	$100	150
Transportation: taxi to airport & back home, from and to airport in Cuba	$100	50
Trip Preparation: fix suitcase, clothing items, sundries	$50	0

Activities/sightseeing: Isn't this why you go on vacation? Whether you want to visit the local pearl divers, or see an opera, you want to anticipate fun activities. Sightseeing might mean paying the entrance fee to a famous art gallery or theme park. In order to get a good read on how much sto put into this category, ask family members, including yourself, for the *one* thing that will make this vacation for them. You might be surprised.

While on that vacation in Ottawa, the son said he wanted to see the Parliament Buildings, the little daughter wanted to swim in the hotel pool, the Mom wanted to see a former Prime Minister's residence and her husband wanted to take pictures of everything. Easy to please some people. They all *did what each one wanted to do, with a good attitude, and everyone came home delighted.*

Airfare: The best research says airfares are cheapest in January and February, and six weeks before the date you want to go if the flight isn't too full. If you can wait that long, good for you. Know that airfares begin to go up the closer to the travel date you want, and are at their highest when there are the fewest seats.

Financial Hint: Before you get flight insurance, check to see if you are already covered by any other insurance you have. If you're using a secured credit card, where you put the money on it *before* you spend it, you might have travel insurance. Also, check with the airline to see their cancellation policy for illness or accident. Some allow you to get a credit towards another flight with only a small financial penalty if you cancel for those reasons, medically backed-up. Be a good shepherd of your resources and get those facts before you book travel insurance which can be pricey.

Evening Entertainment: When the sun goes down, how do you plan to spend your vacation evenings? There are theatres, pubs, nightclubs, and in-room movies. These all cost money, so acknowledge it and place some in this subcategory.

Food: If you're not doing an all-inclusive vacation, food will be a large number in your spending plan. Figuring out how many breakfasts, lunches, dinners and snacks you'll need to eat, times the number of people, will help clarify the overall cost.

While breakfast comes in at about $10 a person, including tax and tip, lunch is often more expensive than expected. So, double that. Dinner is usually the blow out meal, yet not much more expensive than lunch, strangely. If this isn't how much your family really spends, be glad!

Figure out what your numbers are. Then it's easy to see the truth about how much the vacation food will cost. Oh by the way, don't forget snacks. Even walking down the street licking an ice cream cone will set you back $5-10 bucks. You want to factor that in.

Don't get disheartened. You will have saved enough money to pay for all of this before you go. In addition, you'll feel pride in being able to pay and leave a smile on your face.

Hotels/Resort/Cruise: This will be another big expense. You may be staying in more than one hotel if you move from city to city, or you may be staying in a hotel plus a resort or cruise. Really? Think this is fantasy? It is not. It will be you soon enough.

Financial Hint: Check out the prices of cruises. Because meals and entertainment are included, they can be a bargain. If you do choose one, be careful of the prices for drinks, and the gambling. If you keep that down, you can have a surprisingly inexpensive luxury vacation. Maybe not today. Still, it will be sooner than you think as you learn to manage your money with Help.

On Route Expenses: Will you have to snack at the airport because you have a wait? Will you need to buy food on the airplane since they don't give free meals anymore? Or will you forget your novel and have to buy something to read? Best to set money aside for this.

Mini-Emergency Fund: The Mini-Emergency Fund is for the items you have to buy you didn't expect to have to buy, for example, aspirins; or, it's for items you forgot at home, like the suntan lotion on the bathroom counter. It is also a bit of a slush fund in case you under guesstimated how much things would cost.

Souvenirs: Aside from the photographs, you may want tangible memories of your trip. It's helpful for you to make a list of the things you might like as a souvenir before you go, like an item of clothes, a piece of art, or local music. Then you're looking for that right thing and not trolling the stores, getting out of control, buying lots of things, none of which you really want.

If you have kids with you, will you fund their souvenirs or make them use their allowance or savings? If you pay for their souvenirs, what is the financial limit? Get clear first in your own mind and then in theirs. Is $20 reasonable, given the overall spending plan, or $5? And what about a moral boundary? This refers to what you think is healthy for the kid to have, so you may say no to a knife, but yes to a book about knives. As well, do you want to bring back something for your favorite sister or the friend who always brings back something for you?

Here are two easy souvenirs:

1. **Food:** any small specialty item from the area. Be careful you are allowed to bring it back into your country.

2. **Local Craft:** Things like knitted scarves, quilted placemats, or hand-carved animals are good value and wonderful memories.

Transportation: rental cars, local busses, or taxis to catch your flights or to get to a recommended restaurant at the waterfront, are part of a vacation. If you must do any of these, allocate money to it. It will clarify how much is still available for other categories.

Trip Preparation: What if, when you get your suitcase a couple of days before the trip, you suddenly remember the lock is broken. Getting it fixed quickly will be hard enough without having to worry about the cost. Or what if you realize you don't have the right number of ankle socks? Or, aggravatingly, your sun hat is missing. You might also be out of suntan lotion. The fact is something is going to come up before the trip which will cost a few bucks. Anticipate this, and at least you'll feel less stress on that account.

Oops!

Is there anything missing from this woman's Spending Plan? Yes, indeed! What about *tips* for maids or porters? It is the norm, and in some cases, like a cruise, an expectation. Before she finalizes her Vacation mini-Spending Plan, she'll need to reduce one or more of the other categories in the first draft of the Spending Plan to allow for tips.

Final Draft VACATION SPENDING PLAN

On route Expenses: airplane or airport	$30 Reduce to $25
Mini-Emergency Fund	$75
Souvenirs	$100 Reduce to $90
Tips	Add in $15
Transportation: taxi to airport & back home, from and to airport in Cuba	$100
Trip Preparation: fix suitcase, clothing items, sundries	$50

In this sample, I figured Tips at $15. Therefore, I reduced On Route Meals from $30 to $25 and Souvenirs from $100 to $90. But, why not use the Mini-Emergency Fund, you say? Because the Mini-Emergency Fund is meant to be a safety net *on* the trip. Lower it too much, and you may find yourself reaching for your credit card. Then you're back into debting, and who wants to do that?

Tracking a Vacation Mini-Spending Plan

Once you have taken care of all the expenses you imagine will occur on your trip, and have a Mini-Emergency Fund for those unexpected ones, tracking your spending will keep you within the total. It's amazing how well this works. If you subtract as you spend, you will see the balance in each subcategory, and this will allow you to enjoy your vacation more peacefully. You won't worry that you are overspending. And you won't. You will still stay within the total amount of money you planned to spend, avoid all credit cards and other evil debting devices.

Tracking is so easy.

o Bring along a regular sheet of paper and a pen.

o Draw several columns, one for each subcategory.

o At the top of each named column, note the amount of money you plan to spend.

o Ask for and keep all receipts, as our minds are distractible when on holiday.

o At the end of each day, subtract what you have spent from each category.

o Note the balance in each subcategory. This will act as a brake to keep you from overspending. And as a pat on the back, seeing how much is still left!

VACATION TRACKING $3000

	Activity	Air	Night Fun	Food	Hotel	On Route	Mini-Emerg Fund	Gifts	Taxis	Tips	Trip Prep
Amount Allotted	240	Pd 425	180	800	1000	25	75	90	100	15	50
	Mon $50 = 190		Mon$ 10 = 170	Mon B-20 L-30 D-45 95= 705							
	Wed $40 = 150		Tues $14 = 156	Tues B-18 L-23 D-57 98= 607							

Tracking spending has a magical way of getting your attention, not allowing the fantasy of being so rich, tra-la-la, that you don't have to ask for prices. It keeps you from overspending in any one category, which would reduce what you can spend in another. If you stop spending when the $90 you allotted to souvenirs is gone, you'll still have money for sightseeing. Nevertheless, if you buy $200 in Souvenirs, you'll have to miss anticipated outings. Saying *no* to one thing allows you to say *yes* to another, which may be more pleasurable. Though saying no to yourself is never easy. Ask God to help:

God, please guide and protect me as I spend my vacation money.

The goal of the Spending Plan for Vacations is to stay within the overall money you have available. If you go over by a couple of dollars in one category, subtract from the Mini-Emergency Fund. As long as your vacation expenses are within the overall amount, you're laughing.

I bet you will come home with money. It may sound crazy, but it will be a reality—a new vacation reality. If you don't spend all the money, put the remainder back into Vacations as seed money for your next trip.

We work to live; we do not live to work. Research and pray about when and where you'd like to vacation, then, enjoy a fabulous trip.

Yes, you can have all of it. Maybe not all at once, but in time, you can enjoy mini-holidays, family visits, and a full vacation. The vacation category of your spending plan is where you get to dream about fun things to do, enlarge your life experience, and savor the reward for all this work you're doing.

How Much?

What will your dream vacation cost? Research and pray. Note the prices; however don't panic. Check out the travel sites, and the travel advisory sites which often have blogs from people who have done what you want to do, and found good places to stay and eat, and maybe good deals.

In fact, you might want to research three or more vacation possibilities. The research phase is free and fun, if you stay calm and don't get obsessed by it! Pray for relaxed enjoyment. Know that your God wants you to have a delightful vacation, so stay calm and carry on.

Once you know how much your vacation might cost, decide how many days you can go. Maybe this year it will be a weekend, maybe next year, two weeks. Happily, it will be to a place you really want to go and in style.

Get-Through-This-Bad-Month

If your Spending Plan is generally good, but you are having a bad month, or an emergency with no Emergency Fund, you will want a *get-through-the-month* mini-spending plan. Do not panic, but do not debt, no matter what. Keep that as your mantra. This problem time will pass and you'll be in balance again in a few days.

Stay out of fear. Remind your self that you have a roof over your head today; you have food to eat today; and you have clothes to wear. Today, you are all right. Practise faith.

If you have any money coming in, stop funding the discretionary categories, like Meals Out, or saving for a new appliance, and use the money for priorities. What are your priorities? How about shelter, basic food, and transportation costs to get to work. If you have to, dip into your Emergency Fund. If that is short, use the money in discretionary categories, like Clothes or Vacation. They are an auxiliary Emergency Fund in times like this.

Now, cancel or postpone any commitments for this month which will cost money. Be brave. Even if it's a friend's wedding, wear what you already have, and postpone giving the gift.

If none of this is enough, look to see if you can sell something. Don't fret about it. Think of it as stored sunshine or a savings account. And remember, you can always buy it back or buy a better one later.

If you prefer, you can use this item as security for a loan from a friend or family member. Give it to them and ask for an appropriate amount according to its resale value. Agree to repay the amount by a certain date, or they keep the item to do with as they wish. Be rigorously honest about this. It will not do for them to insist you keep the thing. Write a receipt with the agreement details, leave the item in their care, and walk away a proud adult.

After you've done all this, and if you still cannot meet those primary obligations, speak to your landlord or mortgage holder immediately and explain the situation and that you may be late or need help. You may need to call your utilities providers, too.

If you are short of money for food, remember food banks. It is a temporary stop gap meant to help out. No one will question you there. Most who work there were users of the service in the past. Then, when you are flush, you can donate for the next family who needs it.

During this time, remember this: on no account go into more debt, especially loans from friends or family as tempting as that may be. You and God can handle this. Ask for financial direction:

God, please show me the next right step to live a realistic, peaceful financial life this month.

If, happily, you have enough funds to cover the basics, and a bit leftover, consider the other priorities this month, for example, do the kids need something for school? Put the balance where it is most needed for this month.

If this situation is not just a one-month shortfall, but likely to be a crisis, as in, your job is at risk, or the bank has threatened foreclosure, refer to the Crisis Response Drill in Chapter 7, *Save Your Life.*

As soon as the money eases up, restart your normal spending pattern, funding your Spending Plan as before. The only category which needs repayment is your Emergency Fund. Begin to add as much as reasonable to that until it is full again. It's your future sanity saver.

Other Big Annual Events

There may be other big annual events unique to your family. Make a list of them, and plan for each by naming a category, and funding it from your income, even in small amounts to start. Stop worrying; be happy. It will all turn out much better than you think.

ONE-TIME EVENTS

A Good Life includes big events, like babies being born to you or friends and family, weddings, either yours or others, and a host of other events, like bar mitzvahs and christenings. How did you handle these expenses in the past? You debted. You had no choice because you certainly didn't have the money.

At first, you may not want to put much into far off categories. You may say it will take decades to save enough to get there. Don't be so sure. Once you have declared your intention by putting a little of your money where you mouth is, maybe you get more on your tax refund than you anticipated, or you get one of those government refund checks to compensate you for our very high electricity bills. As you begin to take care of your money, you may even find good luck comes your way. Not a leprechaun, exactly, more like invitations from friends, good turns done you by strangers. It happens.

In the next two years, can you expect any of the following events: a baby, a funeral, illness expenses, retirement, university/college tuition, or a wedding? In order to be happy about these, not mired in money worries, start a little fund for each. Save a little from each paycheck now, and expect more to come. Expect a miracle. They happen.

Babies

If there were ever an event which needed a savings category, it's having a baby. There is nothing like the tug on the heartstrings when baby needs something, and the purse strings snap open! However, now, you will handle this calmly and enjoy it thoroughly because there will be money in a category for Baby.

The first child makes the biggest dent in the budget, never mind changing your life for the good, but forever. This is why you need to start saving two or more years in advance. The second kid is a bit less expensive, though not free. And even if you're only the grandparents, you'll likely contribute time and money to these babies.

Cribs, diapers, toys, clothes, food, activities, even medical costs happen at the very time your income may go down if one parent chooses to stay home with the child. Best be prepared. If you start with small amounts, even $1, for pregnancy, birth, and baby's first year, and increase it when you can, you will feel fantastic.

Baby Spending Plan Categories

Some of these subcategories will be one-time expenses, like buying a dresser, while others will be ongoing, like diapers. Once you pay for the one-time expenses, redirect those amounts to the ongoing subcategories.

Activities: Mommy and Me social classes, Mommy and Me swimming, even Mommy and Baby movies. You will want to get out of the house, and to assure yourself about the superiority of your darling compared to the other kids. Mothers can be like that. You'll totally understand the saying, *She had a face only a mother could love* once you have your own baby. No kid is cuter than yours, no matter what she looks like, period.

Back to Activities—They stimulate your baby which all research says is crucial in the first three years for certain areas of the brain to develop well. You want bucks to do activities. First, check free ones at your library, community center, or church. If you run out of those, this will be an ongoing expense, especially as the baby grows older.

Babysitting: for those times when you can't bring the baby, like someone's party or a work-related event, yours or your partner's, you'll need funds to pay someone. The costs can range from $10-20 an hour. If you're on a tight budget, this can be out of range.

Of course, if you're a fierce mother who will not let anyone else take care of your baby when you're not around, your babysitting costs will be zero. But then, you will have to miss some events. Your willingness to learn to trust someone else to watch your baby is going to make your life less stressful. The baby will learn to know the babysitter, and you will get to have time alone with your spouse. It may be a short evening, though even the anticipation of all-adult time will be worth its weight in gold.

You might want a local teenager to come in to entertain the baby while you do something in the house that requires your full concentration. You have to pay for that. In any case, babysitters can cost more than you think. Put some money into that fund.

Bedding: Might be washcloths, crib sheets, light blankets, heavy blankets, and other things which research on baby websites will mention. Or, how about the Family Bed? Many groups recommend this idea, while others criticize it. It amounts to having the baby between you and your partner for several months. It certainly makes nighttime nursing way easier if you plan to do that. Though this is not for everyone, it does mean you won't have to buy a crib or much bedding.

If you do need bedding, cost it out by comparing three different websites. Then face reality, and put a little into the Bedding subcategory.

Clothes: For the first few months, this may mean nothing more than sleepers, shirts, socks with elastic around the ankle—hard to find—and a snowsuit if the baby is born in the winter. The few outfits you'll need you'll get as gifts. In fact, if you have a maiden aunt, she'll flood you with clothes.

Maternity clothes, though, can be a big cost. Eventually, none of your old clothes will fit, especially your coat. If you're sure you'll have more than one child, it might be worthwhile to invest in a set of new maternity clothes. Of course, by the time you're ready to get pregnant again, the styles may have changed. Will you feel comfortable in your old maternity wear?

If style is the last thing on your mind, buy used. Or, borrow ones from someone else if you can. Some mothers get sentimental about their maternity clothes, especially if they had a good pregnancy, and don't want to let them go, and cannot think about wearing someone else's used clothes. If you're one of those, acknowledge it, accept this is who you are, and start saving for maternity clothes. Clothes for the baby are an ongoing expense, but maternity clothes are a one-time thing.

Diapers: Diaper costs drive parents crazy. You need big bucks in this subcategory. On the other hand, here is a news flash from back in the day: diapers do not have to be paper. You can hire a diaper service, so your baby can wear soft cloth diapers, delivered to your house, in ample supply. The diaper service takes away the soiled ones to launder and at that time, gives you a fresh, clean batch.

Even farther back in the day, women used to buy their own cloth diapers, wash them in the hot cycle of their washing machine, and have an ever-ready supply. Rubber/plastic pants kept outer clothing dry. Revolutionary, or reactionary, but far cheaper! This is a big, ongoing expense until the child is about three. Face it.

Food: The baby's food is free for the first six months if you nurse. Breast-feeding support comes from the wonderful La Leche League, a group of mothers who take special training on breast-feeding. They are a great source of help on mothering, too. They even take calls in the middle of the night. Try that with your GP.

Of course, if breast-feeding is not your plan, factor formula and the purchase of the bottles into your Baby Spending Plan. This will be both ongoing and one-time costs.

Food for later may mean strained baby food unless you blend up your own. It's easier than you think. You blend up whatever the rest of you are having for dinner. You freeze small portions in ice cube trays and heat them up for meals. Feeding junior your own cooking gets him used to the spices you use. Makes for less mealtime fuss when he gets older. And the cost is far less. Despite that, if you want to buy baby food, factor that in.

Furniture and Paraphernalia: Crib, dresser, changing table, and the rocking chair for late nights—essential! stroller, high chair, and car seat. Prepare for sticker shock! Strollers seem to be in a class with Cadillacs. You can get an umbrella stroller which is lighter, and cheaper, though it isn't as baby comfortable. By the way, if you can get one, buy a stroller where you can position the handle to see the baby's face. It is reassuring on hot or rainy days.

If you don't like the idea of the family bed, you may want either a bassinet which you can position right by your bed, or if you want the baby in her own room, that means a crib. A changing table is good because it's the right height for this constant job. And often the change table has a couple of shelves underneath where you can place diapers and clothes. A dresser isn't necessary right away. Still, when you get one, if it is an adult size, you'll never have to buy the child a dresser again. You can paint it white to look better in the nursery.

We bought each kid a solid wood dresser with cabinet doors on top, and drawers below. It lasted them through their babyhood, childhood, teen years, and then they took their dresser when they moved out for the last time.

To save money, buy used, maybe at consignment stores where there is often pretty good quality. Or, ask to borrow from other mothers. Alternatively, beg your family or friends to throw you a baby shower. Make a list of all the things you think you need and want for the baby, then let your friends and family sign up for what they might be able to loan you or give you. Your circle will be pleased to know they are getting you what you want, and it will be very helpful to your budget.

Keep in mind, though, you can pare furniture back to the essentials. In the old old days, babies actually slept in dresser drawers. Fortunately, these costs are one-time and you're done.

Gifts: These are not gifts for your baby, rather for other mothers. It seems like whenever you decide to have a child, so do all your friends, or you make new friends with other pregnant women in your prenatal classes. These gifts can certainly come out of your regular Gifts for Others category, but this gift-giving frenzy might tax even that. Having a little pot for a $15-20 gift will make you feel better.

Pregnancy Prep: The Prep category may be painting the baby's room, pre-natal classes, mommy massages, and even paramedical costs, like support stockings. You might stretch this category to include a weekend away for the nervous or tired parents before or after the birth. These can be expensive.

Mini-Emergency Fund: As with every spending plan, you'll need this subcategory because there is no doubt you will have forgotten something. *Oops* won't cut it when there's a baby involved. Don't go under $100 here. You'll be glad, several times over.

Religious Ceremony: If your culture goes in for a big meal at a restaurant 30 days after the birth, or a church or synagogue ceremony at some point, you'll need to pay for the clergyman, the food, and the new outfits, including yours and the rest of the family's. We do that, don't we?

Base this category on what your wishes are, and fund it generously. You will always remember it.

Toys: You won't have to spend a lot of money for toys, after all babies do have their toes. For the first few months, these will be hugely entertaining for them. After that, buy toys at garage sales for a tenth of the store cost. Once disinfected, they are as good as new. This is how many daycares get their initial stock.

If it's books you want, the library has tons of them. Additionally, your kitchen has a plethora of toys, from plastic measuring spoons to plastic cups banged on highchair trays. The pictures you see of a baby banging pots with a wooden spoon could have been taken in any kitchen. Such noise! Such power! Such glory.

How Much?

First, since this is going to be a substantial amount of money, you need to give yourself a long lead-time. If you think in terms of two years before the first hint of the pregnancy, you'll be able to start saving small amounts and get bigger once you know you're pregnant. If you're pregnant now, start now!

Here's how to get a realistic number for your Baby Mini-Spending Plan:

- Research the prices on all the baby things you want. Say that totals $1200.

- Divide the total by the number of paychecks you have until the birth. (Guesstimate when the baby will be born and I do realize it is simply a guess.) If you save $30 a pay for 2 years, you'll have a nest egg of about $1500.

Here is a sample Mini-Spending Plan for the Bundle of Joy covering the first six months.

Baby Mini-Spending Plan for Six Months

Savings		$1500
Activities	$100	1400
Babysitting	$100	1300
Clothes/ Bedding	$150	1150
Diapers	$250	900
Food	$200	700
Furniture	$300	400
Gifts	$60	340
Pregnancy Prep	$150	190
Mini-Emergency Fund	100	90
Religious Ceremony, e.g. Baptism, Bris	$75	15
Toys	$15	0

Track what you spend in each subcategory by subtracting each purchase or expense, and keep a running balance to see how much you have left to spend. This is similar to Vacation spending tracking.

Tracking Record

ACTIVITIES			Balance: $100
April 1	Baby and Mommy Swimming 8 sessions	$40	$60
July 3	Baby Gym 5 sessions	$25	$35

A child costs a lot of money. However, the peace of mind of knowing you have a nest egg for baby expenses will fuel your joy. You will feel like a competent parent. Those feelings aren't easy to come by, so take them when you can get them!

College/University

Tuition. It could be yours or one of your kids. In either case, it hits like a tornado on the checking account. Saving a little bit for a long time is insurance you will be able to afford what you want: the university of your choice, residence, rent, trips home, etc.

Not all those ads about the high cost of higher education are exaggerated. The total amount of money to go to a local university is at least $24,000 for a four-year degree. If your child goes out of town, it is $40,000. College is about $1,000 less a year. Ain't it awful?

Is Education Debt Good Debt?

Some financial counselors say education debt is good debt, more of an investment. Tell that to your child when they have to eat Kraft dinner every night because they are paying off their student loans for 15 years, or not paying them off and racking up penalties and fines, and a ruined credit rating.

Most students borrow in the range of $20-40,000 to get a degree. These debts are especially crippling since the first jobs they get are at entry- level salaries.

By the way, did you know you cannot discharge student loans by going bankrupt? Well, there is one way: if you stopped attending school more than seven years before you filed for bankruptcy, you *might* be able to include them. All unsecured debt is bad. You have to repay it, one dollar at a time, plus interest, for years. This debt will hobble life choices for more than a decade.

All is not lost. You *can* get a higher education without debting one cent.

11 Ways to Avoid Student Loans

Many ways to avoid educational debt do not involve being a scholarship student. People of average intelligence can also go through school debt-free. Yes, they can. It may take patience;

however, at the end of the day, when you've earned the degree, there will be no debt payments.

These tips apply whether you are the student, or you are funding your child.

1. **Work first and save up**. Arrange to work for a year and save enough money to pay for what you have not been able to save.

2. **Night classes**. You can take night classes and work during the day. Sometimes, people are better students when they are older, making more mature decisions about doing the schoolwork, or choosing the courses they want. Since time is on your side once high school is over, you can slow things down and pay as you go.

3. **Part-time**. You can go to school part-time and work. There is no rush to complete college. Any numbers of students are mature students, ages 25-65+, so no one will be out of place if they take a little longer to finish school. And if you are lucky enough to work for a company which encourages continuing education, they often pay all or part of the tuition.

4. **University Employment**. If you or your kid gets a job at a local university, after a certain tenure of employment, employees and their children can attend tuition-free or at reduced tuition. Plan in advance.

5. **Co-op Programs**. Some universities, in some of their programs, arrange for students to work as part of their coursework, and earn money. The University of Waterloo in Ontario has the biggest co-op program in the country. Students can earn $30,000 - $75,000 by graduation. They work 4 to 6 co-op work terms, gaining 16 months to 2 years of work experience, and job placement is about 93 %. Wow.

6. **Scholarships and Grants:** Scholarships: Apply for every scholarship under the sun. If your child has any learning disabilities, play that card now. If your family has undergone any crisis, financial or otherwise, see what you can do to find support from the government or the schools themselves. If your company helps with education expenses, tap them. Grants: These are good because there is usually no academic requirement. Sometimes grants are attached to loan, though. Take the money, but don't spend the loan portion. It's debt, plain and simple. And hard and long to pay back. Return it as soon as you can

7. **Bursaries.** Apply for bursaries, which require financial proof of low income, although not academic standing. If you want bursaries, you would be wise to apply for OSAP. Since you do not have to repay bursaries, you want to get them if you can.

8. **Work-Study programs**. Work-study requires some proof, often OSAP qualification, that you don't have much money. Then the school will give you an on-campus job at which you work between classes. The best place to work on campus is usually the Library because it pays the highest, and has a union. Although, there are many on-campus jobs. They schedule the hours around the students' class times, and often have an upward limit of 15 work hours a week so the student has time to study. Though they may pay only minimum wage, it is a relatively painless way for you or your child to earn money to help fund tuition.

9. **Go Local**. You can also stipulate your child will not go out of town to school. If education is uppermost in everyone's mind, there are local universities or even those where commuting of an hour or so each way is possible. It will save about $4,000 - 6,000 a year in campus rent and living expenses. That's a year's tuition. While there is the loss of independence, students who live at home often do better

scholastically their first year since there are no new distractions. Especially if their friends are going out of town. Keep online education in mind, too. Almost all institutions are setting up courses off campus. It may take a while, but as a young man I knew said, *I'm starting medical school late, and won't be finished until I'm 40. But, I'll be 40 anyway!*

10. **Reconsider Higher Education**: Is a university or college education so vital? Have we let snobbism skew our view of the real world? If your kids are good with their hands at all, consider apprenticeship programs where students learn on the job and earn money while they learn. Have you checked out how much electricians make? These are usually smart women, too. Plumbers make a good living, as do heating and air conditioning technicians. If your child is not great at academics, why force a square peg into a round hole?

11. **Save *while* the student is in school**. A little every month will add up to help with tuition for the following year.

You do not have to go into debt for higher education. Save yourself that 15-year pain.

EDUCATION *INCOME* PLAN

You need a multi-year perspective for an Education Income Plan. The schooling takes four to five years to complete. You can continue putting aside money even while the student is in the process of earning their degree. You can save all year to help with the next year's expenses. There are months in there where the student can work and earn money. In addition, there are different scholarships, grants, and bursaries which come into play.

For example, in the first year schools offer entrance scholarships and residence grants. In the following years, academic excellence can bring about scholarships or grants.

Savings Vehicles

Registered Education Savings Plans or RESPs. The government contributes to these until the student turns 17, the amount dependent on how much *you* put in. Therefore, save as much as you can. Of course, anything is better than nothing. Start small.

We started saving $9 a month. It grew so that each of our kids received around $2,000 a year for four years. We saved a little for a long long time—14 years!

Summer Jobs. Your student will need to earn money in the summer to contribute to their education. It's sobering for them, and teaches responsibility, too. The rich would be wise to do this, too. It's character building. However, that's not your problem, is it? Not yet, anyway. Student summer earnings can top $4,000 since they can work from May to the end of August. Even if they spend a little money on summer fun, which they should, they can save a good chunk towards their education. These earnings do have to be reported on their OSAP application for the following year. Still, they'll be money ahead.

Paycheck Savings. Keep putting aside a set amount from your paycheck once the student is in university. You are no longer able to save into RESPs once they turn 17, but that's o.k. Your money will still buy their books.

Scholarships. You hope your kid will get good enough marks to get an entrance scholarship for the first year and other money for later. Miracles can happen. Keep the faith, baby.

Work and Study: part-time, school-year job. Your student may have to work during the school year in either a school-sponsored Work/Study programs, or a part-time job.

Add together all these streams of income to see a respectable total. Begin the process now.

EDUCATION *INCOME* PLAN

YEAR 1	YEAR 2	YEAR 3	YEAR 4
RESP $2,000	RESP $2,000	RESP $2,000	RESP $2,000
Student's summer savings: $4,000	Student's summer savings: $4,000	Student's summer savings: $4,000	Student's summer savings: $4,000
your monthly savings:$59 x 12=$708	your monthly savings: $59 X 12= $708	your monthly savings: $59 x 12=$708	your monthly savings: $59 X 12= $708
Entrance scholarship $1,000			
Work- study program: $2,000	Work-study Program: $2,000	Work- study program: $1,000* Or Teaching Assistantship	Work- study program: $1,000* Or Teaching Assistantship
Total: $9,708.	Total: $8,708	Total: $7,708	Total: $7,708

*Once students get into higher years, the workload increases, so they may not be able to work as much.

EDUCATION *SPENDING* PLAN

Here is one example of a university or college Spending Plan. First, decide where your kid will live during the school year. If they are commuting from your house, transportation costs will be high, but it's far cheaper overall. Will they live in Residence? Residence is twice the price of an apartment, about $8,000 for the one year; still it does include food, and transportation to school. Since it's usually only for first year students, most kids hook up with a few others, and rent a house or an apartment to share costs after that. That's cheaper.

Remember, students are teenagers. They are going to spend money hanging out with their friends. They are going to buy faddish clothes. You want them to do those things. Also, they will have to buy personal hygiene products, and cleaning products. Well, that last one may be overly optimistic.

The sample Spending Plan assumes the student will live in an apartment for the bulk of their school years.

EDUCATION *SPENDING* PLAN

Item	Cost
Books	$800/school year
Clothes	$300/year
Entertainment	$40/month x 8=$320
Food	$120/month x 8=$960
Gifts, e.g. Christmas, birthdays, anniversaries	$300/year
House Supplies, e.g., cleaning	$10/month x 8 = $80
Hygiene, e.g., shampoo	$20/month x 8 = $160
Rent	$360/month x 12=$4320
Transportation	$150/month x 8=$1200
Tuition	$5,000/school year
Emergency Fund, e.g. unexpected field trip	$200/ school year
Utilities	$60/month/ x 12=$720
TOTAL	$14,360

Books: I didn't believe the books would actually cost $800 a year, until the year they did. Fortunately, it was not every year. Still, better safe than sorry. Any money left over in this category will find a home in another.

Clothes: Quantity not quality is the watchword for clothes at this stage of life. Be careful to factor in a winter coat and boots. These can be expensive, and styles change, don' cha know!

Entertainment. All work and no play make kids dull. Worse, some kids over-study in fear of failing, and burn out. Remind them marks only count if they are planning to keep a scholarship or go on to graduate school. You don't want them failing; however, pushing them to make A's is too much pressure. And A's are very hard to get in university. Encourage them to go out and blow off steam, as long as what they do fits your guidelines of healthy behaviours: no drugs, promiscuity or alcohol abuse. You can draw the line so at least they know there is one. Then again, you can't control them when you aren't there. Tough one!

Food. They have to eat; still they can't afford to eat in restaurants every day. If they don't know how to grocery shop, now's your chance to take them to a discount grocery market and let them buy the family groceries for a couple of weeks, with your guidance.

This mother took her son and his future roommates grocery shopping for their first kitchen stocking for their first apartment. While her son had been grocery shopping a couple of times and bought the family's food, the other lads clearly had not. While he picked up salad, fruit and tuna, the other guys were dancing, literally, in the aisles, grabbing up and hugging items saying, "This bread is speaking to me, speaking to me!"

Tell them they need to consider everyone in the family, and the budget. Give them a calculator and follow, at a distance. Remind them occasionally of your food allergy to strawberries and the cereal their little brother prefers. And show them how to put things *back* before they get to the cashier if they've spent too much. This is an invaluable life lesson.

Gifts: Christmas still comes. Birthdays still come. Their friends may start getting married. Your student will want to have some money for gifts.

House Supplies. God willing, they will clean. Actually, it's better not to think about the mess their place may become. Do not think about it! Anyway, it won't be you cleaning it. Will it?

The week after this woman's son and his roommates moved in, one of the mothers showed up to clean their college apartment! She came every few weeks for the whole school year. Another college student's mother drove 60 miles a week to do her daughter's grocery shopping.

What message is being sent to these kids? They are incompetent to do the smallest things? When *are* they supposed to learn these adult skills? With freedom comes responsibility. That's how you form adults.

Hygiene: Hygiene includes toothpaste, deodorant, and shampoo. Don't forget female products. They don't have to buy these constantly; still when they do, they aren't free. And should they have a supply of condoms? Sorry to bring this up, but sex is a reality at this age. And condoms help keep everyone in school and not pregnant.

Rent. Calculate Rent on 12 months since many landlords insist on a full-year lease. You might be lucky and find someone who will let the kids out after 8 months, which is the length of the school year. This will likely be a flat in a private house.

Transportation: Some universities have deals with the local transit authorities, and students get a discount on the bus. However, do you want them to come home for visits? How often? If your kid's school is a goodly distance from your house, there will be those costs several times a year. Even if your student has a car, especially if your student has a car, there will be expenses.

Tuition: This cost goes up each year by about 5%. By the way, the schools usually let you pay half the tuition at a time, as in Semester 1 and Semester 2. There is no interest charge. Also, did you know many universities have three-year degrees? Unless your child wants to go to graduate school, a three-year degree is as viable in the work world as a four-year. Cheaper, too! College degrees are three years at this time.

Emergency Fund: Cold FX is $15 a box! You don't want them taking that money out of Groceries. In addition to health issues, there may be surprise costs associated with a class, or who knows what. There are many opportunities for life to throw a curve ball, so it's best to recognize that and have a little fund set aside for the unpredictable.

Utilities: These are an unpleasant fact. Ask if their new place pays any utilities. If not, your student will want internet access, maybe cable, plus all the usual, like heat, water, electricity. Figure them into the cost.

How Much?

If your child is good at school and wants to become a professional, or wants a higher education because they simply want to learn, start saving for it now. There are ways to complete a higher education which will see them getting the degree without any debt. Make that your absolute goal. They will kiss your hands in thanks at the end of it all. Even $1 will start the savings ball rolling. Keep the faith. You can do this.

Funerals

In the midst of joy, sadness. In such emotional situations, I've seen women practically throw money away. They buy gifts for people, or stand them to dinners or drinks without regard for the cost.

When this woman's husband died of cancer, she wanted to pay for everyone's meal when they went out with her after the funeral. Her friends said they wanted to and should pay for her. But, she said, "I've lost the most important thing in life. Money means nothing." Since she had a three-year old to raise, now as a single parent, she needed her money. Fortunately, her brother restrained her.

There are five stages of grief: denial, bargaining, anger, depression, and acceptance. Women usually go back and forth between stages. It is not a linear process. However, it is a necessary process, and spending money will not change the loss.

How Much?

Keep in mind Ruth Mulvey Harmer's book, The High Cost of Dying which you can download free. There is no need for an expensive casket, expensive flowers, or expensive parties or burial clothes. If you do not have the funds, the debt you accrue will add pain to your loss.

Prepaid Funerals: Funerals cost a lot of money. Most people do not have pre-paid funerals, and few outside of the funeral industry recommend them. You may move out of the geographic area, and then what? You will get the money back that you've paid, although it will have earned little interest, and will not likely pay for the full funeral expenses in the new city.

Pre-paid Burial Plot: These costs go up every year. If you feel more peaceful knowing where you will be buried, or want to relieve your family of that decision, you can prepay only the burial plot. This is about half of the overall expense. It will ensure this price does not go up.

Life Insurance: It is recommended that you have a small life insurance policy to cover funeral costs.

Death Benefits: The government also provides money in a Death Benefit which you can access, about $1200.

Initial Financial Coping: Keep your spending after the funeral as normal as possible. If you have an Emergency Fund, it will help you over the initial hurdles until you get your thoughts together. If there is to be an inheritance, it could take weeks, months, or even years before you get it all. Ask for Spiritual Guidance before spending decisions:

God, please guide me, and help me to see clearly.

Whatever guidance you think you hear, speak to your support pals before drawing any financial conclusions, as you may be mentally foggy at this time. Experts say to avoid making any major decisions for one year after a death. As rough as this situation is, one day at a time, you can cope by asking for Help, and believing things will get better, in time. And, they will.

Illness

Illness can affect your family income and bring more heartache than we care to think about. However, there are ways to minimize the pain, in advance.

If you're living in Canada, you can thank Tommy Douglas from the old Saskatchewan Co-operative Commonwealth Federation (CCF) Party, now the New Democratic Party. He brought in socialized medicine. It covers almost every important medical need. The government pays for the doctor and hospital; however, there may be other costs, such as home nursing and prescription drugs which private insurance pays for, or you do. Investigate any health insurance you have, such as from work, or privately held policies, like critical care insurance. Check your coverage details today.

If you're sick right now, here are some things you can do to get income:

Financial Safety Net while Sick

- Check to see if your life insurance has a paid portion. You can cash that in.

- Research government programs like Employment Insurance which provide money for critical illness.

- Cash in any RRSP's or RESP's.

- Sell things, like big screen TVs, musical instruments, tools, furniture or jewelry. When you get back on your feet, you can re-purchase them or something similar. Ask someone to help you hold a garage sale. You'll get to de-clutter at the same time as you get a cash infusion.

- Work part-time if you have the energy. Call temp agencies which allow for flexibility if you cannot come to work due to feeling sick.

- Get all the details of sick pay benefits from your work.

- See if one of your professional organizations has group health insurance policies for which you still qualify.

Even if you're not ill, get to know the facts in your financial safety net. It will bring you comfort when your mind goes to the dark place. Along with that, you will have the figures written down, and be able to act right away if illness strikes.

How Much?

Unfortunately, there may be a loss of income in addition to more expenses. If you can no longer earn the salary you had before you got sick, your Emergency Fund will help you keep going for several weeks. Then, you can use any balances in your savings categories, like Clothes, to start paying for basic expenses.

Hopefully, you'll be back on your healthy feet sooner rather than later, and be grateful for all the financial footwork you have previously done. Lowering financial stress will increase your chances of a happy health outcome.

Retirement

Seen on a coffee mug: Retirement: the hours are great, but the pay stinks.

We all hope to retire one day, and it is possible to have an abundant retirement. A Retirement Spending Plan brings the same promise as any other: peace and prosperity. It follows the same pattern as your monthly plan, with a few notable exceptions, like no work expenses!

Even if retirement is far away for you, if you make deposits to any offered company or government retirement plans at any level you can, you will feel responsible, and more secure.

Government Contributions to your Retirement:

If you're closing in on retirement, and you haven't saved much, consider getting a job at a company which has a pension plan. For example, police departments, schools, and the civil service still have Dedicated Benefit Pension Plans, the gold standard for pensions. You get a guaranteed amount of payout monthly once you retire. Plus, you do not have to be a police officer or a teacher to work in these places. You can work as a secretary, a computer person, or in many other capacities. Look over your skills and their websites, and consider applying.

Fortunately, in North America, we have government pension plans which will augment your retirement savings. Canada Pension Plan pays up to $900 a month. You qualify for CPP if you have contributed to it. In other words, if you have worked and paid CPP taxes, you will collect CPP. If you take it before age 65, you will receive a reduced amount. If you wait until you're 65, or even older, your payments will increase to the maximum. Depending how long you think you will live, taking it early might net you more money overall. The Canadian government also has the Old Age Pension plan. This is about $600 a month now. You must be at least 65 to begin to collect. That age is going up, a la the States.

This is all good news. Living solely on a government pension is not super generous, and it may mean you won't get a dog because of the expense; then again, with these funds as a base, you can start saving more to fund a retirement lifestyle to which you can look forward. Remember, $5 a pay is $120 a year, and earns interest. It's a start, isn't it?

STANDARD RETIREMENT ADVICE FOR NON-STANDARD PEOPLE

If you're a standard person, this is what sensible financial advisors tell you to do for a comfortable retirement. However, most of us are not standard folks.

Standard Advice	Appropriate For you?
If you have credit card debts, pay them off before you retire. Do this before you begin to invest.	You *do* have credit card debt and/or other debts as well. For you, it is important to pay them off, ideally before you retire. But, for you, it is also important to enjoy a comfortable life at the same time. If you deprive yourself to pay your creditors, you will start to get sloppy with money again. The human spirit can stand only so much restriction. Pay your debts in an orderly fashion, yes, but at a rate that allows you to live a pleasant life now. With God's help, you will do it before you retire, or manage fine afterwards.
Set up a six-month Emergency Fund.	Stick to three months of expenses. Remember, you are also saving money in various categories which can augment your Emergency Fund.
Keep emergency money in a high-interest savings account with no penalty for withdrawals.	Do such accounts exist anymore? Leave some of your Emergency Fund in a Tax-free Savings account, but the rest in various categories. You can access that money quickly if you have to.
Don't panic when the market drops. If you're investing monthly, market selloffs help you because you're now buying additional shares at lower prices.	Can you *really* look the other way when the market is falling? If not, admit it, and make sure you have more Guaranteed Investment Certificates, and bonds which are stable. The interest rates will be lower, but so will your blood pressure. You are who you are.
Take any yearly tax refund you get from investing in RRSPs and plow the money back into more RRSPs.	All work and no play make Jill a dull girl. Life is to be enjoyed along side the need to be responsible. Remember the Rule of Thirds. While you invest some of the refund back into RRSPs, you will use some for pleasure. Buy the TV you have been wanting, put some of the money towards your dream vacation, or take the family bowling and out to dinner.
Plan to take out 2 - 3% of your capital a year when you retire. For example, if you're 60 and expect to live for 30 more years, taking 2-3 % of your money out will allow it to earn enough interest to last 30 years.	Check out www.liveto100.com and see how long doctors think you might live. Even if you make the lifestyle changes they suggest, you might not live longer, but at least it will give you a wake up call on how long you need your money to last. In Canada, once you reach 71, the government will begin to tax RRSP money, so you will have to cash in some. You can seek the advice of your financial planner as to how to invest that money. You probably don't need their advice on how to spend it!
Live below your means. Don't get caught up in 'bigger is better'. Buy used. Do without the frills like cable TV, or fancy vacations.	Ah, come on. How Scrooge-y can you be? You can have an abundant retirement doing what you love, if you start using the tools in this book now.

How Much?

With the standard government payouts, you are on your way to paying for the basics. A year before retirement, begin by reducing your Spending Plan by 25%. This will allow you to get used to a different level of spending slowly. Six months before you retire, reduce it further to match your new retirement level of income.

Accountants are always harping on the magic of compound interest. And they are right. If you save $120 a year from the age of 30 until you're 65, that's $5 a pay, you will have a lot more money than if you dump thousands into an investment at age 50. Except, in our earlier years, we don't feel we can spare money for retirement investing. We need to live *now*.

While that is a normal response, you're kidding yourself. You will get old. You will not be able to work forever. Start a Retirement category, even if it's at the smallest, tiniest amount, $1 a pay. Then use windfalls and the good luck that comes with spiritually managed finances to save more.

Weddings

If you have kids, they will likely get married. If *you're* single now, you're likely to get married. From my mouth to God's ear, right? These ideas apply whether it's your own wedding or one for your kid.

The Vision

The first principle, as always, is to envision your dream wedding. If it's a destination wedding, or a snazzy dance at the yacht club, or a fun party at a community center, write that down. Even draw it. Have fun with the vision.

If this is your *own* wedding, your vision controls everything. If this is your child's wedding, not so much. Ask them for their vision. Help make it come true while not ignoring your own desires, and the overall spending plan.

Saying a brief prayer before each meeting or outing will help. Pray alone, or in concert with anyone else who's present and willing:

God, we ask for your help in making these decisions for the wedding of xxx. Relieve us of the burdens of our egos and perfectionism. Help us to focus on the greater good of the families involved. Help us to do the work, but leave the outcome to you.

If you think your child will pay for their own wedding, you might be right, but you might be wrong. Or, if you think the parents of your child's intended will pay half, you might be right, and you might be wrong.

Recently, a friend had to contribute $20,000 to have the wedding her daughter dreamed of while the parents of the groom insisted they could only contribute $5,000. In addition, then, they wanted to invite more guests than her. A warning to be careful of expectations of 'the other side'.

Who Pays?

Here is the time to talk about who should pay for this wedding. If the kids are working full-time, should they contribute?

One employed bride divided the $20,000 total into four categories. She and her fiancé each contributed $5,000, and the parents each contributed $5,000.

In another case, our friend was told the groom's parents had no money to contribute. So she had the working couple pay for the whole wedding. Then she and her husband gave a sizeable cash gift.

Different strokes. Whatever works. In any case, if you give the couple a certain amount of money to spend, it is easier for them to stick to a budget rather than having fantasies dictate to the exclusion of reality. That can turn into a spending frenzy!

One thirty-something bride bought three wedding gowns over the internet, none of which she could return. She did wear one of them, but she had to give the other two away. The closer to the wedding she got, the more she began to spend. Fortunately, she had a financial friend who stopped her before she went into debt.

You have probably watched those wedding TV shows. The money becomes a non-issue in their desire to have the best wedding ever. Repeat this mantra: *a wedding is just party; the marriage is what counts.*

If you are the parents, make it a condition of your contribution they not go into debt for their wedding expenses or honeymoon. They will thank you later, though maybe not until their next lifetime.

Wedding spending is in such large sums, it can disorient even the fiscally sane, making it easy to slip into debt. Any wedding debt is bad. Does the couple want to move forward in married life with a small nest egg from a few cash gifts, or start it with a debt burden? Even one dollar of debt is a burden which *they* are going to have to pay, not the parents. .

Remember the old axiom: Pay $100, expenses $99.99—Joy! Pay $100, expenses $100.01—despair.

Tell them that one! These days it's common to give the money for the wedding to the kids and let them make the decisions. Know, once you have given them the cash, it is their money. If you're lucky, they may include you in the decision-making because you're so wise. Or not.

INCREASE FUNDS

If faced with a financial shortage for the wedding, there are three ways to remedy it. The first is to bring in more income, the second is to reduce the expenses, and of course, there is a third ace up your sleeve. Pray for a miracle!

1. Cash Shower

Given many young couples are already living together and have all the kitchen stuff they could ever want, a new idea has become popular: fund raise for the wedding party from the guests. Instead of having people give items you have placed on a Gift Registry, ask guests to give cash.

Some cultures already do this, so it isn't much of a stretch in those communities. On the other hand, if your group isn't used to this, it can seem crass. Younger guests think nothing of it. Others will not co-operate, and that is their choice.

One woman threw an engagement party for her daughter, asking guests to help the young couple with their dream honeymoon. However, instead of giving money, one cousin gave a plain glass bowl. Some people are like that. The other guests used it for their envelopes. The couple received over $1,000, which they did use to help pay for their honeymoon.

The risk here is that some people set aside a total amount to give for the all the wedding events, and so you may end up with smaller wedding gifts.

2. Cash Wedding Gifts

Some cultures give cash for wedding gifts. Many Ukrainians in Edmonton have a big glass bowl in the center of the room, and people bring up their gift and the Master of Ceremony announces the amount. Not surprisingly, the gifts tend to be large. However, when it's their turn, the community returns the favour.

Whether or not this is your tradition, it's likely the couple will get some money for wedding gifts. Should they count on that to help pay for the wedding? Here's the problem: they may not get as much as they hoped. It used to be people gave gifts equal to what they thought it cost you to feed them at your venue. It also used to be people sent a gift when they got a wedding invitation even if they could not attend. However, there is a more budget-minded philosophy afoot these days: *if I don't eat, I don't pay; and your party choices do not determine my gift level.* This means don't expect your guests' gifts to cover the cost of your wedding.

On the other hand, more people are giving cash gifts. Though it won't pay for the whole shebang, it helps.

3. Cash Bar

Given some people get drunk at weddings, and can spoil the evening, maybe a cash bar isn't such a bad idea. Many people drink what is available, so if you put wine on the table, or have servers go around offering red and white wine, that will be plenty for most guests. For those who have to have a cocktail, they can purchase drinks from the bar. This will save you a lot of money compared to an open bar.

One woman who could not afford to have an open bar at a family celebration provided one bottle of white and one bottle of red wine for each table of eight. However, out of curiosity, she checked with the bar at the end of the evening to see how much liquor her guests had purchased. They'd bought $600 of drinks. The meal had cost $2,000. That was nearly one third. Besides, only a few guests did all the drinking. She was relieved she had arranged for a cash bar.

Another woman had an open bar. When she went to pay the bill, she almost fainted. It cost as much as the whole meal.

Another option that has been used is to provide each guest with one or two drink tickets. Those who don't want to drink often give theirs to people who do. Drinkers don't like this much, but it is an attempt at both generosity and restraint.

REDUCE YOUR EXPENSES

There is a more camouflaged solution when there is a money shortage for a wedding: reduce the scope of the event. For example, if your wedding costs seem 20% above your spending plan, you might downsize one or more things until you get to the right overall wedding price tag.

The Food

Remove one course of the dinner, especially if you're serving soup. That fills people up very quickly. Alternatively, maybe the dessert table can be more modest since people will have eaten a big dinner. Think of all the food that will go to waste to help you make that decision.

The Music

Hire a smaller band, or a DJ. Or find a venue which provides a DJ or band within the price.

The Pictures

Reduce the number of hours the photographer will attend the wedding. On the other hand, if your guests are willing to be pseudo-photographers, and some people love that, place a disposable camera on each table. You'll get shots even a professional photographer would have missed.

Invite Fewer People

Alternatively, you could simply reduce your guest list by 20% --- 10% for the bride's side and 10% for the groom's side. If that causes fits, try the old way of doing things: invite some people to the dinner, and others to the dancing and dessert table later. The dates of the bridemaids and groomsmen could fit into this category, and work friends.

When to Start Saving for Weddings

Once you know the cost of the wedding, save from each paycheck, balancing that cost against other expensive events, like Confirmations, Bar Mitzvahs, high school graduations, university fees. You are practicing parallel savings, so the wedding fund may have to start small, very small. All the same, even $5 a pay adds up.

Is it realistic to be saving for their weddings from their birth? I don't think so. Start around the time they are juniors in high school. The little dears might get married during their twenties. It happens. In that case, you will have 10 years to save. And if you want to save $10,000, you'll need to put aside about $40 a pay from the time they are 16 years old to meet your goal.

If you only have five years to save, or two years, do the math. It might be a number hard to swallow; however, it's a lot better to save something upfront than pay off the credit cards and interest for years after the event. If you have already debted for a wedding, turn to the section on debt repayment.

Parents' Personal Spending Plan

Parents need a separate wedding Spending Plan, a little stash for your own expenses. For example, will you want to give the wedding couple gifts at the showers, engagement party, or the wedding? Will you have to buy new clothes for these events? Will you want to get your hair done, nails, etc, for each event? Will you want to host a party? What about the out of town guests' dinner? How about the costs of airport parking and gas to pick up the out of town guests, and maybe entertain them? In addition, what about the things you don't even know about yet?

If you choose to save $10,000 overall for the couple's wedding, you might keep $2,000 for your own expenses. If you have money left over in your stash, you can give it to the couple, start the next kid's wedding savings, or take a much-needed weekend holiday to recover from it all!

Once you have your dollar amount set aside for yourselves, say, $2,000, divide it up into various subcategories:

- Clothes for you, for your spouse, for your other children.

- Gifts for the shower, the luncheon, etc.

- Beauty treatments for you, for your spouse, for the kids.

- Transportation Costs for Out of Town guests.

- Entertainment for Out of Town guests.

- The life-saving Mini-Emergency Fund.

What does a Spending Plan for a Wedding look like? Numerous wedding books and websites detail what you need, so I won't.

How Much?

No matter whose wedding it is, you will be spending a large sum of money. In major cities, as of now, the average wedding costs start at $185 per person. That includes everything from the dress to the cake. If you think your wedding should have 100 guests, you can see what you need to save. This can take awhile.

Now, given your best guess, how many people do you think you will have at your wedding? Big families can mean many guests, yet small families can also have many guests. Will you invite business associates, book club friends, second cousins, children under 10? Come up with an estimate for total number of guests. Let's say 100 people.

With your vision in mind, and the number of people attending, you can now research and pray to stay calm, and joyful. How much for a wedding in Hawaii? Mexico? Banff? What does it cost to rent Casa Loma, The Jewish Community Center, the Doctor's House and Church in King City? What will your ideal menu cost per person? Then there are favours for the guests, the bridal party, your clothes, and merrily on and on. You can borrow wedding planning books from the library to see costs, and ideas. Open it one section at a time, or you may feel overwhelmed! Don't forget the wedding planners who can get you discounts and almost pay for themselves.

Total this up, on paper, and see how much your share will be, and how much you need to save from each pay to get there.

Remember, a wedding is just a party. The marriage afterwards is what counts. Going into debt for a wedding is not an option. Starting any married life with that burden is crippling. Would you go into debt for a party?

Along the way, pray for a Miracle. Keep your eyes open, and notice things coming to you easily and with a modest price, or even free. Thank your Higher Power each time. You got a Miracle!

SPIRITUAL SOLUTION:
Back Talk

W hat if you *don't* feel you should go on a vacation, or experience celebrations? As with so many high expenses, your feeling of being unworthy can rear its ugly head. Your self-talk whines like this: *How can you spend so much money when you're in so much debt? How can you consider going away when your parents/ kids/ friends/ partner/company needs xxx? Selfish! Bad! Die!*

You need to *talk back* to those distorted thoughts. Try something like this: *I work hard, and I deserve this. I'm saving for it, not reducing other categories which take care of everyone and everything else.*

Or, simply: *Thank you for sharing your thoughts, Voice, now shut up!*

If you still can't get that Voice out of your head, apply a screen. Ask your God to filter your thoughts. That usually brings on no thoughts at all, which is a welcome relief. Then, you will get distracted, and you are safe.

God, please filter my thoughts. I don't want to go down that old route. Fill my head with your thoughts instead.

As you become more prosperous, you'll have many lovely choices. God wants you to be happy. Like a nurturing parent who gets joy out of seeing their child happy, so God gets a kick out of seeing you. Remember, if you fund the big, important things in life, you will have years of pleasant anticipation while saving for future happiness. Give yourself that pleasure.

9

MAKE THINGS RIGHT

Power Up!

*B*e sure to read this chapter to the end *before you takes any action.*

Everyone makes mistakes. A mistake is *an incorrect, unwise, or unfortunate act or decision caused by bad judgment or a lack of information or care.* So you made mistakes around money, *you* are not a mistake. Believe this: given your circumstances and your childhood, you would have done better if you had known how. Fortunately, you now have a new set of guidelines for your money life, and you are doing better.

Yes, you will pay off every negotiated cent you owe, in time; however you will no longer deprive yourself of your needs. You will be amazed to see that this approach creates the best life you have ever experienced, and pays off your debts at the same time. That is how a spiritual money management system works. Why would a loving God want anything else?

Let's give you a boost by noting your progress. If you answer Yes to *any* of these questions, you are on your way to getting out of your financial mess:

Checklist: HAVE YOU *STARTED* TOWARDS A DEBT-FREE LIFE?

- Have you written a Money History to see the forces which acted on you?

- Have you outlined your debting triggers and what you will now do instead?

- Have you paid attention to your dreams, written them down, analyzed them to be sure they are enduring?

- Have you created a One-Day-Soon Spending Plan which will bring about a comfortable life?

- Have you listed your income sources, and noted where more can come into your life?

- Have you scheduled your bills, and renegotiated them to free up income for savings?

- Have you created multiple Savings categories to fund a rich life, full of purpose and enjoyment?

- Have you tracked your past spending for a realistic Spending Plan?

- Have you massaged your categories so they fit into your present income, reducing or increasing as appropriate?

- Have you included categories in your Spending Plan for big future events, and present pleasures?

- Do you know how to create a mini-Spending Plan?

Debt Repayment

A Debt Repayment Plan negotiates only two things: the *total* you will repay, and *how long* you will take. None of that has anything to do with your self-esteem or worth as a woman. These are financial transactions, period.

You will soon know exactly how much debt you owe, and then begin to repay each as a regular part of your Spending Plan. First, you will use your money to fund your comfortable needs, and then use money left for debt repayment.

I know this is backwards to some experts. Their thought is you need to repay all your debts *as fast as possible* no matter what sacrifices you have to make. However, by now you and I know that will make you debt again. The human spirit can take only so much deprivation before it rebels. My way suggests you live a pleasant life at the same time as you repay debt.

Master Debt Record

At this moment, all you need to do is make a *list* of your creditors to whom you owe unsecured debt. Not your mortgage or car loan, unless either is in arrears. Include family debts and any theft. Yes, record any money you have taken unlawfully. Create a table with 10 columns. First, write down the approximate amount you think you owe each.

Master Debt Record

Creditor	Debt								
VISA	$8,000								
Back taxes	$4,000								
Mom	$13,000								
TOTAL	$25,000								

Take a deep breath, and *add* it up. Though the number may be large, very large indeed, note this: it is no larger. Until you write it down in black and white, the number can seem to grow in your head.

Next, add contact information to your debt record, that is, phone number, email address and city address. Call each creditor and get the exact amount they think you owe, including arrears, fines and fees. Ask God for the courage:

God, please give me the courage, the willingness and the words to get the facts from my creditors.

Accuracy is the goal. If Mom says you owe her only $12,000 and swears this is so, take her word for it and reduce her debt number from $13,000 to $12,000. Miracles are happening already!

While you have each creditor on the phone, get more facts: interest rate, payment due dates, minimum payment amounts, and who you spoke with.

Master Debt Record

Creditor	Debt	Interest Rate	Min. Pay't		Payment Date	Address	Phone	Contact Person
VISA	$8,000	18%	$150		1st of month	123 Bloor Street	555-1212	Sherrie
Back taxes	$4,000	11%	$83		15th of month	1024 Yonge Street	555-3141	Dwayne
Mom	*$12,000*	0%	$0		1st of month	Known	Known	Mom
TOTAL	24,000							

You may not agree with one of your creditors about the debt amount. That's o.k. Note the amount *they* think you owe. You can dispute it later if you have records to prove them wrong.

Correct your debt total if you received information different from your original total.

Debt Repayment Funds

The next step is to see how much money is available for debt repayment. After funding your bills and savings categories to a reasonable amount, how much money do you have left for debt repayment? If there is absolutely none, try these options:

1. If you haven't done some tough negotiating with your service providers, like the phone company, it's open season on them now. Lower those bills!

2. Review Chapter 4, *Claim your Income* to get more funds.

3. Don't start depriving yourself again, but shave a few dollars off the more abundant savings categories. Put that money towards debt repayment.

4. Use one-third of every windfall for debt repayment.

Debt Repayment Strategy

What is the best process to eradicate debts? Well, there are as many strategies as there are financial gurus. For example:

- **Snowball**. Pay the minimum payments on every debt. If you have extra money, start applying it to the smallest debt. When the smallest debt is paid, apply that money to the next smallest debt, and so on. Unfortunately, if you do not have enough money to pay the minimum payments on all your present debts, first, this strategy does not work.

- **Pain Relief**. Repay the debt which bothers you the most, perhaps a family or friend debt about which you feel guilty, or the creditor who is pressuring you the most. This plan also only works if you have enough money to continue paying the minimum on the other debts, or you'll have the rest of your creditors hounding you.

- **Preferential Treatment**. Apply *most* of your debt repayment money to the highest interest debt before all other debts. But, creditors are a jealous lot. If any of them find out what you're doing, each will put on the pressure to become the preferred one.

- **Proportional Payments**. This is the most workable approach and one your creditors trust. It treats them all equally. You pay each creditor a share of the available debt repayment money, proportional to how much you owe each. The biggest debt gets the most money; the smallest debt gets the least. Everyone gets something, although not necessarily their minimum payment.

It is a slow and steady way of improving your credit rating, too. As the creditors see your payments coming in consistently, on time, they accept that though it may be slower than they'd like, you will eventually pay off your debt. This is how you rebuild a reliable repayment track record.

Steps to Proportional Debt Repayment

Step 1. Write down the amount of money you have available for debt repayment after completing your Spending Plan. Eg. $125

Step 2. Fill in the Debt Record table: the name of the creditor, how much the debt is, the interest rate, the minimum payment they expect, the date the payment is due, their address, phone number and contact person for each creditor. You probably know Mom's phone number.

Step 3. Be sure to list *all* your debts, institutional and personal. Get it all down in one place. Don't panic. Your debts may be high, but they are no higher. And, they will be gone, sooner than you think.

Master Debt Record

Step 4. Using a calculator, divide Debt 1 which is Visa at $8,000, by the total amount of debt: $24,000.

8,000÷ 24,000 =.333
Multiple that number by 100
.333 x 100 = 33.3
Round down = 33%.
Write the answer under *Pay't %,* as in the table below.

Step 5. Divide Debt 2 which is the Back Taxes: $4,000, by the total amount of debt: $24,000.

4,000 ÷ 24,000 = .166
Multiple that number by 100
.166 x 100= 16.6
Round up= 17%.
Write the answer under *Pay't %* .

Step 6: Divide Debt 3 which is Mom: $12,000 by the total amount of debt: $24,000.

12,000 ÷ 24,000 = 0.5
Multiply that number by 100
.05 x 100 = 50%
Write that answer under Pay't %.

Step 7. Multiply the amount of money available for debt repayment times the Pay't %:

Debt 1: $125 x 33%= $41.25
Round down to $40 for simplicity's sake, and your sanity.
Therefore, out of your $125 available for debt repayment, you offer Visa $40 a month. Write that number in *Pay't Amt.*

Debt 2: $125 x 17% = $21.25.
Round that down to $20.
Therefore, out of your $125, you offer Revenue Canada $20 a month. Write that answer under *Pay't Amt.*

Debt 3: $125 x 50% = $62.50
Round that up to $65.
Therefore, out of your $125 available for debt repayment, you offer Mom $65 a month. Write that answer under *Pay't Amt.*

Master Debt Record

Creditor	Debt	Interest Rate	Min. Pay't	Pay't %	Pay't Amt	Payment Date	Address	Phone	Contact Person
VISA	$8,000	18%	$150			1st of month	120 Bloor Street	555-1212	Sherrie
Back taxes	$4,000	11%	$83			15th of month	1024 Yonge Street	555-3141	Dwayne
Mom	$12,000	0%	$0			1st of month	Known	Known	Mom
TOTAL	$24,000								

Debt Repayment Money Available per Month: $125

MASTER CREDITOR CONTACT LOG

A master Creditor Contact Log allows you to make note of all the agreements you make with each creditor, verbal or written.

Put your Creditor Contact Log in one binder or file folder which you can find easily. Create the template before you begin contacting anyone. Here are samples:

Creditor	Contact Person	Type of Contact	Date	Action Agreed On	Start Date	Written confirmation & date
Visa	Liz Columis	Phone	Aug 9	Columis agreed to lower payments from $150 to $40. I sent confirmation of agreement by email Aug. 9.	Sept 1	Rec'd reply email from Columis Aug 9
Back Taxes	Mike Park	Phone	Aug. 13	M. Park will accept lower installment pay'ts from $83 down to $20. I sent follow up letter Aug. 14	Sept 10	Letter Aug. 14
Mom	Mom	Email	Aug. 21	I agreed to send postdated checks for $65, starting in Sept. I mailed 6 today. Then, I sent follow-up email Aug. 21	Sept 1	Email Aug 21

MASTER CREDITOR CONTACT LOG

Individual CREDITOR CONTACT LOG

Additionally, an individual Creditor Contact Log for each Creditor adds more clarity. You see the theme, here: *clarity*. It is such a relief from vagueness and worry. After you have created the one-page Master Log for Creditors, make an individual page for each creditor. Put them all in alphabetical order, in the same binder or file folder as the Master for easy access.

Use this record to track any *inappropriate creditor behavior*, too. Note dates and times of late or early calls, insults, threats, and any language that was demeaning, and who said it.

Individual CREDITOR CONTACT LOG

Creditor	Contact Person	Type of Contact	Date	Action Agreed On	Start Date	Written Confirmation & Date
Visa	*Liz Columis	Email	Aug. 11, 2xxx	I will send postdated checks for $40 for 6 months from Sept. Sent checks out Aug. 14	Sept 1, 2xxx	Sent email asking for receipt confirmation Aug. 12.
	Jim Stiles	Phone	Aug. 21			Confirmed receipt of post-dated checks.
*Problems: Columis called my home on Sunday Aug. 9 at 7 am.						

Order of Debt Repayment

Once you have money set aside for debt repayment, which creditor do you tackle first?

Mortgage/Rent

Speak to your mortgage holder or property owner first. You don't want to be out on the street.

Mortgage Arrears Options

- Ask your bank to tack missed payments onto the end of your mortgage. They will sometimes do this for two payments.

- Request your mortgage lender add all missed payments to the mortgage balance and spread them over the remaining mortgage repayment period.

- Open a line of credit with another institution, using your house as collateral, and pay off the arrears. Once you have repaid the arrears, negotiate with your lender for a lower interest rate. If they won't cooperate, find a new lender who will give you a lower rate.

- Obtain refinancing to pay off the arrears if you are in a power of sale, more commonly called foreclosure. Although challenging to obtain and not widely available, there are specialty mortgage brokers that offer mortgage foreclosure loans. These loans have a higher interest rate than what you enjoyed on the loan in default. However, you do avoid losing your home.

Because we see more American news than Canadian around foreclosure, know that Power of Sale is Canadian and different from U.S. Foreclosure rules.

Power of Sale	Foreclosure
Borrower remains the title holder	Property gets transferred in the name of the lender
Property sold using a realtor most of the time	Property sold in auction most of the time
Borrower remains responsible for any losses the lender may have	Borrower is not responsible for any loss of the lender
Any extra money from the sale goes to borrower	Any extra money from the sale stays with the lender

Of special and unfortunate note is that in Canada, if the bank sells the property for less than the mortgage owing, the *borrower* is responsible for the difference. That's you! You cannot walk away from a property here.

Rent Arrears Options

- Contact Welfare to see if you qualify for social assistance.

- Ask to add an extra amount on each month's future rent, like $100, until you have repaid the arrears.

- Offer paid services, like maintenance, babysitting, or using your apartment as a show unit until you pay off the arrears.

Income Tax

Contact Revenue Canada next. If you owe back taxes, the government can seize your property, garnishee your wages, or do other things to get the money.

- If you are behind in your taxes, including GST, you can negotiate with the Canada Revenue Agency or CRA. They are quite helpful, actually. They want the money you owe, and will help you make a payment plan, often allowing you to repay over 12 months. They may even lower the debt total. Unfortunately, whatever the unpaid balance, penalties and interest continue while it remains unpaid. The CRA will not arrange this if they think you cannot afford to make the payments.

- If you neglected to file last year, or for the last several years, and now feel paralyzed, relax a little. Canada Revenue wants your return, so if you file voluntarily, even late, there will be no fines. It's called tax amnesty or tax pardon. You'll have to pay any tax owing, with interest, but that's it. Besides, what if you are entitled to a refund? It happens.

She was 7 years behind in her tax filing. She hired a house declutterer to help her organize her paperwork. Then she lugged boxes of information to her tax professional who had outlined what to bring. Over the next few months, he filed her back taxes. In the end, she got a refund of over $10,000.

- Start the process with professional help. If you are several years behind, or have a complicated situation, that is likely your best bet. You might be able to pay their fee from the refund you get. Alternatively, start a savings category for their fee now, and hire one when you're ready. Ask them to double-check your last few completed filings, too. If you did them yourself, you might have missed something, and be entitled to a refund there.

Utilities

Next, contact the gas, electricity, and water companies to avoid them shutting off your services.

- Don't panic. These utility companies rarely cut off services during the winter.

- Give each of them a call and explain your hardship situation, including the measures you're taking to resolve it.

- Request that each company add an extra amount on each month's future bills, like $25, until you have repaid the arrears.

- Keep copies of any correspondence.

Credit and Loans

- Finally, begin to pay credit cards, store cards, lines of credit, and personal loans. No matter what the harassment, stick with Proportional Debt Repayment. You will pay these debts off, to the full amount you negotiate, though it might take longer than they'd like.

- Call, email or write to all these creditors to explain your situation, including the measures you're taking to resolve it.

- Keep copies of any correspondence.

You have created a Spending Plan which revealed how much money you have for debt repayment after taking care of yourself. If you have not done this step, please consider going back to Chapter 5, *Spend the Proceeds*, and doing the work to clarify your numbers. This very basic information is necessary before you begin to negotiate.

PRACTICAL SOLUTION:
Winning Negotiations

Now that you know how much money you have available for debt repayment and what proportion of that money each creditor will get, you are ready to negotiate to get your debts lowered. Yes!

It may surprise you to learn you can ask for a lower interest rate, a reduction of the total debt amount, and/or relief from further interest and penalties. You can negotiate department store credit cards, collection agency debt, medical bills, credit cards, and other unsecured personal loans.

Why would creditors negotiate with you when they are in a position to insist on getting *all* their money back? You have one enormous advantage: you have the money. Though you don't have it right now, you're still the source. This puts you in the driver's seat, and creditors know it. As long as you assure them you will be making regular, timely payments of the new, agreed upon amount, some prefer to negotiate a lower total rather than getting far less if you go bankrupt. However, others say they are happy if you go bankrupt because they will at least have a guarantee of some money. You'll have to convince them you can and will pay the new amounts regularly and in a timely fashion.

Let them know your situation as soon as you realize you don't have the money to pay your bills. Early intervention offers many benefits. Your creditors can offer solutions to the problem if they are aware of your situation. They may eliminate late charges, offer the option of paying only the interest, or even defer your payments. While you're still able to enjoy their good will, they will continue to take care of your account instead of sending it to a collection agency. It is easier to negotiate with the company.

Negotiating Tools

Now, with the help of your God for courage, you're ready to face your creditors. Before you make a call or send an email, try this prayer:

God, please give me the courage and the words to negotiate the best possible arrangement for all concerned with this creditor.

Gather your tools:

- A script of what you will say. *See below.*

- Master Debt Record which lists all your creditors and the amounts you are offering

- Your financial statement—your Income and Spending Plans

- Past Correspondence, if any

- Your Master Creditor Contact Log to note all agreements.

12 Negotiation Tips

1. Call a financial friend before you make one of these creditor calls. Tell her what you plan to do. After you have done it, call her back and give her a report. It will make you feel supported, and more courageous, to know you have someone rooting for you.

2. *Never* agree to pay more than you can afford. The last thing you want is to negotiate a payment and then not be able to live up to it. Only negotiate the total amount you will repay, including interest, not the length of the repayment period.

3. Do not let the collection agent try to lower your monthly payments by extending the length of the loan. That way you will end up paying the full amount, plus extra interest. Stick to your pre-planned monthly amount, and your planned

time of repayment. Be persistent about your position. Use the broken record technique if the creditor tries to make you change your offer. That is, repeat the same statement clearly, no matter what the creditor says. For example, *I can pay $90 a month, and will do so on time, until I repay the debt. No, I can only pay $90 a month, but I will do so on time until I repay the debt.* By the way, this also works on nagging teenagers.

4. Begin to negotiate as soon as you can with your credit card companies if you're late over 90 days. This magic number of 90 days is a red flag to creditors. They think it means you're likely to debt again, and for this long, again. While it is bad for your credit rating to be 90 days in arrears on your bills, creditors are more likely to settle with you. If you have no other assets, a lawsuit against you will net them nothing; therefore, if you offer to pay them something, it is better for them. Do not presume your creditors will automatically freeze the interest on your debt. Ask them to do this or your debt will continue to grow as you're making the repayments.

5. Try to contact the original creditor before the debt goes to a collection agency. It is much easier to negotiate with the original creditor now than a collection agency later. Be assured no one can garnish your wages except the government and only with a court order. You would have received notice in writing if it were true. Most creditors will not take you to court if you really don't have the money. The creditor knows court action is expensive for them and simply counterproductive.
If one of your creditors is the Government, you often find their staff is reasonable and cooperative. If that is not your experience, ask the ombudsman to intervene on your behalf. The Taxpayers' Ombudsman is an independent and impartial officer who reviews complaints from people who

believe they have been treated unfairly or unprofessionally by the Canada Revenue Agency.

6. Don't over-explain. Tell the creditor what you *can* do, rather than what you can't do. Make some type of offer. They'll either agree or make a counteroffer, and you can proceed from there. Expect a *few* rounds of negotiation. Don't allow yourself to become discouraged. Most successful negotiations take place over a matter of days or even weeks, with several rounds of offers and counter-offers.

7. Do your best during negotiations to uncover your creditor's bottom line, the absolute minimum they'll accept. Historically, credit card companies were not willing to settle for less than 80 percent of the total amount due. However, more recently, some have been willing to settle for 50-70%. However, don't *ask* the creditor how much they will accept for *monthly* payments. Tell the creditor how much you can pay. Never offer to pay more than you can afford.

8. Try to space repayments throughout the month. Perhaps, commit to half being due in the first part of the month, and the other half due in the second half of the month.

9. Ask to speak with a manager or supervisor if the agent denies a request you make for any reason. The telephone agent often does not have the power to negotiate. Do not feel intimidated by the person with whom you are negotiating. Remember, the money they want is in your control. You have the right to seek bankruptcy protection where they may get no money. You're in the driver's seat.

10. Get all settlement agreements in writing, signed, and dated by both parties. Keep copies of letters, emails, statements, phone call notes, and other papers in your files. During the conversation, take notes on what the other person is telling you. When you have ended the conversation, send a

confirmation letter or email stating what you have agreed to do so there will be no confusion on either side, or possible denials in the future.

11. Do not lose sight of the fact that if you can afford to settle an account by paying a lump sum (as opposed to a payment plan), you'll have more negotiating advantage with any creditor.

12. Let the creditor know you're trying to take responsibility for your past credit history and regain control of your financial situation. Remember, too, for the collection agency, this is simply business. They earn a commission based on what they can collect from you. If you have money, they want it to get their own paycheck.
    This is nothing but a business transaction to both of you. You owe the company money. You intend to pay back the money. The only variables are the final amount you negotiate to repay, and how long that will take.

NEGOTIATION SCRIPT

Here is a written script you can keep in front of you during the phone call. It will prove a lifesaver. Being nervous can make you say things you don't mean to, offering to pay more than you can afford to reduce your anxiety. Also, if you're expecting resistance from a creditor, a script will keep you on track, and allow you to repeat yourself until the creditor accepts your terms.

Be sure to rehearse this script 2-3 times, maybe with the phone to your ear. This will boost your confidence.

Before You Begin Negotiations:

1. Ask to speak to a Manager. Do not divulge any information at all except to a Manager. If you do, you will end up in a fruitless discussion with someone who has no power to grant your wishes. Do not give the first person who answers the phone your name, your account number, or any other

information. Simply repeat your request to speak to a manager.

2. If the person on the line says s/he is the manager, I'd doubt that. It is rare a Manager who answers first. Politely, repeat yourself as often as necessary.

Here is an example of what you might say:

Negotiation Script

I'd like to speak to the Manager of the Department, please. **If there is any resistance to getting a manager, repeat your request.**

I'd like to speak to the Manager of the Department, please. I cannot discuss my situation with anyone else.

If there is no way you are going to talk to a manager, you can start to negotiate with the person on the phone, but the minute the agent refuses to agree to any request you make, insist again on speaking to a manager. When the manager answers, continue with the script.

My name is ----------------------. **I'm calling about Account number --------------. To whom am I speaking?** (Write down the name in your Creditor Contact Log).

My records show my total debt to your company (or XYZ Company) is $_____ and the interest rate charged on that debt is ____percentage. My minimum payments are $_____ a month, due on the _____ of the month. Is that information correct?

Due to many circumstances, my account is not up-to-date. For this, I apologize. I wish to assure you I fully intend to repay this debt.

I'd like to request relief from additional *interest and penalties on the debt, starting now.* (Wait for a response. Whether it is positive or negative, continue with the script.)

I'd like to point out I've paid a substantial amount of my bill, and have been a good customer of XYZ Company in the past and will continue to be so in the future. (If the Manager did not grant your first request for immediate interest and penalty relief, repeat your request):

I'd like to request relief from further *interest and penalties on the debt.* (Wait for a response. If it is positive, say Thank you. If it is negative, go on with the script.)

I'm getting financial help, now, [You are. You're following the suggestions in this book, and from God]. *I'd prefer to negotiate a repayment amount which I can handle, and which I will pay consistently and on time until I clear the debt.*

Once I've paid off some of my smaller debts, I will arrange for larger payments to you.

Given my income, expenses, and debt situation, I know I qualify for bankruptcy protection, but I do not wish to take that route at this time.

The principal amount remaining on the debt is $_____. *I'd like to ask you to remove the interest and penalties accrued to this time.* (If the response is positive, say Thank you. If it is negative, continue with the script.)

Based on my present net income, living expenses, and in fairness to my other creditors, I can pay off the principal of this debt, only, on a monthly basis of $_____ and will continue to do so, on time, for _____ months until the principal is fully repaid.

(Or, if this is possible for you) *I can send you a lump sum payment today for $_____.*

Once I've made timely payments for six months, I'd like to ask you to amend your comment on my credit report to show I make my payments on time, and on a consistent basis. Will you do that?

I promise to keep in touch with you as often as you think necessary, keeping you advised on any changes in my financial situation.

I'd like to repeat what we have agreed to, and I will send you a confirming letter (or email) to be sure we both have understood clearly.

You have agreed to stop adding new interest and penalty charges to this debt.

You have agreed to reduce the amount of the debt to the principal only, removing past interest and penalty charges.

You have agreed to amend my credit report after six months of good payment history, showing I'm repaying the debt on time, and in a consistent manner.

I've agreed to pay $___ a month, on time, for _____ months to repay a total of $_____.

I will send you a confirming email (or letter) to be sure we are both clear about the agreement.

Thank you.

Responses to Expect

Theirs: Their response may be to refuse your offer. Still don't give up on your plan. They may threaten you with legal action, although we know they have to send notice in writing first. Consult Legal Aid if you get a letter indicating legal action.

Even after negotiating with you, some creditors may contact you, saying the amount you're paying is not enough. But, as long as you pay a minimum of $1.00 monthly, bill collectors cannot refer your account to a collection agency. Keep all correspondence in your Creditor file. Continue to pay the amount you can afford.

If any creditor becomes abusive on the phone, tell them you will not accept abusive language or threats, and you will continue communicating with them only in writing--letters or emails. Make that note on your Creditor Contact Log. However, if they insist this is not how they communicate with clients, it is better to keep up the phone contact, though insisting on civil treatment is your right. If they don't change their ways, tell them you will complain to the Office of Consumer Affairs. They don't want that black mark on their record, and they will tone things down. Be prepared to write a formal complaint if they misbehave again. See a sample complaint letter later in this chapter.

Since you are repaying your creditors proportionately, the most money going to the highest debt, and paying them what you can afford without ruining your health with overwork, or depriving your family, you are doing the best you can at this time. Will these amounts seem paltry to your creditors? Possibly. Despite this fact, stick to your guns. Pay steadily, month after month. Soon enough, they will regain confidence in you.

However, if your best efforts to negotiate do not reach a satisfactory agreement, let them know you will consider formal Debt Resolution. This means Debt Settlement, a Consumer Proposal or Bankruptcy. They don't like those. They may become more amenable to your plan as a result.

Yours: you may feel sweaty and shaky because you're afraid of the creditor's anger. You may find your voice quakes. If you rehearse this script often before making calls, you will be calmer. After all, you're doing the best you can at this time, and you're going to repay the newly negotiated amount. It will take longer than they would like, that's all.

Then again, do these amounts seem paltry to *you*? If so, realize Time is on your side. You will pay off all your debts, eventually, and live a pleasant life *at the same time*. It's one of the miracles of spiritual finance.

If a Creditor Calls You

Sometimes, you feel strong enough to deal with creditors calmly, other times you don't. Where possible, have a phone which reveals the name of the caller. Answer if you feel strong, don't otherwise. In any case, do not make promises you cannot keep. Do not make any decisions without taking 72 hours to consider them. During that time, speak to a financial advisor, whether it's a formally trained person or a friend or family member who knows your situation. Airing the dilemma can help you think more clearly about what to do.

If a creditor calls you and you're unprepared to speak to them, that is, your script is in another room, or you're too tired and can't think clearly, tell them you have to speak to your financial advisor before making any commitments, or you need more information before deciding on their request. Set a date for a return phone call, and make sure you keep that date. They will have written it down and be expecting to hear from you. Make the call even if you have no new information yet, or cannot make a commitment. It strengthens their trust in you.

DEBT RESOLUTION PLANS

If your debt is so high you cannot make the minimum monthly payments on your present income, and have not been able to negotiate them lower with your creditors, you can reduce your debt with one of three plans: Debt Settlement, Consumer Proposal or Bankruptcy . Trustees in Bankruptcy arrange both Consumer Proposals, and Bankruptcy. A trustee can also negotiate Debt Settlement, or you can do that yourself.

Debt Settlement

Debt settlement requires a lump sum of money to a creditor to clear your debt. It is often lower than the debt on record, but, to tidy their books and get quick money, some of the big banks allow collectors to settle for 65 percent of the principal and interest owing on debts less than $5,000. Debts that are more expensive settle for 80 to 85 percent below the owed amount.

Unfortunately, this isn't a viable option for women who are experiencing financial hardship and have no lump sum. However, if you *are* able to come up with a large single payment towards your debt, you will be able to negotiate to pay less than you owe. Do this on a creditor-by-creditor basis.

Don't feel bad about paying less, as if you are defrauding the creditors. Realize that a large part of your debt is their fees and fines for late payment. You probably paid off the principal long ago. So, if you are in a position to pay a lump sum, negotiate hard to reduce the total. They want the money, and you have it.

There is a somewhat controversial idea which I want to mention which is a corollary to debt settlement. It is making use of the Statute of Limitations on your debt. Depending on the province you're in, it can be anywhere from 2-7 years. That means, after the required time has elapsed, the debt cannot be collected.

Don't get too excited, but get a little excited. Some conditions apply:

1. This does not apply to money owed to the government

2. This does not apply to secured debt, in other words, a house mortgage or car loan.

3. Non-payment of such a debt will affect your credit rating.

4. If you pay the debt voluntarily, even $1, or acknowledge the debt *in writing (which includes emails)*, the debt time-period resets and the debt remains.

5. If your creditor sues you and you fail to file a defense, the debt remains.

I say this method is controversial because it is controversial to me. It means that you might legally avoid paying a debt you actually owe. Is that right? Those who like this method point out that if the debt is quite old, as in over six years old, it has likely been sold to a debt buyer, and so your original creditor will never see the money. In fact, the debt might have been sold to a debt buyer if it's older than six months. So, it will depend on how much the debt weighs on your conscience. That is what is important.

Each province has its own period after which the statue of limitations kicks in, and its own requirements of the credit bureaus to remove the bad debt notation from your credit file.

Limitation Periods by Province

Province	General Limitation Period for Consumer Debts	Length of Time on Your Credit Report
Alberta	2 years	6 years
British Columbia	6 years	6 years
Manitoba	6 years	6 years
New Brunswick	6 years	6 years
Newfoundland & Labrador	6 years	6 years
Northwest Territories	6 years	Not Specified
Nova Scotia	6 years	6 years
Nunavut	6 years	Not Specified
Ontario	2 years	7 years
Prince Edward Island	6 years	7 years
Quebec	3 years	Not Specified
Saskatchewan	2 years	6 years
Yukon Territory	6 years	Not Specified

For a detailed discussion of this solution, I recommend Mark Silverthorn's book, *The Wolf at the Door*. There is a ton of help here if you are considering this debt resolution strategy.

I am not recommending this method or anyone's services. Research and pray before you move in that direction. In the meantime, take the question to a financial buddy. Work it through so that you feel not just relieved, which the prospect of getting rid of any debt would do, but *peaceful* about the decision.

Consumer Proposal

There is another solution to get out from under heavy debt. A Consumer Proposal is an agreement with your creditors, negotiated by a Trustee in Bankruptcy, to pay a percent of your debt based on your income.

The Trustee in Bankruptcy negotiates it, though this process is not going bankrupt. The advantage over bankruptcy is you can keep your assets, like a car, and if you get a windfall of money or higher wages, your negotiated debt repayment will not increase.

Consumer Proposal Details:

- Must be *less* than $250,000 in debt

- Once electronically filed with the Federal Government, protection is in place immediately. Creditors are notified within five business days at which point all harassment must stop.

- Once filed, unsecured creditors have 45 days to vote for or against the proposal or put forward a counter-offer. If approved by the majority of creditors, all the other creditors must agree, too. Two weeks later, the Proposal gains court approval.

- Settlement offer must be "sweeter" than the creditors would receive in a bankruptcy

- If creditors reject the Proposal, the debtor may opt to file a Bankruptcy or attempt to settle with the creditors directly in an informal manner.

- You need to attend two mandatory counseling sessions during the Consumer Proposal (the first within 60 days, the second within 210 days)

- No monthly income statements are required

- Tax refunds go to the debtor

- Proposal can be 1-5 years. Trustees will recommend that you pay down the proposal earlier and of course, creditors welcome it.

- If three payments are missed then the Consumer Proposal is considered "annulled", the protection is immediately lifted and the creditors have the legal right to pursue the amounts owing to them.

- Three years following completion of the Consumer Proposal payments, the debtor's credit rating can begin to improve.

Source: A. Farber and Partners, Trustees in Bankruptcy

You will pay a monthly amount to the Trustee who then divides the money between the creditors. Consumer Proposals do affect your credit rating, but not as strongly as a bankruptcy. Often, credit-reporting agencies keep this information on your records for only three years, assuming you pay your monthly repayment on time, as opposed to seven years for a bankruptcy. In addition, if you get a better job, and earn more, or come into money through an inheritance, after the Consumer Proposal is in force, you do not have to pay more to your creditors.

You can see why many women prefer this method to bankruptcy. All the same, sometimes bankruptcy is the best solution.

Bankruptcy

Bankruptcy is like a get-out-of-jail-free card. You can use it no more often than once in 12 years. It is a way to wipe the slate clean of most debts, with the exception of some student loans, child support, and debts from fraud. For a complete list of what is covered by this arrangement, google bankruptcy .

Though the minimum amount of debt needed for filing bankruptcy in Canada is over $1,000, very few people with

$1,001 in debts go bankrupt. In a 2005 study, the average person filing bankruptcy in Canada had unsecured debts of $50,000. A Trustee negotiates how much you will repay of your debt. It's usually a small amount, based on your assets and income, though it is something. The Trustee will use that money to repay your creditors in proportion to the amount you owe each, and to pay them.

One woman owed $54,000 in unsecured debt. Her bankruptcy settlement was $1800.

However, Bankruptcy forces the liquidation of your assets, such as a house. On the other hand, if you do not own a house or other assets, this might be a good solution for you.

Personal Bankruptcy Details:

- Any person who owes more than $1,000 in debt is eligible to file a personal bankruptcy in Canada. Ideal candidates are those who need rapid financial relief.

- The more you earn, the more you will be required to pay.

- You are required to surrender certain assets in order to be absolved of your debts.

- You will receive an R9 credit rating, which is the worst rating. Depending on your province, it will remain on your credit report for 6-7 years for the first banlkruptcy, 14 years for the second. If, during the repayment period, you get a higher-paying job, or come into money, such as an inheritance, the amount you repay your creditors will go up.

- You are required to complete a monthly budget for all income and expenses, as well as supply copies of your pay stubs to your trustee.

- You will lose all tax refund(s) and/or credits owing to you.

Source: Hoyes Michalos & Associates

You get relief from the bulk of your debt in a bankruptcy, yet one in ten Canadians who declare bankruptcy once, do so again. If you do not learn a *new* way of managing money, you may be one of them. On the contrary, if you are following the suggestion in this book, you are on your way to financial stability.

SPIRITUAL SOLUTION: 'Fess Up

L earn this apology pattern and it will serve you well in many arenas for the rest of your life.

1. Admit you were wrong: you can do this in a letter, an email, or face to face. People appreciate this acknowledgement.

2. Apologize: Saying *sorry* and that you messed up is an age-old way of expressing humility.

3. Promise not to do it again: No one believes an apology without the assurance that you won't repeat the offense.

4. Make full restitution: That means, make it right. If it's money owed, pay it all back. Restitution can relieve you of guilt, and the desire to self-sabotage.

Admit It

This is what it takes: ignoring the behavior of everyone else involved, including the government or your company, did you do anything inappropriate, ethically or morally, around money? It might be theft, cheating, hiding facts, sneaking, manipulating, blaming, or excusing any financial behaviour as all right when you knew it was not.

1. Admit, at least to yourself, though others may have contributed to the problem, your behavior wasn't ideal. That can be hard to swallow, but swallow it anyway.

2. Prepare to admit this to any members of your family affected by your debts. They need to know the extent of the money owed. You have a written list with all the details. Show it to them. Tell them in order for you to break the

pattern of debting, and gain peace and ultimately prosperity, you need to correct your past financial mistakes.

3. Before you admit to a large debt with a creditor who does not know about it, you may need to seek legal advice.

4. Now, admit your mistake, in person if possible, or on the phone, to each creditor using a script similar to this sample:

Good morning, Mr. _____: I am getting my finances in order. When I worked for your company in 2xxx, I did this: I took petty cash funds of $540. I am deeply sorry for this. I have now learned a far better way of dealing with my financial issues and will never do such a thing again. I want to make things right.

Apologize

Next, if you feel shame or simple embarrassment, apologize sincerely yet don't grovel. Apologize for what you did, not who you are. A simple *I'm deeply sorry for this* with the appropriate body language and face expression will communicate volumes to your listener.

However, some women give conflicting messages: they mean what they say but their body language or facial expressions aren't consistent with the verbal message. If this is your problem, look in the mirror to see if you look like you're expressing your genuine feelings. Practise your script until your physical self is consistent with your verbal message.

Promise

After the apology, give people your word, you intend never to do this sort of thing again. They don't want to be re-victimized. Given you have probably broken previous promises to yourself and others around money matters, the only real guarantee you will cease and desist is with God's help.

God, please give me the willingness and the courage to have integrity where money is concerned.

Repay

Restitution is in kind. If you stole money, you repay with money. If you stole goods, you replace them, or pay the money to replace them. Even if you've borrowed money and haven't paid it all back, you will need to repay it, even to children. And no matter what the injured party's reaction, and most times it is neutral or positive, you will feel less guilt, more a woman, and more optimistic about your future. Really.

Here is how you repay and not get fired. Replace the stolen items with new ones you've purchased. If you stole, you will have to repay that debt, too.

> *One man wanted to make restitution, but he stole money from drug dealers. He didn't want to give them money with which they would buy more drugs and sell it on the street to kids, so he decided to give the full amount as a charitable donation to a drug rehab center.*

In order to have a future of peace and abundance, you have to make restitution. If you cheated a large corporation like a department store, you still want to get that off your back.

> *This woman stole clothes from a high-end store in Alberta, but she now lived in Ontario. She knew she might be sent to jail for the theft and evading the law. In the meantime, this secret was driving her to erratic behavior in many areas of life; she knew she had to face it. After much prayer and counseling, she got a lawyer. The day she was leaving for Alberta, she was so scared, her whole body was visibly shaking.*

> *To her shock, and immense relief, the judge ordered her to repay her debt, no jail time. Moreover, the store congratulated her for being willing to repay what she owed them, and removed the fines and penalties.*

You can simply send them a note with a check for the amount. You can leave the note anonymous if you want. The corporation wants its money. Or else, you can fess up face to face.

One woman chose to make face-to-face restitution to a bank. They greeted her warmly, and toured her around the office, introducing her as an honest and courageous person. The company had had people leave a check, or even cash at their door, but no one had had the guts to show up in person.

CAREFUL DEBT PAYING

Vanishing debt can also be surprisingly *disturbing*. You have been under the gun for so long, it feels normal. Freedom from debt pressure may actually make you nervous! So, get nervous for a while. All change has an adjustment period. You will start replacing the feelings of chaos to a peaceful freedom as you pay one debt after another. In time, you will begin to trust yourself again.

You will see you are self-disciplined in debt repayment; therefore, you can be self-disciplined in other areas. You were able to negotiate with your creditors, so you will be able to negotiate in other situations, meeting your needs and your responsibilities. You have accepted responsibility; that is an act of maturity, and you have gained peace of mind as you got out from under the abuses of creditors. You are living a model, money-management life. Besides, most importantly, you have learned how to take care of yourself which wasn't happening before, which is why you got into debt in the first place. Putting your Enduring Dreams first, within your present income, is what makes miracles possible and a pleasant life guaranteed.

You are in the process of changing your mind, literally. You are opening up to new ways of doing things, foreign ways. Don't be scared. You are being guided, now. You are on a positive wavelength.

10

SLAY THE DRAGON
Power Up!

*T*his professional couple owed $8000 to MasterCard, $9000 to Visa, a $25,000 student loan to a bank, $2300 to his brother, and $1000 for furniture to the credit union at her company: a total debt of $45,300. Then they hit the wall. They could no longer make their minimum monthly payments. They were paying the MasterCard by borrowing from Visa, but their Visa credit was almost at the max. The bank refused to lend them money for a consolidation loan as they were so far in debt. She ignored letters from their creditors because she couldn't cope with them. The bills were in a box under their bed. As a result, their phone had been ringing relentlessly with calls from collection agencies.

Few life situations are as stressful as this-- collection calls at all hours, insulting language and demeaning innuendoes, even threats. These can make women so miserable, they consider leaving the country, or worse, think of suicide.

Bill collectors seldom care what your circumstances are; they want the money. This is how *they* are paid. Agents often use intimidation, complex legal language, and early, late and frequent phone calls which harass you, your family and your colleagues. They may deny they received your payment. Plus, even while you are in negotiations with them, they will be adding late charges to your debt. No matter who your creditor is, you have the right to respectful treatment, protected by the Ministry of Consumer Services, Consumer Protection Branch. You're conducting a business transaction, that is all. Your personal life style or character is not in question here. From now on, expect and demand civility.

Agency Trauma

Debtors and collectors run up against each other in so many bad ways, so often, the government has enacted a law to get civil behavior operating. In Canada, it is the Collection Agencies Act. This Act regulates calling times, frequency of calls, and requirements for mailing correspondence prior making telephone contact.

In Ontario and Alberta, most debts have a limitation period of two years. Most other provinces have a limitation period of six years. After this, no one has the legal authority to collect the debt, though it will remain on your credit report for 6 or 7 years, depending on the province. The collection agency might try to collect after that time, but they cannot garnish your wages or place a lien on your property unless they have a court order, of which they had to advise you in writing.

In-House Collection Departments

Some larger businesses have in-house collection departments where the agents are employees of the same company to which you owe the money. Banks are often in this category. It is cheaper for them to have their own people collect the outstanding debt because they don't have to pay the hefty commission to an outside collection agency, sometimes more than half of the debt.

Since the agents are likely on salary, though they need to show progress on getting your account paid, they are not likely to be so aggressive. They will likely work out repayment terms more suitable to you because you were a customer of theirs once, and are a potential future customer.

If their own collection department cannot collect your money, they hire or sell your debt to outside collection agencies.

Outside Collection Agencies

Once a debt has passed a given period and not been repaid, your creditor will hire or sell your account to an outside debt collection agency. Either they sell the debt at a discount, meaning your original creditor has lost as much as 50% of what you owed them, or the original company will pay a hefty commission, also about 50%, once the collection agency gets you to pay.

Though you owe the money, at no time should they treat you disrespectfully. You owe money, not your self-respect. Unfortunately, Credit Collectors have a long history of disregarding their own Code of Ethics.

Collection Agency Ethics

Though debt collection is a regulated business, some collection agencies play rough, illegal games. While the dictionary defines ethics as "standards of conduct and moral judgments", collection agencies define them as "whatever it takes to get the money." Then again, if you have been dealing with collection agencies, you already know this.

Here are the limitations under which collection agents should act:

- No more than three contacts a week after reaching you by speaking to you on the phone or leaving a voicemail or answering machine message.

- Calls must be between 7 am and 9 pm. None can be earlier or later than stated.

- No calls on Sunday before 1 pm or after 5 pm.

- No calls on statutory holidays which are Boxing Day, Canada Day, Christmas Day, Family Day, Good Friday, Labour Day, New Year's Day, Thanksgiving Day, the Civic Holiday, Victoria Day, and any other day fixed as a holiday by the government.

- No telephone calls or personal calls frequent enough or of a nature to be considered harassment once they have contacted you. Some debt collectors will call ten times in ten minutes. This is harassment.

- No profane or abusive language, such as *you deadbeat, dirt bag, thief, credit criminal,* or *liar.*

- No threats they can't carry out. A letter to you will have corroborated any court action against you. They cannot threaten legal action if you don't pay the entire debt at once.

- They must have the creditor's written permission to recommend or initiate legal or court action. The client, not the collector, must notify you in writing.

- No calls at work if you state your employer does not allow personal calls.

- They must notify the debtor in writing that the original debt holder assigned them to your account.

- They may get no information other than a debtor's address or phone number from the debtor's employer, friends, relatives, or neighbours.

- They are not to imply or give false or misleading information to anyone who could damage the debtor or the debtor's family.

- A collection agency cannot publish anything about you and your debt payments.

Post these guidelines near you and complain if the agent is not following them. Collection agencies ignore their own code of ethics simply because they can. Few women ever complain of their mistreatment since they don't know their rights, or are too ashamed of their situations. They suffer the abuse in silence. Well, it is time to stop that!

Are These People Human?

All the same, consider this: debt collectors are people under pressure to produce. They need your money to keep their jobs. You can see why they will do whatever it takes to make you pay up. Aside from the money angle, some agencies fire the person who has made the lowest level of collection in the month, or embarrass them in front of their colleagues if they are not collecting enough.

If a stressed agent explodes at you when you resist paying up, realize they have to make 250 calls a shift, and create computer notes on each one. Their supervisor monitors these notes. Agents who fall behind in their calls hear about it. On top of all that, the collection agency does not pay agents overtime. Since nights and weekends are times when debtors are home, agents work without pay in those hours. Also, they are not at home with their own families.

Though it's good to understand the agents, it does not make it all right that they treat you badly. *Warning:* These people are not your friends and do not want to help you even if they are being nice. Nice is a manipulative technique! Sorry, but these are facts.

Your Rights

Knowing your rights can give you the courage to deal with bad agents, and make them clean up their act.

You have the right to:

1. Hang up on collection agents if you do not want to talk to them, either when you first answer, or in the middle of a conversation

2. Refuse to tell them where you work, whether you have a job, what bank accounts you have, or which bank you use.

3. Protect your spouse or partner from being included in the debt collection if they did not co-sign the debt. S/he does not have to pay for any of it.

4. Ask them to identify themselves, and the agency's name when they phone. Then say only this: *Number 1*. And hang up. If they call again, say: *Number 2*. And hang up. If they call back, say: *Number 3*. *That constitutes the three contacts you can make to me in one week.*

5. Insist they call you by your last name, like Ms. Brancks. The agent will want to use your first name while insisting you call them by their last name to create a dominance situation where you're the inferior.

6. Confirm all agreements in writing before sending any money.

7. Pay by money order instead of a check to keep your banking information private.

8. Take some control by asking for the collector's registration number. The government does not allow them to operate without a registration number.

THREATS, LIES, and MANIPULATION

Though you are genuinely getting your financial life in shape, collection agents seldom care. They want the money and that's it. They may even use illegal means to harass you into paying on their schedule and in the amounts they want.

Collection agents might threaten you with everything, including jail. Remember, threats are only that, and the reality is unless you have received notice in writing of impending legal action, threats are simply part of a nasty bag of tricks.

Both Outside Collection Agencies and Internal Collection Departments can be difficult. Be ready to counter any of these.

I'll Ruin Your Credit Rating!

Think about this: why do you need a good credit rating right now? Are you planning to move? Are you thinking of buying a large item, like a car? If not, no need to worry about it today. No one checks your credit rating if you want to go to the movies. MacDonald's won't turn you down for a Happy Meal. Your friends won't refuse to kiss you on New Year's Eve. You can rent a car, stay at a hotel, or buy airline tickets without anyone checking your credit rating. Do not get in a panic if a creditor threatens to ruin it.

If you presently have an R1 credit rating, that's good. It means you always pay on time, or not over one payment past due. On the other hand, if you already have an R9 credit rating, that is not so good. It means creditors have had to write off debts because they were never repaid. Still, these ratings are private, hidden from most of the world. Do not be intimidated by this threat. If an agent says they will fix your credit rating if you pay up, know they *cannot* do this. Once you're getting collection calls, credit bureaus note that on your file. Nevertheless, there are legitimate ways to improve your credit rating. First, you have to understand it.

Credit Scores

Your credit score judges your financial health at a specific point in time. In other words, how much of a risk you are for lenders as compared with other consumers

Credit-reporting agencies, Equifax and TransUnion, use a scale from 300 to 900 with 900 being high, or good. Good by their definition means you are a low risk for loan default. Most lenders decide on the lowest score you can have and still borrow money from them, and at what interest rate.

Credit Score Abbreviations

"I" is for installment credit, like a car loan. The lender gave you credit on an installment basis, where you borrow money once and repay it in fixed amounts, on a regular basis, for a specific period until the loan is paid off.

"O" is for open credit, like a student loan. Here you borrow money, as needed, up to a certain limit and the total balance is due at the end of each period. You do not have to start repaying student loans until you're out of school.

"R" is for revolving credit, like credit cards. You make regular payments in varying amounts depending on the balance of your account, and can then borrow more money up to your credit limit.

R Scale

If a borrower always pays on time, their rating will be coded R1. R4 is a red flag. It means the borrower is more than 90 days late with a payment. At this point, creditors may turn down further credit. They think the borrower might make one payment, then not pay again for another 90 days.

At R5, 120 days of non-payment, creditors may write off the loan. An R7 means the borrower is getting outside help, such as credit counseling or a debt management program. R9 occurs if a debtor does not repay a loan and the creditor writes it off as a loss. Creditors list bankruptcy as an R9. Special note: moving without giving creditors a new address will get you an R9. They think you have skipped out on them.

R0	Too new to rate; approved but not used
R1	Always pay on time, or never over one payment past due
R2	Pays in more than 30 days from due date, but no more than 60 days
R3	Pays in more than 60 days from payment due date, but no more than 90 days
R4	Pays in more than 90 days but not more than 120 days, or four payments past due.
R5	Account is at least 120 days overdue, but is not yet rated as R9
R6	No rating exists
R7	Making payments through a special arrangement to settle debts.
R8	Repossession. Voluntary or involuntary return of merchandise
R9	Bad debt; placed for collection; moved without giving a new address.

Source: Equifax Canada

New creditors always check past payment history to decide whether to approve a new money request. They often overlook minor delinquencies, like having paid a bill a couple of months late, or having one or two bills past due.

Credit Rating Clean Up

You can clean up your credit rating yourself, calmly, over time. First, know that after six years, credit bureaus erase any recorded debt problems from your credit history.

Make sure the credit rating agencies have removed any black marks on your report. Make sure the information on each is accurate. There might be a note on your report which should have been placed on another person's report. Or, a note might have been left on it when the credit agent should have removed it. Any number of women have found small errors, like bills they had paid in full, still showing a balance due. Make sure you challenge them on inaccuracies, and then check back later to see if they have made the corrections.

Check your credit report from both credit rating agencies, TransUnion and Equifax, as scary as that might be. It will be free if they snail mail it to you.

While you are requesting the removal of false negatives on your report, start paying on all your debts, on time, and consistently. At the same time, begin a little savings fund. Once you have $500 in the bank, borrow the same amount from them, using your savings as collateral. This is a secured loan, backed up by the same amount of money in cash in a savings account. Now, repay this loan consistently, and on time over a year. It is an easy thing to set up an automatic withdrawal from your savings account so the bank repays the loan without your having to mail a check. You'll never make a late payment!

During this time, don't make too many applications for credit in a short span of time - and that includes things like mobile phone contracts. Lenders translate that as desperation. Space out applications.

Don't pay the loan back quickly. Lenders want to see a steady record of timely repayments over months. While you are paying down this new loan, new lenders will see your new loan record. This will build a better credit history.

All the same, how do you get credit if you have messed up your credit rating?

Can Bad Credit Get Credit?

Appliances: If you need to buy a big-ticket item and need credit, and you have a poor credit rating, you might have to go to a secondary lender, not a bank, but a company with a private source of funds. They will loan you the money to buy an asset, but at a higher than bank interest rate. Despite that, if you need to buy the item, accept the loan interest rate. Make your payments faithfully, in full and on time, for 12 months. Then go back to the lender and renegotiate, pointing out you now qualify to have this loan re-financed based on your good payment record.

Mortgage: If you are shopping for a mortgage with a poor credit rating, know lenders look seriously at stability of address and employment. If you have this, you may be able to get normal mortgage rates. You'll get the best rates through mortgage brokers who can shop your file around to various lenders. The difference between a standard lender and a mortgage broker is you may have to pay a broker, though this is not always the case. Sometimes, the lending institutions pay them. Be sure to make a special note of your stability to your mortgage broker.

New Apartment: If you need a new apartment, try to avoid a credit check altogether by finding a landlord who doesn't do credit checks. That's usually houses, condominiums, townhomes, duplexes, and small apartment buildings owned by a single property owner, not the large complexes. You can search your local newspaper, or online at Kijiji or Craigslist.

You may be asked for a larger than normal deposit if you have a poor credit rating. You can even offer to put down a little extra to cover any property damage. Your new property owner may feel more secure renting to you that way.

Soften the negativity of your credit report with a prior letter that explains the situation that caused your financial problems to persuade the property owner to rent to you. Divorce, medical bills, and job loss are common situations that lead to bad credit. Make sure your letter describes how you've cleaned up your finances and why you can handle the rent now.

Reference Letters from past property owners, your bank, or your employer also increase landlord confidence. And don't forget to turn on your charm. Pat their dog.

Employers: While it is true some potential employers do credit checks if you will be dealing with cash or valuables, or will be a financial executive, if your overdue debts are under $5,000, this is not an issue. A Human Resource Management report found most organizations focus on credit history of four to seven years overall. Consequently, even if you've improved your credit lately, you may still have to explain indiscretions from bygone years to the person making hiring decisions. The fact is many HR people can't make sense of the complex information on credit reports except for notes on Bankruptcy. Furthermore, no employer expects a perfect report. Worry a little less.

If your overdue debts are higher than $5,000, and if you think a potential employer will check your credit rating, this is the time to be upfront. Bad things happen to good people, so it's better to alert the HR person of derogatory information which is on your credit report before they see it. If you don't, they wonder what else you are hiding. But, emphasize your new financial system.

A poor credit rating is a lesson in learning to pay bills on time. That's all. You have learned. What doesn't kill you makes you stronger and get on with your life.

You'll Be In Jail by Christmas!

Bad collection agents use spouses and even the children in the family to manipulate women to pay faster than they are able. They may call in the early afternoon, before parents are home, and tell the child who answers they will put Mommy in jail if the bill isn't paid. Mommy is likely so humiliated, she may borrow money to stop that collector's calls.

Avoid this by telling the kids to check call display if you have it, or by setting up a call code with your children. Have a one-ring call; hang up, then another call right after as a phone code so the children will know when it's you calling. Otherwise, they need not answer the phone before you're home.

If you're concerned this threat sounds legitimate, ask the collection agent to send you a letter outlining the actions they plan to take. They must send all appropriate, pending legal actions to you in writing. Ask them for the date on the letter if they say they sent one. If the agency is unwilling to put it in writing, or can't give you the date, it is a bluff. The reality is if your debt is under $200, no legal action will take place. It is not cost effective for the collection agency. The agent says it only to scare you. Then again, no matter how high the debt, remember, there are no more Debtors' Prisons! Our society does not put women in jail for debt.

We'll Garnishee Your Wages!

Any reference to a matter this serious means the courts are involved. The agency will have to use lawyers, send you notice in writing, and go through many steps before this can occur. Unless you have a letter, and you can ask them for the date if they say they sent one, this is another empty threat to scare and manipulate you into paying more on the debt than you can afford.

Should you actually get a letter like this, contact a lawyer, perhaps through the Lawyer Referral Service which arranges 30 minutes of free consultation. Alternatively, call Legal Aid.

This Is Your Police Department. We Have a Subpoena for You

Collection agents might flat out lie, pretending to be someone they are not to scare you into paying more than you can. They are trying to intimidate you, so you'll call the collection agency and promise to make any payments they want. Know this: notices of court action are sent to you in writing, not through a phone call.

In order to get you to expose your personal information for future manipulation, some agents will play nasty games. Remember their goal is to get you to pay more than you can manage, and on their time schedule, without consideration for your family's well-being. Tell them nothing. These agents are typing every word you say into their computer notes, monitored by their supervisors. They will use this information against you in the future.

Go on the alert when you hear ---

I want to help you.

Doesn't it bother you to be burdened by this debt? Just pay it and you'll feel so relieved.

Tell me what the problem really is.

How is the rest of your family doing financially? They probably want to help you out of this mess.

Tell me all about it. Isn't that terrible? Then what happened? Then what did you do?

The agent is pretending to listen compassionately to your situation while they will use what you tell them to your detriment down the road. Look at this scornful list found on a collection agency's website.

The Funniest and Strangest Excuses debtors give for not being able to pay:

The check is in the mail

I already paid

I don't have any money

I'm divorced and my ex is supposed to pay that bill

There was a problem with the service, or product

I'm sick and can't work

I don't have a job

My wife (husband) handles that

I'll try

You're harassing me

I'll pay in full when I get my tax refund

I can't get a loan

My insurance company should have paid that

While you are explaining sincerely, and they are laughing. These people are not your friends. However, if you still think your collection agent is the exception, maybe you're right. Most are not. Collection agents are known for trying to shame:

You are aware your kids are watching your actions. What kind of an example are you?

I'm disappointed in you.

Oh, come on. I know many women who are out of work. They make an honest effort to pay their bills.

Caution:

- Agents will probe for personal information only to find ways to get you to pay. Remember, your children's ages, your extended family issues are fodder they will use down the road to get money from you. Don't answer any of their questions.

- Don't tell them about your job or your spouse's job. They are trying to find out if you have the ability to pay or not pay.

- Don't tell them when you get paid. They will call you around that time, knowing you should have money, ignoring you have family expenses.

- Don't tell them if you own any property. They will pressure you to sell it.

- Do not tell them if you have any loans or credit cards. They will want you to get a cash advance and pay them with it, or borrow more money and pay them. Remember their only purpose in talking to you is to get your money.

- Don't tell them about any family members who may be able to help you out of this debt. Of course, they will use this information to pressure you to borrow from them.

- Don't tell them if you have found temporary work. The minute they smell money, they will pressure you to give it to them.

- Don't reveal you don't want your spouse to know about any of this. They will threaten to tell him/her all about it to force you to pay more than you can afford.

- Don't reveal you're afraid of losing your house, car, or anything of value. They will make note of this and use it to threaten you in future calls.

- Don't tell them you take pride in paying your bills on time. They will use this to shame you and then manipulate you.

- Don't tell them you work hard to maintain a good credit rating. They will threaten to destroy your credit rating. A threat like this is intimidating, but not fatal.

PRACTICAL SOLUTION:
Complain

Y ou do not have to put up with abuse or ridicule. Paying a debt is a financial transaction. It does not involve your humanity. Remember, while you may owe someone money, you do not owe anyone your dignity. You have unconditional self-respect.

If bill collectors and agencies are hounding you, you have rights and they have responsibilities. Deal with the problem directly and insist they treat you as an adult who is working on paying off financial obligations.

Assert yourself. They'll back down. They actually do know the rules, but break them because they can get away with it. No longer with you. If you think a creditor has broken their Code of Ethics in dealing with you, complain to the Ministry of Consumer Services, Consumer Protection Branch 1-800-889-9768.

Complaint Log

This is important: be sure and keep a record of your complaints and follow up to be sure the collection agent is taking the corrected action. Your record should contain this information: The date you complained, the type of communication, like a complaint letter, email, phone call or text message, the name of the company and the name of the person to whom you spoke, as in: *Steve Wright from Sears Collections Department.*

Briefly summarize the abuse, what the person said in response to your complaint, date of the response, and what result occurred. Note any other concerns in Comments. Keep track of your complaints in a file. Note each time you send a message or receive a reply.

COMPLAINT LOG

Date	Letter, email, text, call	Company & Person Contacted	Problem	Date of Response & Summary	Results	Comments
Nov 11, 2xxx	Email	Sears, Allen Wright, Collections Manager	Jim Nord, in Collections called 5 times before 6 am at home, and 7 times at work.	Nov. 25, 2xxx Emails: Wright apologized. Nord apologized. Promised to stay within legal guidelines	Calls from Nord now within legal hours. No more calls at work.	Wright will advise his staff my boss does not allow personal calls at work.

Complaint Letters

Let creditors and the government know about unethical collection agents. The Ministry of Consumer Services is set up to receive and *act* on consumer complaints. Here's what to do:

Request for Ethical Treatment from In-House Collection Department

If the company to whom you owe the debt has their own collection department, and they are harassing you, complain:

a. **Call** the Manager of the Collections Department of the company to whom you owe the original debt, for example, Sears. State your complaint.

b. **Record** the details in your Complaint Log.

c. **Send Letter #1** as follow up, like the sample below.

d. **Next Step:** If you do not get a response, and the abuse continues, complain to the CEO of the company, Letter #4, and to the government, Letter # 5. Yes, do it. You do not deserve to be treated badly.

Letter #1. COMPLAINT LETTER TO IN-HOUSE COLLECTION DEPARTMENT

Jan. 6, 2xxx

Manager's Name
Manager, Collection Department
Sears
124 Blog Street
Toronto ON

Sears Account No. _____

Dear _____: (Manager's Name)

You have referred my arrears account to your staff member, _____. Mr. _____ has been attempting to collect the full balance of my delinquent account on behalf of Sears. On numerous occasions, I tried to resolve the account by a repayment plan which will pay off the debt in full, on a pro rata basis with my other creditors. Mr. ------- has declined this plan.

This agent has repeatedly called both my wife's workplace and mine. Further, on Dec. 29, 2xxx, he called our home at 6:50 a.m.

Please tell him and all your staff to stop calls to my wife's workplace and mine, as our bosses do not allow us to take personal calls. Also, please advise them the Collection Agencies Act prohibits calls made prior to 7 a.m.

I will report any further incidents of this nature to the Ministry of Consumer Services.

I appreciate your quick written response.

Sincerely,

Letter # 2. A Request for Ethical Treatment from Outside Collection Agency

If the company to whom you owe the debt has hired an outside collection agency, and they are harassing you, complain:

a. **Call** the Manager of the Outside Collections Agency. State your complaint.

b. **Record** the details in your Complaint Log.

c. **Send a Letter** as follow up letter like the sample below.

d. **Next Step**: If they do not treat you properly after complaining, do *not* wait. Write the CEO of the company which was the original debt holder, Letter #4, and the government, Letter # 5.

Letter #2 COMPLAINT LETTER TO OUTSIDE COLLECTION AGENCY

Jan. 9, 2xxx

Manager's Name
Manager, Collection Department
XYZ Collectors
658 Long Street
Toronto ON

Dear _____: (Manager's Name)

RE: My file No. _____

Sears File No. _____

Sears has referred my file to your agency for collection. Mr. _____ has been attempting to collect the full balance of my delinquent account on behalf of Sears. On numerous

occasions, I tried to resolve the account by a repayment plan which will pay off the debt in full, on a pro rata basis with my other creditors. Mr. ------- has declined this plan.

Mr. _____ has phoned my home and work on numerous occasions. On Dec. 29, 2xxx, he phoned my home at 6:50 a.m. and disturbed my whole household.

Several times, I've asked Mr. _____ to stop calling my wife and me at work; however, he has ignored our requests.

Please be advised I will contact the Ministry of Consumer Services regarding your employee's misconduct if the harassment does not stop.

I'm asking that you no longer call my wife or me and that you continue all contact in writing.

I await your prompt written response.

Sincerely,

Letter #3. Complaint Letter to Creditor Who Hired the Collection Agency

If the collection agency does *not* stop harassing you, remember they work for your creditor, the original debt holder. Therefore, their unethical actions reflect on the debt holder. In this example, Sears hired XYZ Collectors to recover your debt. Sears is paying the collection agency, so they are the agency's boss. Complain to the Manager of the Collections Department at Sears:

a. **Call** the manager of the Collections Department of the company to whom you owed the original debt, that is, Sears. State your complaint.

b. **Send a Letter of complaint** as follow up to the phone call addressed to the manager at Sears.

c. **Record** the details in your Complaint Log.

Letter #3 TO CREDITOR WHO HIRED THE COLLECTION AGENCY

Jan. 15, 2xxx

Manager's Name
Collections Department
Sears
124 any Street
Toronto ON

Sears Account No. _____

Dear Collections Manager:

You have referred my arrears account to _____ Collection Agency. Mr. _____ has been attempting to collect the full balance of my delinquent account on behalf of Sears. On numerous occasions, I tried to resolve the account by a repayment plan which will pay off the debt in full, on a pro rata basis with my other creditors. Mr. _____ has declined this plan.

Mr. _____ of their office has repeatedly called both my wife's workplace and mine. Further, on Dec. 29, 2xxx, he called our home at 6:50 a.m.

Since this collection agency is working on your behalf, kindly advise them to instruct their collector to stop all calls to my wife's workplace and mine, as our bosses do not allow us to take personal calls. Also, please advise them the Collection Agencies Act prohibits calls made prior to 7 a.m.

Please let the collection agency know I will report any further incidents of this nature to the Ministry of Consumer Services.

I appreciate your quick response in writing.

Sincerely,

Letter # 4. Complaint Letter to Original Creditor CEO

If you've complained to the above people, and gotten no improvement in treatment, go higher up. Contact the office of the CEO of the original creditor (e.g., Sears).

a. Send a Letter to the CEO, similar to the example below.

b. Send a Copy of your Complaint Log, attached to the letter.

c. Record the new details in your Complaint Log.

Letter # 4 COMPLAINT LETTER TO CEO

Jan. 22, 2xxx

CEO's Name
Chief Executive Officer, Sears
120 Any Street
Vancouver BC

Sears Account No. _____

Dear Chief Executive Officer:

This letter is to inform you of some of the difficulties I'm encountering with XYZ Collectors. I've contacted your collections department manager, Mr. _____ but have had no satisfactory response.

Mr. _____ of XYZ Collectors has been attempting to collect the full balance of my delinquent account on behalf of Sears. On numerous occasions, I tried to resolve the account by a repayment plan which will pay off the debt in full, on a pro rata basis with my other creditors. Mr. _____ has declined this plan.

Mr. _____ has repeatedly called both my wife's workplace and mine. Further, on Dec. 29, 2xxx, he called our home at 6: 50 a.m.

Since this collection agency is working on your behalf, kindly advise them to instruct their collector to stop all calls to my wife's workplace and mine, as our bosses do not allow us to take personal calls. Also, please advise them the Collection Agencies Act prohibits calls made prior to 7 a.m.

Please let the collection agency know I will report any further incidents of this nature to the Ministry of Consumer Services.

I appreciate your quick response in writing.

Sincerely,

Letter # 5. Complaint Letter to Ministry Of Consumer Services

If you get no reply either from the XYZ Collections Agency or from Sears and the harassing behavior *continues*, the next step is to send a letter of complaint to the government office which handles consumer complaints: the Ministry of Consumer Services, Consumer Protection Branch.

a. Send a Letter similar to the sample below.

b. Copy your original letters to Sears, and/or XYZ Collections Agency and attach.

c. Copy your Complaint Log and attach.

d. Record the details in your Complaint Log.

Sample #5 COMPLAINT LETTER TO THE MINISTRY OF CONSUMER SERVICES

Date

Address

Dear Consumer Protection Branch, Ministry of Consumer Services:

This letter is to inform you of some of the difficulties I'm encountering with XYZ Collectors. Their employee, Mr. _____, harassed us. Mr. _____ has been attempting to collect the full balance of my delinquent account on behalf of Sears. On numerous occasions, I tried to resolve the account by a repayment plan which will pay off the debt in full, on a pro rata basis with my other creditors. Mr. _____ has declined this plan. He continues to phone me at both my home and workplace.

On Sat. Nov. 12/ XX, he called my home at 6:50 a.m. demanding payment in full and threatening legal action. This disturbed and upset my entire household.

I am enclosing copies of letters I have written to resolve the problem and a copy of my Complaint Log. Please investigate this matter.

Sincerely,

If enough women put in complaints, an industry sorely in need of clean up may be improved. To complain of inappropriate treatment, see the website for the Consumer Protection Branch or call 1-800-889-9768.

SPIRITUAL SOLUTION:
Emotional Freedom

Dealing with creditors can feel unsafe. After all, these people may threaten to *take* what they want. And since fear is such a prevalent emotion when it comes to your life, how can you feel safe? There are no people, places, or things, which can save you from fear except God.

EMOTIONAL FREEDOM

God wants you to get out of the tough situation you're in, feel happy, and show other people it is possible to recover from crushing debt problems with your dignity intact. Try this prayer:

God, please transform the unpleasant feelings into peace of mind. And give me the courage to take action.

1. Ask for relief from negative feelings, like *fear and worry:*

First, acknowledge the feeling. *Yes, I feel fear.* Then, validate it. *Would most women in a similar situation feel this way? Likely. Then, I'm normal.* Finally, ask God to transform your negative feelings to neutral, or better yet, peaceful feelings.

2. Create an emotions' list.

To relieve negative feelings, write a brief list of all you are feelings, and why. You might think you are only upset about your creditors, but you may *also* be upset about finding more grey hair. The mind is a mighty puzzle, as complex as a maze. To get at the several things which are bothering you, and air them so they no longer make you miserable, create a numbered list of everything you are feeling. When you sigh deeply, give that its own number.

If you start to cry, give that its own number, too. Beside each feeling, briefly explain why.

Here's an example.

Dear God:

Please guide my thoughts and my pen. As You know, I am very upset. I feel

1. Worried. I don't have all the rent for this month.

2. Worried. I don't have enough gas money.

3. Scared. I hurt my ankle, and it's not healing well.

4. Sad. No one called me on my birthday.

5. Big sigh.

6. Worried. My contract is up in three weeks and I don't have a renewal.

7. Frustrated. My brother won't help me fix my car.

8. Ashamed. XYZ agent is calling me non-stop.

9.

Continue to write down your various feelings, and repeat feelings until you see a shift. After maybe 30, or maybe 50 emotions, you will start to see a positive turn. For example,

27. Hopeful. My boss likes me and wants to talk about my work next week.

28. Relieved. I still have a bus pass which is valid.

This whole process won't take you more than 15 minutes, but the relief you will feel will be immediate. Women I have counseled have used it even in the middle of events.

One woman was so distressed during a memorial service, she ducked into the bathroom, and wrote an Emotions List there. In no time, she felt better enough to rejoin the ceremony, more emotionally stable.

Here's where you are heading now: towards a debt-free, peaceful, and abundant life. Once you have made restitution, forgive yourself around debt. You have made mistakes, yes, but you'd have done better if you'd known how. Now you know better, so you can do better.

Once you forgive yourself for the money, you will learn to forgive yourself for other things. Self-forgiveness is the greatest gift you will get from working on your finances.

11

PROSPER STILL

Power Up!

I f you want to know a person, find how they spend their money. A Spending Plan hints at how you spend your life. You're starting a new life, now, a preferred life, and your Spending Plan should reflect that.

Then again, what else is involved in this new life? You're now connecting to a source of power which you may have known about yet never experienced to this level. Karl Jung, the famous Swiss psychiatrist, called it the Collective Unconscious. This Source of wisdom and power connects you to every other person and their experiences. Everyone can tap into this Source. God is the answer to all your problems, once you learn to access the information. Absolutely, there are practical solutions to your financial difficulties, and you've been trying those throughout the past chapters.

Even so, if you hope to keep yourself solvent, spiritual help is the only permanent solution.

PRACTICAL SOLUTION:
Persevere

You have to keep doing the new things you have learned so far:

- **See your Money History**
- **Skip New Debt**
- **Create a One-Day-Soon Spending Plan**
- **Claim your Income**
- **Create a Monthly Spending Plan**
- **Tame the Bills**
- **Build Savings Categories**
- **Save for Predictable Life Events**
- **Repay Creditors**
- **Tame Collectors**

If you use these strategies, they will work for you. You sleep everyday. You eat everyday. You may even take vitamins or medicine everyday. Think of this process as equally routine, and equally important.

However, how can you get yourself to make the right decision to *follow* this new process? Human beings can rebel from doing what is good for them like school kids on their way to school, dragging their backpacks along the pavement. The only way out of this resistance is to ask for Help! from God. This Source can do for you what you cannot do for yourself. This is a fact.

When you don't want to keep your Spending Record up-to-date, that is, you're too busy, too tired, too bored, and certainly too intelligent, ask God to help you remember it is a priority, and that it will take no more time than brushing your teeth. Ask for Help!

Higher Power, please give me the willingness to take care of myself around money.

When you'd rather run out and get that coat because you want it because you just do, ask God to help you look at your Spending Plan and see if there is enough money in the Clothes category. If yes, hey, if it's something you have been wanting and you price-checked a little, go get it! The Spending Plan is about Permission not restriction. Say this before you go into the store:

Higher Power, please guide and protect me around this purchase.

On the other hand, if the right amount of money is not in the Clothes category, now, ask God to help you remember more money is coming in a few days, when you next get paid.

Higher Power, please give me the patience and the faith to wait around this purchase, knowing more money is coming.

Remember, if it's the right coat for you, it will be there when you go back to buy it later in the month. Thank this Source for the money that *is* in the Clothes category and the money in Vacation, and Entertainment, as well as Groceries and Phone. Try this prayer any time rebellious thoughts intrude:

God, please filter my thoughts, and help me feel gratitude for what I have today.

YOU ARE NOT ALONE

Once things start getting better for you, you may think you have conquered your money demons finally. Unfortunately, it doesn't work that way. Because you're one who has chronic money problems, you still have that tendency. It's like having one leg a little shorter than the other. Nothing you do will change it, though you can improve the way you walk with shoe lifts. Yet, if you remove the helpful device, you will still have one leg shorter than the other, and you will go back to limping. And the older you get, the worse the limp will get. Sorry.

OUTSIDE HELP

There are face-to-face groups and online support where you can hear heartening stories of recovery and prosperity experienced by women similar to you.

Financial Buddies

The only form of permanence in this world is repetition. The solution to keeping your newfound, hard-earned solvency and peace of mind is to keep thinking and behaving in these new ways, and share them with others.

God wants you to experience lasting financial security, dream fulfillment, and joy. You help by helping others which, in turn, reminds you of what you knew but may have forgotten. They will help others learn what you taught them, and so on and so on, and so on. It couldn't be more win-win.

You may think you have nothing to teach yet. Your life isn't perfect, and your finances are still in the recovery stage. However, your saner financial behavior and your more peaceful life are the best examples you can give to your children, your family, and your friends.

Though going it alone has been your hallmark, it's time to share your journey with like-minded people. Think through your family and friends. Are there any women you know who are also struggling with finances? There has to be someone. This is where you and she get together and form a pact. From now on, you are going to support each other emotionally and intellectually around finances.

You are each doing this for selfish reasons. You will benefit from the cooler head of the other. While you may be confused about your money, she won't be. And vice versa.

You may say this would be embarrassing, so think about it this way: you're both in the same boat. If you know a few women like this, gather them together and propose this support network.

12-Step Groups

You use money on a daily basis. There is no getting away from purchasing things like food, clothes, and shelter. The temptation to overspend, and fall into debt is ever present. Still, there is help in the 12-step society. Two groups which specialize in money issues are Debtors Anonymous and Underearners Anonymous. Debtors Anonymous has been successful in turning debtors' lives around for more than 30 years. Underearners Anonymous focuses on building self-esteem high enough to earn what you deserve.

As a service to other groups, Alcoholics Anonymous has a help line which can give you a contact phone number for the money groups. Also, Googling the name of the group as listed here will get you onto their local websites. They even have free online groups, and phone meetings. If you'd like to hear recovery stories from 12-step members, try this website: www.xa.speakers.org/ and click on *The Lights Are On*. Look for testimonials from Debtors Anonymous.

Websites

The Canadian Government has several pages of information designed by the Financial Consumer Agency of Canada. Another unbiased, not-for-profit source of help is Credit Counseling of Canada. Be sure to use that name exactly as written, though, since several for-profit groups have tried to pass themselves off as this organization. You can access my website at www.stopdebting.com If you find other good sites, let me know and I'll post them on my website.

Blogs

There are many financial blogs. Most are for people with a normal relationship with money, needing practical guidance on spending and investing. Some focus on getting out of debt with practical suggestions. Trying to find ones which combine the practical and the spiritual isn't easy. Dave Ramsey does have a spiritual base of fundamentalist Christianity, though you will have to overlook the marketing of his other products within it. Suze Orman, Gail Vaz Oxlade, and others have blogs which are practical, but with few spiritual suggestions.

You can access my blog on my website at StopDebting.com

Listen:Meditate

Meditating is listening to God; prayer is speaking to God. To prepare your mind to receive God's advice, meditate first, and then pray.

Meditation will connect you to God's wisdom about even the smallest things. Many books teach how to meditate, and much research touts its effectiveness for emotional stability. Meditation also improves intuition. Rightly-trained intuition will guide you.

It's like trying to navigate a dark room full of furniture. You can do it. It will take a long time as you have to feel your way, and it may be painful because you'll most likely bump into furniture, but eventually you'll make it to the other side. Mediation is the light switch. Once the light is on, you can get through the room easily, efficiently, and less painfully. Daily meditation turns on the light in your day.

Some women who tried meditation once and didn't get immediate results gave it up as a bad job. However, meditation works like exercise works. You build up the muscles over time, and not without a little pain. Well, meditation doesn't hurt as much as lunges, but remember exercise works for every body when done consistently, and in the right way. Meditation is the same. It will work for you if you do it consistently and in the right way.

What is consistent? The more you do it, even for short periods, the more effective it will be. Most women end up meditating daily. How long do you exercise in a given session? Many experts agree you need 30 minutes of exercise for full benefit. Other experts say 12 minutes should do it. That is, if you do it consistently. As far as meditation is concerned, more often and shorter is better than less often and longer. You're building meditation muscles. So, try for 10 minutes to start. Then again, and this is important, it is better to meditate for *one minute* than not to meditate at all. You will get benefits even from that. It may not seem possible, but it is true. Many women I know meditate for longer than half an hour, or have a morning and evening session. Once you start getting results, the frequency and duration is up to you. Give it a good try, say, three months.

How to Meditate:

Meditation does not have to involve chanting, incense or candles, unless you want it to! There are many books on how to go about meditation. For the finer points, I'd suggest you go to the library and see what you can find. In the meantime, try this simple method:

- Set a timer for how long you want to meditate that day.

- Sit in a quiet room where you have privacy.

- Sit up as straight as feels comfortable.

- Place your feet on the floor.

- Let your hands rest comfortably.

- Close your eyes.

- Breathe in God.

- Breathe out Peace.

- Let your breaths come and go.

- Ask God for Help: *Help me to see clearly.*

- Now, focus your thoughts on a money problem you're having, and ask God for a solvent idea.

- If you get an idea, great. If not, continue to breathe, letting your mind drift.

- When the time is up, thank God.

- Send Love to those in your life who need extra support at the moment.

- Then go about your day.

You will feel a little more peaceful. Later, you may even get an inspiration about what to do regarding financial issues. Sometimes, however, it seems your mind dwells on nonsense: a grocery list, something someone said to you yesterday. However, of the hundreds of thoughts, the millions of thoughts you could have had, why those? Look carefully at each thought and then ask God to clarify the message for you.

If you see no visions, hear no ideas or think no thoughts, enjoy the silence! This rests your mind, and calms your inner turmoil. Some say this quiet is really the goal of meditation.

When the timer goes off, thank God for being with you. If you were to speak aloud, you may notice your voice is lower, calmer. You may feel as if you have had a brief nap. These are all good things! Take special note of how your day goes. Are you more patient? Do you smile a little more?

If not, say, *not yet*. Just as one session of exercise will not flatten your tummy, one meditation session will not bring you inner peace. Still, little by little, you will get benefits, and be on the way to stronger mental health, and resilience. And better decisions.

One Note: If you're lucky enough to get Guidance, check it out with someone you trust. Our minds can invent nonsense, too. If your buddy agrees the action makes sense, follow the advice. No one, even God, likes to be asked and then ignored.

ASK: PRAY

Does prayer actually work for regular women like you? Scientists have been investigating the power of prayer quite vigorously over the last 20 years. In fact, from 2000-2006, the U.S. government spent more than $2.3 million on prayer research. There have been four times as many studies done on the connection of prayer with healing in the last 10 years than in the previous several decades. Why the sudden interest?

It seems the weight of anecdotal evidence of miraculous recoveries of people prayed for, whether or not they knew it, has encouraged medical researchers to take a closer look at this phenomenon. Naturally, scientists want to find out if prayer works in healing, so it can become a complementary treatment to the high tech methods presently in use.

In a 1988 study by Dr. Randolph Byrd at San Francisco General Hospital, 393 coronary care patients receiving prayer along with medical care suffered significantly less congestive heart failure, fewer cardiopulmonary arrests, used fewer antibiotics and diuretics, and had less pneumonia than the control group.

On the other hand, a more recent 10-year study concluded in 2006 found prayers offered by strangers, in this case, the congregations of three different churches, had no effect on the recovery of people who were undergoing heart surgery. Worse still, the study found patients who knew they were being prayed for had a higher rate of post-operative complications like abnormal heart rhythms. Researchers suggested this result might have been a type of performance anxiety, that is, those who knew they were receiving prayers expected a better result than they were getting.

One problem other investigators found with this and other similar studies is the scientists could not know if the families of the control group were praying on behalf of their patients. Nor could they be sure if the patients prayed for themselves, as people under the knife often do.

To combat study contamination of this sort, scientists began to experiment on microbes, plants, and seeds. In one of these studies, Jean Barry, a physician-researcher in Bordeaux, France, used a destructive fungus, Rhizoctonia Solani. He asked 10 women to try to inhibit its growth merely through their positive intentions at a distance of 1.5 meters. The control petri dishes and the influenced dishes were treated identically otherwise. When the examiner compared the growth in the experimental dishes, the fungi dishes sent positive intentions showed retardation in fungus growth in 151 out of 195 dishes, far more than in the control group. The University of Tennessee replicated this study. They found significant results when positive thoughts were sent up to 15 miles away.

This does not mean all scientists are convinced of the power of prayer. Still, thirty medical schools in America are now offering courses in faith and medicine.

Feel the Refreshment

Prayer is one way to ask for help with your problems, and feel confident your burdens will be lifted from your shoulders, even if for a welcomed few minutes. Hand all the details of your struggles to God right now. You deserve the break.

If you want a quick, effective prayer, and don't know where to start, say, *Help*, as often as feels right. God will know what your most pressing issue is. You will feel relief soon.

If you're still stuck on the idea you're talking to thin air, that nothing good is there or no one is listening, remember you can define God any way you like. Try what some women do: think of God as Nature, or Love, Beauty, Clarity, Reality, or Outside Help. Just create a positive image. You pray to this force.

Think about your financial situation, and try this prayer:

God, as you know, I'm worried about my money situation and scared sometimes. What would You have me do? Please guide me to bring about the best possible outcome.

If you started crying when you said this prayer, so much the better. You are under so much pressure right now about money problems, and other things, you need a healthy emotional release.

Do you need to be part of a religion to pray? While many women are open to spirituality, some do not like organized religion. Fortunately, you do not need a religion to pray. What is more, you do not need to do prayer in any particular way, but there are techniques which will help you get better results.

How to Pray

- First, you can pray anywhere. No church, synagogue, or mosque has a lock on it. Many women enjoy praying in nature. It's so expansive. However, people also pray in airplanes, bathrooms, and foxholes.

- You can pray aloud, or in your head.

- It doesn't have to be a formulaic set of words, though many women do enjoy the familiar lilt of memorized prayers. The repetition of phrases is soothing.

- You can begin to talk to God in a casual way, using your own words. For example, if you're worried about your child, you might say: *God, as you know, I'm a worried about Steven.*

- Then go on to tell God what your worries are.

- Alternatively, you can write down what you're worried about in a letter to God. This is a form of prayer, too. You will feel some relief getting that stuff out of your head and on paper where it has a boundary.

This man was an alcoholic from the time he was 13. He caused untold misery to his family for five years until one night his father told him he could not live with them any more. His father sent him packing across the country, alone. After bumming around in the same old way for a couple of years, he finally found a recovery program, got on a healthy path, and became a successful businessperson. Unfortunately, he had a bad turn of events and lost his business to his partner, and he got mad at God.

He was in such emotional distress, he went to a retreat center. The monk in charge of the monastery asked the problem, and the man told him God had abandoned him. So the monk said," Well, if you had a problem with a supplier, what would you do?" The man said, "I'd call him or write him." The monk said, "Well, you can't phone God, so why not write Him a letter?"

That night, he wrote this note: 'Dear God: I wanted this and you gave me that.' And he signed his name. Then he went to sleep. In the middle of the night, he woke up with this thought: 'Do you trust Me?'

He thought through his life. He remembered all the times he was drunk and could have been maimed or killed by cars, or thugs, or the winter weather. He had survived. And he realized God was always taking care of him.

After the retreat, he saw his old business was not meant for him anymore. A new idea came. It was a business sorely needed at the time. He franchised it, and now several other people have become successful, too.

The temptation to tell God what to do is hard to resist. If you have a sick loved one, of course you want to pray for their recovery. Yet, the best use you can make of this power of prayer may be to ask for the courage to face the situation no matter what the outcome. I saw a wonderful church marquee: *Faith isn't denying a bad situation; it is bringing God along to help face it.*

If God is a power greater than you, God knows what to do in every situation, better than you do. Let God do Its work and you do yours. Your work is to pray. This adds positive energy to the weaker energy of the person in trouble.

If you're still not sure, God will intervene in your life, that's understandable. I mean, your life feels dangerous, scary right now. And maybe God hasn't done for you what you wanted, and you figure It either doesn't care, or isn't there.

Read this anecdote, and see how you feel at the end of it.

This woman always took the bus home after her midnight shift. There were always one or two other passengers, and the bus was bright, so she wasn't nervous. One night, and for the first time, a car was waiting at the bus stop when she got off. She'd never even seen a car in the area at that hour of the morning in the several weeks she'd been using the bus. She assumed the man driving was waiting for one of the passengers, and she disembarked, and the bus drove away. She had to cross the street, and walk past a wide ditch and an empty field before she got to the start of the houses. Her house was in the next block. She got home in the normal manner that night, and thought nothing more of it.

The next night, the car was there again. This time, when the bus pulled away, the car started up. She crossed the street, and the car turned in her direction. She glanced back through its windshield and saw a man staring right at her, with unblinking eyes. She took stock of her situation: the ditch and the field were too long for her to be able to get past them before the car could cut her off. It was 1: 30 in the morning. There was no one around to save her.

As the car drove nearer to her, she started praying. First, she prayed to her dead mother. Then she prayed to her old boyfriend who was big and strong, but who lived out of the country. Then she started to pray to God. As the car pulled next to her, unexpectedly, another car turned onto the street. It forced the would-be attacker, who stared daggers at her, to drive on, and it kept right on his tail until they were out of sight.

She raced home, and never took that bus again.

Do you have a story like that, one in which the outcome was so positive and so surprising, it seemed like a miracle? Can you find any evidence of this kind of help in your life? Write it down. And the next time you feel afraid, re-read your journal. You will live with more faith in the future.

Exercise: Think of one time in your life, from the past, when things which could have gone very wrong, turned out well.

Example CRISIS STORIES

Situation	What Happened	How It /Could Have Gone Wrong
Taking late bus home. Approached by man in car.	Another car came behind him and forced him on so I could get home safely.	I could have been raped and beaten, maybe murdered.
Cars behind me were skidding on a crowded, icy road. I had been rear-ended twice in the past. I had gotten back to work from being disabled by the last accident.	I prayed for protection, and the two cars behind me slid on either side, leaving my car unharmed.	I could have permanently disabled from one more rear-end collision.

SPIRITUAL SOLUTION:
Your Virtues

I n the grand scheme of things, the job of each of us is to become a more loving human being. When we fall short, God gives us strengths to offset our weaknesses. Knowing your strengths and admitting your weaknesses creates a program for you to follow: focus on your strengths, your virtues. This will create abundance in your life and that of those around you in the form of calm, happiness and prosperity.

Exercise:

To improve, you first have to become aware of your weaknesses. Here is a list of well-known character flaws and virtues. Evaluate yourself. Place a checkmark either closer to the virtue or to the defect.

SPIRITUAL VIRTUES	1	2	3	4	5	6	CHARACTER FLAWS
Agreeable							Disagreeable
Assertive							Passive, Withdrawing
Balanced Emotionally/ Spiritually							Smug, Complacent
Calm							Worried
Caring							Indifferent
Cheerful							Depressed
Confident							Fearful, Apprehensive
Considerate							Selfish
Consistent							Inconsistent
Content							Envious
Cooperative							Domineering
Courteous							Rude
Discreet							Gossiping
Forgiving							Resentful
Generous							Selfish
Helpful							Self-Indulgent
Honest							Dishonest
Hopeful							Despondent
Humble							Arrogant
Industrious							Lazy
Kind							Cruel
Loving							Indifferent
Making Use of Gifts and Abilities							Disinterested in yourself
Open-Minded							Smug, Stubborn
Outgoing							Withdrawn
Patient							Irritable
Perceptive							Judgmental
Prompt							Procrastinating
Purposeful							Aimless
Realistic							Impractical
Relaxed							Tense
Responsible							Unreliable
Sincere							Deceitful
Stable							Panicky, Violent
Thankful							Ungrateful
Thoughtful							Self-Pitying
Tolerant							Small-Minded
Trusting							Suspicious
Trustworthy							Gossiping
Willing to Admit Faults							Self Righteous

Source: Blueprint for Progress: Alanon

Did you mark more flaws than virtues? If so, you're being too hard on yourself! However, if you didn't note *any* flaws, you're not being honest, folks! Now, pick one, two, or three flaws at most. Look at the opposite virtues, and make those the focus of your meditations for the next three weeks. Begin to practice them in your daily life and check to see how you did at the end of the day. You'll be amazed and proud of how you improve.

A Happy Beginning

Think of God like your GPS. If you are getting lost, it tells you, and recalculates the route to get you back on the path. Despite its willingness and ability, after several tries to get you on the right path and being ignored, the GPS gives up and tells you where you are. However, God is not that impatient.

If your God guides you to do something good for you and you refuse, even simply by ignoring the advice, God will bring you another opportunity, but one which isn't as easy to refuse.

You have certain lessons to learn in this life in order to become the most loving woman you can be, and God wants to help you do this. If you learn from the first lesson, you will walk the easy path and learn to cope well with this type of problem. But, if you dodge it as too hard, you still have to learn the lesson, but now it will be harder to dodge it, and harder to live with the problem.

This woman had a problem with the personality of her mother who was too controlling, almost a bully. So, she spent as little time with her as possible. But, she herself didn't learn to stand up for herself in the right way at the right time. So, what do you know, she got a boss who was like her mother. And it was a good job and she needed the money, so she couldn't quit. She was terrified to face down her boss. She turned for courage to her God. Guess what? Her boss backed off!

PROGRESS SELF-TEST

1. **Do you now recognize you have a chronic problem with money?**

2. **Though you may still be in debt, are you digging yourself out of the hole?**

3. **Are you saving for wonderful things like vacations and weddings?**

4. **Do you now have an Emergency Fund, even if it is tiny?**

5. Do you know how to increase your income and how to spend on both your needs and wants?

6. Have you lowered at least one of your bills?

7. Around creditors, are you calm and business-like?

8. Are you repaying your debts in a consistent manner, at a level you can afford?

9. Do you now have at least one person you trust to talk to about the little money decisions which used to baffle you?

10. Are you helping someone else who is in your old financial situation?

11. Do you turn to your own definition of a powerful God for help with purchases, and life decisions?

Simply reading all of this book means you have made progress. Seeds of ideas have been planted, and some have now even begun to flower. Permanent change comes slowly for most women, but it comes.

No matter how much debt you're in, there is a way out, permanently.

Step out onto that happy road with God at your side, my friend. You are no longer alone.

PRAYERS

Courage

God, please guide me to right thinking about who to invite into our home, and give me the courage to do it.

God, please give me the courage to negotiate with this service provider, and please give me the words.

God, please give me courage, protect me, and give me the words to negotiate the best possible arrangement for all concerned with this creditor.

Gratitude

God, please filter my thoughts, and help me feel gratitude for what I have today.

Health

God, please help me take loving care of my body with the exercise best for me.

God, I want to live in a safe, lovely and healthy place within my means, and I know this is Your will for me. Please guide me.

Money

God, bring me a feeling of peace as I record comfortable amounts of money in my categories.

God, as you know, I'm worried about my money situation and scared sometimes. What would You have me do? Please guide me to bring about the best possible outcome.

God, please bring me wonderful work where I do wonderful service in a wonderful environment for wonderful pay.

God, please show me the next right step to live a realistic, peaceful financial life this month.

My Partner

God, please help me forgive (your partner), and guide (your partner) and myself to right thinking and right action around our money.

Peace

God, I've had a terrible day. I feel bad. Anyone going through the same thing would feel as I do. But, please, transform these negative feelings into peace of mind.

God, relieve me of the habit of self sabotage, and restore me to the hopeful, healthy, and abundant life You want for me.

God, we ask for Your help in making these decisions for the wedding of xxx. Relieve us of the burdens of our egos and perfectionism. Help us to focus on the greater good of the families involved. Help us to do the work, but leave the outcome to You.

God, please transform these unpleasant feelings into peace of mind. And give me the courage to take action.

Shopping

God, please guide and protect me as I shop on this site, or *in this store or mall.*

God, help me find the perfect gift for So and So that fits within my Spending Plan.

God, please guide and protect me as I spend my vacation money.

Bibliography

Bach, D. (2007). *Smart Women Finish Rich.* Toronto: Doubleday Canada.

Bryan, M. a. (1993). *Money Drunk Money Sober.* New York: Random House.

Cain, S. (2012). *Quiet.* New York: Random House.

Chilton, D. (1989). *The Wealthy Barber.* Toronto: Stoddart.

Chilton, D. (2011). *The Wealthy Barber Returns.* Toronto: Financial Awareness Corporation.

Cooper, S. (2009). *The New Retirement.* Toronto: Penguin.

Debtors Anonymous. (1999). *A Currency of Hope.* Needham: Debtors Anonymous.

Dubner, S. D. (2009). *Freakonomics.* New York: Harper Perennial.

Freudenberger, D. H. (1981). *Burn Out.* Toronto: Bantam Books.

Godman, M. (2001) *Confessions of a Former Bill Collector.* National Wellness Group.

Hill, N. (1937). *Think and Grow Rich.* Soho.

Mundis, J. (1996). *Earn What You Deserve.* New York: Bantam.

Mundis, J. (2012). *How to Get Out of Debt, Stay Out of Debt & Live Prosperously.* New York: Bantam Books.

Orman, S. (2006). *The Nine Steps to Financial Freedom.* New York: Random House.

Ramsey, D. (2003). *Total Money Makeover* . Nashville: Thomas Nelson.

Shulman, M. (1966). *Anyone Can Make a Million (in the stockmarket)* (First Edition edition ed.). New York: McGraw-Hill.

Silverthorn, M. (2010). *The Wolf at the Door.* Toronto:McClelland & Stewart.

Stanley, T. J. (1996). *The Millionaire Next Door.* New York: Taylor Trade.

Tyagi, E. W. and Isabelle Warren (2005). *All Your Worth.* New York: Free Press.

Tyagi, E. W. and Isabelle Warren (2003). *Two Income Trap.* Cambridge: Basic Books.

Spicer, R. (Director). (2005). *Til Debt Due Us Part* [TV Series]. Canada: Slice.

Vicki Robin, J. D. (2008). Your *Money or Your Life.* London: Penguin Books.

Vaz Oxlade, G. (2011). *Debt-Free Forever.* New York: Harper Collins.

Walsh, P. (2007). *It's All too Much.* New York: Free Press.

INDEX

www.ingramcontent.com/pod-product-compliance
Lightning Source LLC
Chambersburg PA
CBHW071446200326
41519CB00038B/1742